HOLY WOMAN

Louise Omer is a writer born on Kaurna Country, with essays, criticism, and poetry published in *The Guardian*, *The Saturday Paper*, *The Lifted Brow*, and more. Beyond Australia, she has lived in Scotland and Ireland, and has a heart connection to many lands, seas, and people.

HOLY
WOMAN

a divine adventure

LOUISE OMER

SCRIBE
Melbourne • London

Scribe Publications

2 John St, Clerkenwell, London, WC1N 2ES, United Kingdom

18–20 Edward St, Brunswick, Victoria 3056, Australia

3754 Pleasant Ave, Suite 100, Minneapolis, Minnesota 55409, USA

Published by Scribe 2022

Typeset in Adobe Caslon Pro by the publishers

Printed and bound in the UK by CPI Group (UK) Ltd, Croydon CR0 4YY

Scribe Publications is committed to the sustainable use of natural resources and the use of paper products made responsibly from those resources.

978 1 912854 97 4 (UK edition)
978 1 957363 05 9 (US edition)
978 1 925849 23 3 (Australian edition)
978 1 922586 45 2 (ebook)

Catalogue records for this book are available from the National Library of Australia and the British Library.

scribepublications.co.uk
scribepublications.com
scribepublications.com.au

For all the women who came before me.

To all those who will go beyond me.

'If God is male, then the male is God.'
Mary Daly

'The best slave
does not need to be beaten.
She beats herself …

Years of training
are required for this.'
Erica Jong

'I'll tell you what freedom is to me. No fear.'
Nina Simone

Prologue

My Husband had keys to the church. On Sundays, we would arrange the stage, set up chairs, sing and dance and hug; after, wash coffee cups and sweep the silent chapel. Then Tuesday meetings, Wednesday Bible studies, Saturday barbecues. Writing sermons, checking on newcomers, buying supplies, fundraising, and planning events.

When I left Him, everything stopped.

I no longer went to church, and then, I didn't want to go. Faith stuttered and died. When I removed myself from routine, expectation, and ideological reinforcement, I discovered my religious habits hadn't felt right for a long time. I just hadn't noticed.

In the space left by broken responsibilities, questions blew on a hot wind, questions that had long lurked at the edge of dreams and threatened my entire world.

Why was my beloved God male?

Why were Bible stories mostly about men?

Why was Eve responsible for the Fall of Man?

Why were there abusers in the church?

And how could I reconcile all of this with my feminism?

He'd confessed: He wanted to be alone. Before we had the Talk, I was a wife, a Pentecostal, a preacher. But these roles weren't as solid as I thought; they dissipated in the swirl of that horrid wind.

He wanted to be alone. What should we do? After the Talk, He'd wanted to go to therapy together, get advice from church leaders. But at this crossroad, I discovered a new truth that lived between my ribs, glowing like embers: *I want to leave.* Everything within me had been brittle and dry, like the Adelaide Hills at summer's end. My Husband's rejection sparked certainty inside my body, and now I was aflame.

Sometimes, what we want is so buried, so against our identity, that it's unknowable to ourselves. Yet when it's offered, we rise, propelled by a fire of inner volition. I followed the smoke scent.

My Husband and I sold our furniture. He kept the car. I moved the leftovers of my life — books, clothes, a bicycle — to my auntie's house, and took odd jobs at a bookstore, a festival, a chain cafe. I wept against train windows, and cycled across town, sobbing. Grieving the life I'd planned, the status that came with a man, my tribe.

Nothing was clear anymore. God's voice fell to silence. But the fire between my ribs whispered: *Leave home. Go in search of answers.* This inner knowing told me I needed to cross borders of land and sea to liberate my mind. *Leave everything you know to become who you truly are.*

A journey into the unknown begins with a single step into the dark. But I never would have begun if I'd known how much I'd burn.

after

Australia

I yanked open the screen door. Nag-champa incense, chatter in the kitchen.

'Hello-o?' Auntie Liz called out, her tone both welcome and rebuke. I was late for my date with a nun.

Framed in the light of the doorway, my dark curly hair was splayed in Medusa-tangles, my mascara smeared, my heeled sandals clutched in a weak, shaking fist. I hoped there was no spew on my mouth from when I'd asked last night's one-night stand — my first ever, at twenty-eight — to pull over on the drive across town.

I sat at the wooden kitchen table, apologising, breathless. Gurrumul's songs played soft in the lounge room. Auntie Liz's goddess drawings hung on the fridge.

'Hi, Margie.' I smiled apologetically at the nun I'd invited to brunch. My auntie had worked with the Sisters of Mercy in the nineties. Auntie Liz thought her old colleague Sister Margie Abbott might direct me to some answers.

Everyone else's plates were maple syrup–smeared. Uncle Sal picked up a spatula to serve me ricotta-orange hot cakes. For the last three months, our Sunday pancake ritual had tempered the loss of my thirteen-year-old churchgoing routine. But today I shook my head in panic.

'Not hungry, are you?' His eyes glittered beneath wavy silver hair.

Auntie Liz poured me coffee with a smirk, and said, 'We were just talking about Margie's trip to Ireland, Louise.'

Lively coils of wiry white hair sprang from Margie's head. No habit, no black gown; just cargo pants and a bright-blue Patagonia jacket. She emitted a stoic, pragmatic sensibility, like a straight-backed rural farmer, but held her body with light, natural ease. The author of several books, her latest was *Cosmic Sparks*, which suggested rituals to unite hearts with the earth. I'd summoned no ordinary nun.

Margie grinned at Auntie Liz. 'Two years ago, I went on a goddess pilgrimage for my seventieth birthday. It was a wonderful tour through the sacred places of Ireland and the British Isles: Iona, bike riding around Newgrange, and then off to Glendalough. I had a friend to stay with in County Kerry.'

I slow-breathed through my nose, trying to calm my nausea, as she described stories embedded in the Irish landscape. Méabh, Queen of Connacht. Éire, the mother goddess for whom Ireland is named. And Brigit, of course, an ancient Celtic goddess; when Christianity came to Ireland, she became an abbess and a saint.

'If you get a chance, do go to Kildare and meet the two Brigidines who tend St Brigid's flame.'

'Louise, did you know Nan's grandmother was born in Ireland?' said Auntie Liz. 'We've got our own Irish heritage.'

'Yes, I remember.' I looked at Margie across the table. Tried to sit tall and say why I'd asked her here. 'I just … It hurts. All that praying, all that singing. To who, you know? A guy.' I'd always prayed to God the Father, Jesus the Son. We even called the Holy Spirit 'Him'. But lately, it felt wrong. I trailed my finger along my mug handle. 'Where am I? Where are the women?'

According to Pew Research Center, there were 2.3 billion Christians in the world. In my religion, women outnumbered men, making up approximately 60 per cent of believers. Which made

1.38 billion Christian women in the world. Not to mention the roughly one billion Muslim and six million Jewish women in the other two world religions that prayed to a monotheistic, male God. Surely, I wasn't the only one with questions — could someone, somewhere, tell me if women can belong in a patriarchal religion?

Margie pressed her lips together. 'A lot of women have these questions. Some of them find answers exploring the goddess tradition. I think St Brigid could have what you're looking for.'

Soon, my nun-guide left for a long drive home. Auntie Liz and Uncle Sal walked her to the driveway, but after an urgent wave at the door, I dashed to the bathroom, where I retched until tears fell.

'Idiot, idiot,' I muttered, gripping cool white porcelain, punishing myself with the memory of last night's mattress on the floor, the smell of an ugly stranger's skin.

As my breathing slowed, Margie's words knitted together. This straight-backed, alternative nun seemed to believe I was at the beginning of a quest. Ireland was the place where goddess traditions and Christianity intersected, and the country held another pull: my mother's family line. Margie's pilgrimage laid out a path for my own.

A cheery beep, the screen door slammed. Someone put the kettle on and still I panted over the toilet bowl, wishing there was a way to divine the future in swirling specks of orange vomit.

I peeled off sweaty clothes and fell into bed, kicking back sheets as fresh air whispered through the window. Auntie Liz had left a jug of lemon water. I poured a tall, luscious glass, then closed my eyes, let noises come as if through a long tunnel. The rainbow lorikeets' vibrant chirps, the back door's *squeak-creak-slam* as Uncle Sal went to tend the veggie patch. My mind separated from my body, and I drifted.

Leave home.

I think St Brigid could have what you're looking for.

Who could resist the direction of a nun? Who could deny a call upon their heart? I'd survived my marriage breakdown, and wanted to be alone and free, wanted to leave safety and follow my questions. I would be a nomad with a red suitcase and a borrowed coat, unlacing Doc Martens at airport security, flying across the world in search of answers.

I would go to Ireland — from there, I would decide my next move.

Six months after I left my marriage, I left the country.

Ireland

Twenty-six hours, four airports; I fled the sun across the earth in one long night. The sky was grey-bright when I exited Dublin Airport in early afternoon, the wind rude and cold. I tugged my suitcase past the taxi rank, climbed aboard a double-decker bus, and contemplated long-haul travel's quiet brutality. My body felt as if it'd been spun by centrifugal force — spleen thrown against spine, stomach against ribs — and spat out.

On Camden St, I pushed open a butcher's back door. An Airbnb host with a salt-and-pepper beard led me three storeys up a thin, creaking flight of stairs ('Geez, whaddya have in this suitcase, bricks?') to my attic room. Clasping a cup of strong black tea, I sat cross-legged on my first of many temporary beds. East of the window, boiler-pipe steam rose into a dark ash sky, though it wasn't yet 5.00 pm. Enormous seagulls circled the city's chimneys.

Among the heavy books in my suitcase was an A5-sized King James Version Bible with a black leather cover and elegant, slim pages edged with gold. But instead of the word of God, I opened

John Bunyan's seventeenth-century novel *The Pilgrim's Progress*, where a man leaves his family to answer God's call. The first person he meets asks, 'Do you see yonder shining light?' The light calls the pilgrim forth and guides him where he's meant to go.

Like Bunyan's protagonist, I'd left community and security behind, convinced God had called me to this divinely designed path. I didn't know how long I'd be away from home. Three months? Six? A year? I only had three nights' accommodation booked, $200 of savings, and the $300 that Grandad had slipped into my hand when I last visited. A few freelance writing projects were lined up, but I'd have to pitch articles on the road. I planned to live on as little money as possible, and depend on providence.

I tucked my feet beneath me, and wrote in my journal:

Rules of pilgrimage
1. *Forsake comfort.*
2. *Seek yonder shining light. At the next stop, you will receive instruction.*
3. *Never steal, even if you have no money.*

Where I travelled would be decided by my quest: if I felt drawn to a concept that addressed women in Christianity, and perhaps Judaism and Islam, then I'd go there. And talk to people. This first stop, to meet St Brigid, was guided by a nun's holy wisdom; I'd received God's instruction and obeyed. I already had a few potential countries on a 'maybe' list. Soon, he would direct me where to go next.

At this point, I still trusted God.

—

'You're new here.'

It wasn't a question. My cheeks burnt at the pony-tailed librarian's patronising smile. I hated looking like I didn't know what I was doing.

'If you could just tell me where the Ussher Library is?'

He pointed to a grey flight of stairs. Heavy coat slung over one arm, I climbed four storeys to the religion section, and was disappointed when I pushed open the door to find undecorated rows of shelves. I'd hoped the research library would look like the Long Room, the famous library where Trinity College keeps the Book of Kells, the famous ninth-century illuminated biblical manuscript. But that was in a different building. Which cost €14 entry.

Piling my arms with books, I found a free desk between students' laptops and energy drinks, and started taking notes. St Brigid was one of three of Ireland's patron saints — the other two were St Patrick, who 'brought Christianity to Ireland' in AD 432, and St Colmcille, alleged to have invented monasticism. Like her saintly companions, St Brigid still had schools and churches named after her in almost every county. Born in Faughart, County Louth, in 450, her hagiographies (saints' biographies) claim she wanted to join a convent to dedicate her life to caring for the sick and poor. But her father, the pagan chieftain of Leinster, had promised her hand in marriage, so she prayed God would make her ugly. When her suitor glimpsed her transfigured face, he refused to marry her. After she took her vows, her beauty returned, more radiant than before. When she asked her father for land in Kildare, he said he'd only give her as much ground as her cloak covered. She unfurled her cloak and threw it across the green: it supernaturally stretched for acres. Thanks to this miracle of God, she built her monastery, where the town of Kildare now stands.

As the monastery's abbess, St Brigid lived a life of justice and evangelism. Most famously, she wove reeds into a cross while sitting at the deathbed of a pagan chieftain and teaching him the story of Christ. The chieftain supposedly asked to be baptised into Christianity before he died. Every January, schoolchildren weave these crosses in preparation for St Brigid's Day, February 1.

But before she was a saint, Brigit was a goddess. (I use 'Brigit' when referring to her as a goddess.) She has had many names, like Bríd or Bríg, and her legends are often contradictory. According to pre-Christian Celtic mythology, Brigit was a triple goddess, incarnated in three characters; stories associate her with poetry, healing, and blacksmithing. Her multiplicity meant stories depicted her as maiden, mother, and crone.

(A note here on the rich history of Celtic tradition. Neolithic archaeological sites like burial mounds and ring forts are found across Ireland. Newgrange is the island's most well-known monument; built around 3200 BC, it's older than Stonehenge and the Egyptian Pyramids. Due to the earth's angle, sunlight enters the ancient structure at dawn during the winter solstice — and no other time of year. Pre-Christian Ireland was an oral culture, so Newgrange's full meaning is guesswork. But it proves the Celts operated with a sophisticated level of astronomy, ceremony, and design. Celtic mythology, and therefore Brigit's stories, connect us to something ancient and powerful.)

All three of Brigit's mythic incarnations have associations with fire: the spark of creativity ignites the song of poetry, a medicine woman uses heat to prepare herbs and brews, and smith-work requires an open flame. Legend says a perpetual fire burnt for the goddess for hundreds of years. In a fire temple attended by priestesses, a taboo against male intruders caused transgressors' limbs to fall off, or doomed the men to madness. Sister Margie Abbott had mentioned that the Brigidine nuns nurtured a perpetual flame of their own.

The flame wasn't the only tradition carried from Neolithic times to today. St Brigid's Day coincides with Imbolc, the ancient pagan festival celebrating the beginning of spring. In a legend that persists today, St Brigid journeyed across the land on the dawn of February 1, bringing the season's expanding light with her.

The Serpent and the Goddess, by Trinity College researcher Mary Condren, traces Brigit's transformation from goddess to saint. As monasteries proliferated in the fifth century, Christian scribes recorded ancient myths, aligning them with monotheistic dogma. Brigit was transfigured into sainthood, Condren wrote, and her supernatural power was ascribed to God.

I chewed a soggy cheese sandwich on a damp wooden bench under a maple tree, my breath visible in the air, and watched tourists queue for the Book of Kells. Sister Margie said St Brigid and the goddess tradition could have what I was looking for. But this implied transforming my spiritual practice to worship female deities from old religions. This was a near-impossible, gargantuan psychological leap. What was God to me? A Supreme Being, an omniscient, invisible presence, an ultimate power who created the world and controlled all things. A divine Father, who created universal laws and was the source of eternal wisdom. With whom I was in an intimate relationship. Thirteen years of faith had cultivated a continual conversation that occurred deep in my consciousness. So how to direct my attention, instead, to a feminine pantheon? How to believe in fairytale characters?

Wind shook wet leaves. And God was love, above all. He loved me: this underlaid my actions, and brought meaning and purpose to each day. And again, I came to that familiar frustration: God was father, man, other. Opposite to me, my body, my history.* I rolled crumb-filled cling wrap into a ball and tucked it in my pocket, fingers pink with cold.

By recommending this goddess tradition, Sister Margie encouraged me to search for a feminine divine: a mystic god-power personified as a woman. Maybe venerating goddesses — even if they were just pictures in storybooks — was a way to remedy the psychological imbalance of a male God.

The next morning, I knelt on the floorboards. Mist drifted beyond the window.

'Please light the way, Lord.'

Unease as I walked into the city centre, last night's dream seeping into waking hours. I had been the protagonist of a play. The audience was waiting, the lights were bright. But when I stepped onstage, I forgot my lines.

I splurged on an americano and croissant, and strolled through St Stephen's Green, a park at the top of Grafton St. Families and friends sat on benches beneath great sycamore trees, watching ducks and swans drift on a green-tinged lake. A laughing woman took photos of her partner extending his hands like a man crucified as grey-brown pigeons lined his arms. I breathed in as I passed, as

---

* For the purpose of using my cisgendered experience as knowledge, I define my womanhood through socialised gender *and* through my body. Transwomen are women. This is true *as well as* the fact that women's experience throughout history has been, in part, defined by our biology.

if I could inhale their happiness.

I caught a coach to Dundalk, County Louth, to meet Celtic-spirituality teacher Dolores Whelan, who for the last decade had organised an annual St Brigid festival on her feast day. She was also involved in the revival of a July pilgrimage honouring the saint. Every year, hundreds of people made the walk from St Brigid's holy well in Faughart to the cathedral in Kildare.

Hundreds of wells are named after saints across Ireland, some decorated with pictures, candles, and ornaments. They might be ringed by brick, or simply be a hollow in long grass, and often mark a place of mythic significance. Before Christianity, the Celts saw wells as a connection to elemental power embedded in the earth. Saints supposedly used them to baptise new converts, and now people visited them for contemplation or healing. Pagan sites became Christian holy places.

At Dundalk bus station, a woman with dyed-crimson hair and a fuchsia coat waved at me from her car. I hopped in and we drove to a garden cafe. Across the table, Dolores had large round eyes and a deep and husky voice, and was about ten years older than my mother. She enunciated words with deliberate care when she wanted to drive a point home, a habit from when she lectured: she taught biochemistry before studying a master's in spirituality under radical Dominican priest Matthew Fox in 1983. Dolores had taught healing and creative spirituality for thirty-five years, and in the last four censuses marked her religion as 'Celtic Christian'.

'Growing up in Ireland,' she told me over soup and soda bread, 'there was an incredible religiosity. It was like everything was governed by the church. It was a really closed society. On Good Friday — there was always a sermon at three o'clock. And because there was communion, ye couldn't eat anything for three hours before. Mam would say to us, *don't be hanging around the house*. And I used to go down to the forest. Now, when I think of Good Friday, that's what I remember: the primroses coming out. A part of my child soul knew that I could find God there. On Good Friday now, I never go to a church, but I spend the day out in nature.' She quoted a line from Patrick Kavanagh's poem 'Canal Bank Walk': 'But this soul needs a new dress woven of blue and green things and arguments that cannot be proven.'

Dolores encountered a sense of the divine in nature. She saw herself as continuing an ancient practice that sought connection with earth, water, and fire. But it wasn't only eco-spirituality that drew her to Celtic practices. Irish Catholicism was authoritarian, she felt, full of commands and directives and punishment. What's more, worshipping a male God felt incomplete. One of the reasons why she ran the festival was because St Brigid was important to women: she was a feminine face of God.

Catholic Ireland, Dolores said, had a strong relationship with the powerful maternal figure. The Virgin Mary, the Mother of God, was prominent in Catholicism as an intercessor; like her, Brigid embodied divine feminine qualities: compassion, nurture, generosity, trust.

'People often ask me, is what you teach Christian or pagan? What I'm teaching, what I'm doing, is both. Sometimes, I think Christianity imagines it fell out of the sky. But it integrates with the indigenous people in every country.'

A teenage waitress cleared our plates.

'Thanks a mill.,' Dolores mumbled. We left and climbed into her car. 'Oh! I forgot!' She dashed back to the cafe, and returned with a jar begged off the staff. 'For the holy water,' she said, before tucking it beneath the handbrake, turning on the ignition, and driving up a windy road. She parked at a peak and directed me to look out towards Dundalk Bay and further, the Irish Sea: an apricot light glowed between the horizon and the clouds. I breathed air so cold it hurt my nostrils. Wind rustled through beech trees.

I followed Dolores' skinny legs under a copper arch spelling 'St Brigid's Shrine'. Across uneven mounds of wet grass, we passed odd-angled gravestones rubbed clean by decades of rain. We were right at the Hill of Faughart's peak, believed in Celtic mysticism to be a 'thin place'. Where elements meet — land and sky, land and sea — the veil between the physical world and the 'Otherworld' becomes thin. I tried to feel something, searched for tingles up my spine, which had always been the physical manifestation of the Holy Spirit. I was used to reaching up, for a God on high. But what if, like the Celtic Christians thought, power buzzed beneath my feet?

Dolores pointed to hundreds of coloured ribbons flapping from a hazelwood tree. On the craggy branches were lengths of blue cotton and yellow silk, some clearly ripped from old clothes, wavering in the wind.

'The legend is that Brigid passes through the country on the eve of Imbolc, the 31st of January. And if everybody leaves out their cloths, she absorbs the dew that settles on it at night. So if you had a sore eye, you would touch your eye with a cloth and tie it to a branch. And you receive healing.'

Tucked in to the side of the hill, was an enclave covered in moss; inside, the stone ring of a well.

'In the Irish tradition and all primal traditions,' Dolores said, 'the well is the gateway to the Otherworld.' Close beside her, I leant in. Was God down there, too? The water seemed immeasurably deep. Fear thrilled from my hips to my shoulders.

'Would you like a blessing?'

I nodded, and she grabbed a long rusted ladle from a metal hook, before reaching into the well.

'We're lucky it's not frozen,' she said. She pulled up her arm, poured water from the ladle to the jar, and dipped two fingers in. Hands resting on my jacket, I closed my eyes.

'So, Lou, we bless you with this water of Brigid's well.' Her voice slow and deep. 'May Brigid guide your spirit's steps, may you know the deep truth of her being and the wonders of her teaching. May your eyes open to see that inner vision.' With each invocation, she anointed the part of my body with holy water. 'Your ears to hear that inner vision, your nose to sense it, your mouth to speak it, your throat to speak it, your heart to absorb it, your solar plexus to give you the strength, your sexual creative energy to allow you to be creative, your knees to help you go forward, and your feet to keep you firmly grounded on the earth. And may Brigid wrap her mantle of protection around you as you continue this important journey in this sacred land.'

She screwed on the lid, and I slipped the jar into my jacket pocket. We walked down the hill in new, awkward intimacy, and she insisted on taking a photo of me at the roots of an oak.

On the ride back to Dublin, the gloaming hour lowered like a velvet curtain. Country homes' yellow windows flashed in deep twilight blue, and I fingered the jam-jar lid. Where did the goddess end and the saint begin? What was superstition, and what was faith? The bus left a trail of my questions across County Meath. When did water become sacred? When it came from the sky, when it clung to my jacket, when I cycled through fog? How did the ordinary become holy?

—

Kildare's cathedral spire stretched into bright blue sky. The town's name came from the Irish *Cill Dara*, Church of the Oak, and St Brigid's cathedral stood where her monastery is recorded as being in the fifth century (though this is disputed by some historians). After Viking attacks and many rebuilds, the church of turrets and gargoyles towering before me was 150 years old.

Heartbeat thick in my chest, I entered the gate and wandered around thick grass, worn old gravestones, and Celtic crosses. I found a reconstructed fire temple. Catholic sources believed that St Brigid adopted the pagan fire and that through her it became the light of Christ. But it had been extinguished by invading English forces in the seventeenth century. Now, the temple was a knee-high stone wall that encircled ten square metres, with stairs leading three steps down to lower ground. In its centre was a pile of blackened ash.

I loved outdoor fires. They meant camping holidays, winter parties, or sometimes a personal ceremony. Before I left for Ireland, I had invited my two closest friends, Gemma and Gul, to Auntie Liz's house. Gul's phone played songs by Selda Bağcan, a Turkish singer and freedom fighter, and Gemma balanced logs atop kindling, scrunched newspaper, and struck a long match. When the flames burnt hot and orange, we pulled up chairs and tore strips from my wedding dress, ripping purple mesh and crimson chiffon. We fed my costume into the fire.

Tucking my hands into leopard-print pockets, I exited the churchyard. The Brigidine nuns, too, had their flame. A global network of Roman Catholic nuns founded by the Bishop of Kildare in 1807, the Brigidines were inspired by St Brigid's role as Carer of the Earth and Healing Woman. Their website claimed she was a model for Christian womanhood and 'the feminine face of God'.

The Solas Bhride Centre's gravel car park hosted a row of metal bike racks by a vegetable garden. In the garden's centre was a copper statue of St Brigid, and at the back were the self-contained hermitages where Sister Margie had stayed. I pushed open a glass door — in an instant, a strong cup of tea and plate of fruitcake were in my hands. Guided by God, I'd happened upon a morning tea.

At a round table, I met some women who'd gathered for reflection and prayer. Brenda, who wrote her postgraduate thesis on St Brigid, led me into a room where natural light spilled through a tall window. The design was circular, echoing the feminist theory of erasing hierarchy to ensure equality of voices. Red-cushioned chairs were arranged in curves.

In their centre was the flame.

Considering its historical and symbolic value, I expected an Olympic cauldron. At least a fireplace. But I squatted and leant my cheek almost to the floor to see a diminutive light in a glass dome. This thing was tiny.

One of the three nuns who lived at the hermitage, Rita, led me to a room heated by the sun. A sweet Irishwoman in her seventies, she repeated the last word of my sentence as I said it, making me feel as if she were finishing the sentence for me, and knew exactly what I meant.

'Yes, naturally you are surprised. Everybody is. Because they are expecting something big, a ball of flame.'

They relit it in 1993. In 2006, the flame was moved to the Market Square in the middle of Kildare. The president of Ireland, Mary McAleese, attended the lighting ceremony. But Irish weather got the better of the gas, and whenever the flame blew out, fumes went up into the sky. This went against the nuns' environmental policy.

'So we have the little naked flame.'

The act of tending was without grandeur. A tall seven-day candle sat in a glass chamber, and when it neared its end, another nun, Mary, would light a new wick with the dying flame. Rita witnessed, and together they thought about all the people who had visited that week, or anyone asking for prayers, or whatever was happening in Ireland or the world.

Born in County Tipperary, Rita took her vows at twenty-one, disappointing her parents, who had hoped she would take over their pub.

'You either became a sister, or you went into the bank, or you became a nurse; college wasn't an option at that time, even in Ireland.' The Brigidine order was established with an emphasis on education. Rita's story echoed the historical appeal of convents: for many women, it was the only pathway to education.

I asked her about the link between pagan and Christian beliefs.

'Our tradition holds that the hill of Kildare — at the site of St Brigid's monastery, on which stands the thirteenth-century cathedral today — would have been a sacred place.' Her croaky voice high-pitched but authoritative. 'Y'know, frequented by priests and priestesses petitioning to gods and goddesses, to protect their herds and to provide a fruitful harvest. A lot of these were sacred places prior to the coming of Christianity.

'We know that Rome advocated a strategy that pagan sanctuaries were not to be destroyed, but they were to be used to preach the new religion. The Celts were a religious people, they believed in another world, and a lot of the same kind of beliefs about life as the Christian message.

'There wasn't a war to bring in Christianity,' she said, her eyebrows furrowing theatrically with the word 'war', as if she were reading a children's book out loud. 'There's an interweaving of the myths and the stories of the gods with the Christian story.'

The train back to Dublin was empty. Green fields flashed, and heaviness seeped through my limbs. Outside Heuston station, the almost-sour fragrance of roasting hops floated from the Guinness factory. I plodded along the Liffey, watching a lone swan drift. Gleaming Clydesdales pulled lavish carriages holding tourists with blankets over their knees among taxis and buses. The sky deepened from indigo to obsidian. On aching legs, I walked to Grafton St, where golden lights spelt *Nollaig Shona Duit* — 'Merry Christmas' in Irish. Shoppers with red noses rushed, clutching Brown Thomas bags in gloved fists. I passed Bewley's glowing tearoom, its curling brass lamps and packed tables; outside, buskers sang acoustic covers, their breath unfurling. A child in lavender mittens and a beanie tugged on her father's hand, looking up at him with an obstinate frown.

I wandered, carried by the crowd's flow. History books, Dolores Whelan, and the Brigidine nuns told me that monks stole pagan beliefs and adapted them. Christianity wasn't just a male God but a system of thought. Colonisation conformed existing beliefs to the imposed doctrine; the old and the new were consolidated. In Irish mythology, female figures accessed independent power, but now they could only request it from Big Daddy. In this way, the goddess was dethroned.

What was with all these women being *under* God? Why was independent female power incompatible with Christianity? For a mad moment, I imagined visiting a department store Father Christmas, sitting on his lap, and saying, 'Help.'

Frozen fingertips throbbed. At Butlers Chocolate Café, a line of shoppers snaked from its golden lights, and I imagined the luxury of a hot chocolate to warm my hands, maybe a marshmallow or two — no. I needed the coins in my pocket for tomorrow's airport bus.

The next day, I examined myself in the bathroom: my knitted jumper made me look bulky. As I stuffed it in my full backpack, my fist knocked something solid: the jam jar! Even in Ireland, they wouldn't let holy water through airport security. I unscrewed it, dipped my fingers in, and dabbed water on my eyelids. Maybe it was time to try praying to someone new.

'Brigit,' I whispered. 'Show me the way.'

I emptied the water down the sink.

Mexico

'*Este lugar es muy peligroso.*' The taxi driver shook his head as he turned onto my hotel's street. *This place is very dangerous*. Tangled black electricity wires hung from colonial facades. Women in skin-tight dresses leant against peeling walls, lit orange by sharp early sun. A man slouched on the pavement gazed with burning eyes.

I had taken Spanish at university seven years ago, and assumed the language would return to me. But only when I checked into the hotel did I realise its name, Mala Vecindad, meant Bad Neighbourhood.

Mexico City's traffic grumble and car horns faded as I slipped between crisp white sheets for a nap. My disappointment in Ireland had led me to reach for the highest female figure in Christianity: Mary, Holy Mother of Jesus Christ. In Pentecostalism, we didn't touch her unless telling the Christmas story, but in Catholicism, she sits beside God the Father.

Researching this figure, I came across the iconic imagery of Mexico's La Virgen de Guadalupe. Central to Latin American Catholicism, her basilica received eighteen to twenty million pilgrims every year (higher than annual visitors to the Vatican), and astoundingly, around twelve million people came over *two days* for her feast day, December 12. I was here to join this pilgrimage and try to touch the robe of the feminine divine.

I snuggled into blankets and scrolled through notes on my phone. Her story was first told in the *Nican Mopohua*, a text written almost 500 years ago by Spanish priests in the indigenous language Nahuatl. Colonialism arrived in the sixteenth century to evangelise the unsaved and annihilate language, culture, and religion. Ten years later, in 1531, the Mother of God appeared on Tepeyac Hill, above the Aztec city Tenochtitlán.

'My abandoned one,' said the woman of perfect beauty with clothing like the sun. She spoke softly to an indigenous man, Juan Diego: 'I am your merciful mother and the mother of all the nations that live on this earth … I will hear their laments and remedy and cure all their miseries, misfortunes, and sorrows.'

He scrambled down the hill to tell the Spanish bishop, who refused to believe the story. When Juan Diego returned to the Virgin Mother, she bade him take some flowers. Nothing naturally grew here among rocks and prickly pears, but she stood in a field of miraculous wildflowers. He gathered them up in his tilma (robe) and dropped them at the foot of the bishop. The holy man gasped: imprinted on the tilma was the image of the Virgin Mary.

This supernatural cloth was still on display in the Basilica of Our Lady of Guadalupe, at the foot of Tepeyac, in the inner north of Mexico City. December 12 was two weeks away. I had fourteen days to find someone to take me on pilgrimage.

I turned on my side, attempting deep breaths despite the inner chorus of '*what the hell am I doing*' cha-cha-ing with the street noise. In the last month, I'd reached out to anyone I knew who had ever lived in Mexico, or knew somebody who did, as well as feminist writers and artists online. I hoped God would steer me in the right direction. Or maybe St Brigid, or La Virgen.

I texted Gemma. 'Have I made the right choice?' It was late in Australia.

I watched the word *typing* materialise under her name.

'There is no right choice. Babe, why are you always scared of making a mistake?'

I woke in time for breakfast in a bright pink, yellow, and green room. While eating *chilaquiles rojos*, fried eggs on corn chips topped with tomato sauce, cheese, and cream, I imagined myself dusty and panting, walking in a group towards the venerated hill.

Mary was never important to me, not being Catholic. But I did wonder what it was like to pray to a female figure. In my mid-twenties, Auntie Liz had sent me a copy of Carol P. Christ's 1978 essay 'Why Women Need the Goddess'. A feminist theologian and later founder of the online journal feminismandreligion.com, Christ campaigned for women to foster a spirituality focused on female divine figures, and led pilgrimages to goddess sites in Crete until her death in 2021. In her essay, she wrote that religious symbolism powerfully influences the way we think. Religions have existed throughout history and across the world, creating rituals and stories to mark life's transitions (birth, sexuality, death) and crises (death, evil, suffering). As those are our lives' most meaningful moments, these beliefs are profoundly important.

I wiped my greasy mouth with a paper napkin, pushed my plate away. Citing anthropological studies, Christ claimed that religious symbols become embedded in our psyches.

As I flicked open Google Maps to figure out what Metro train to catch, I wondered again if I would feel I belonged in Christianity if I could develop a relationship to a female symbol. Would I pray to Mother, or Her? The words felt wrong, as if I were playing a game. God was GOD, while goddesses or holy mothers seemed make-believe.

But I would try. Maybe, here in Mexico, I could kneel at La Virgen's multicoloured altar.

Smog hung low in dirty sweeps across the sky. A local tour guide met me and two other English speakers at the entrance to Plaza de las Tres Culturas, also called Tlatelolco. 'Three Cultures' signified the independent state of Mexico, the Spanish colonial era, and pre-Columbian times. The square was famous for a 1968 government massacre of unarmed student protesters. We stood on many layers of history.

As our tour group explored the site, two men in overalls cleaned the 700-year-old dark stone steps that stood twenty metres high. This was the remnant of a gargantuan pyramid. Tlatelolco was once the centre of an Aztec city-state, and a neighbouring settlement to the larger Tenochtitlán, which was built on an island on Lake Texcoco. These Aztec cities' canals and causeways worked cunningly with the environment to live atop a body of water. The Aztecs — the generic title covering the Valley of Mexico tribes in the Spanish Conquest era — were a dominant, warring clan. When conquistador Hernán Cortés and his army arrived in the

Valley of Mexico in 1519, he claimed the land for the Spanish crown. After a small battle in Tabasco, he marched on Tenochtitlán and was received amiably by Aztec emperor Montezuma II. But the people rebelled. In 1520, Montezuma was killed, stoned by his own frustrated people, or murdered by the Spaniards — depending on who was telling the story. The colonial army laid siege to Tenochtitlán, leading to Spanish victory and utter destruction of the city and surrounding areas, including Tlatelolco.

I looked to my right, where a cathedral rose over the ruins: the Church of Santiago Tlatelolco, commissioned by Cortés and completed in 1609 to honour the conquering of New Spain. The detailed facade was the same dark grey of the pyramid remnants: stones from the temple were used to make the church.

Colonisation's genocide was enacted first through slaughter and destruction and then by enchaining surviving imaginations. White supremacism operates on a belief of racial inferiority; Europeans saw the 'white man's burden' was to 'civilise' conquered nations by displacing their religion and implanting Christianity.

I peered up at the monstrous cathedral, its ornate carvings, its bell tower. Aztec sites were razed. And in their place, monuments were built to Spanish power: God and the king.

I sipped a canned gin and tonic on the hotel's concrete rooftop, celebrating my first lead: a friend of a friend knew someone going on pilgrimage.

I sighed and thanked God for the solidarity of women. Oops, forgot. 'Gracias, Señora.'

The difficult task of turning towards the mother was made easier by her image's ubiquity. She was omnipresent. Six-metre-tall purple-blue murals peeled from pink apartment buildings; she was framed on corner-store shelves and inked into biceps. She gazed from altars embedded in walls, petrol-station shrines, white boxes on street corners flashing green and red. Every rendition the same composition as Juan Diego's 500-year-old tilma: La Virgen on a crescent moon, her body framed by spiking sun rays, her robe dotted with glowing stars. Hands held in prayer, face tilted in serene compassion.

Her iconography held complex meaning. The famous priest Father Miguel Hidalgo carried her image as he rode into battle in the 1810 War of Independence; 100 years later, leader of the peasant uprising Emiliano Zapata held a flag imprinted with La Virgen in the Mexican Revolution. She became the patroness of Mexico. Now, her shrines were found in places associated with the Mexican diaspora: California, Texas, more. She represented an amalgamation: pride in culture, politics, and belief; mestizo and indigenous integrity, and resistance to imperial forces.

I looked across the endless rooftops. I could barely digest Mexico's vibrant sensual assault: cumbia music at tortilla stands, poverty on the street, blue-and-red disco lights at corner stores. Food smelt different, menus were confusing, sometimes I accidentally ordered meat. The meaning of things was strange and unknown to me, and my ignorance made me lonely.

My body was suffering, too. CDMX (La Ciudad de México) was over two kilometres above sea level. Altitude sickness manifested as headaches, shortness of breath, and fatigue. With a population of twenty million, air pollution was high. But nature never felt far away. Altitude sickness became reminder of mountain and sea. Lopsided, semi-sunken colonial buildings were slowly swallowed by ancient lakes. Illustrated instructions in case of earthquakes hung on restaurant walls. When the smog cleared, a dormant volcano stood over the city.

If I was going to go on the pilgrimage, I needed to get in shape. I decided to walk everywhere. The next day's enquiries took me three kilometres to Biblioteca Vasconcelos — CDMX's mega-library, whose six floors of shelves seemed to float in midair, joined only by thin metal staircases.

I leafed through books on La Virgen de Guadalupe. I had questions, many of which challenged the legend's veracity. Firstly, why was La Virgen, who appeared on Tepeyac, not called La Virgen de Tepeyac? Evidence suggested her distinguishing label originated in Spain. Spanish Catholic tradition honoured localised shrines: a Mary in every town, a saint in every village. Cortés was a devotee of La Virgen de Guadalupe in Extremadura, the Spanish region where he was born. He prayed to her before battle.

What's more, multiple historians provided evidence that the design of her iconic image mimicked fifteenth- and sixteenth-century conventions in European religious art. Which implied she wasn't a divine apparition, but was imported.

The word 'syncretism' — meaning the combination of two philosophies — perfectly describes La Virgen de Guadalupe. She was remade as La Virgen Morena, the Brown Virgin, a mestizo mother, a mix of Spanish and indigenous, her skin colour darker than in European churches.

The author and trauma specialist Resmaa Menakem writes that the white body is held up as the superior standard. Revered images show which bodies a culture affirms as the status quo or ideal; the absences demonstrate which are not. While I was angry that the *male* body was the superior standard in Christianity, I'd always taken God's whiteness for granted. All Western images I'd seen of God and Jesus and Mary were white (despite Jesus being born in Bethlehem, in modern-day Palestine). I'd never considered my religion's white supremacy, never recognised the violence Christianity had rained down upon bodies of colour by excluding them from the image of God. And the history of La Virgen de Guadalupe, whose skin colour was the same as her followers, proved how important it was to see an element of our body or identity in the divine.

Elements of her image, too, were intertwined with those from Nahuatl culture. The Aztec religion had a pantheon of gods and goddesses crowned by the Father and Mother Gods, represented by the sun and moon. It made sense that La Virgen de Guadalupe stood on a crescent moon, the symbol of the goddess.

This syncretism was enforced with violent penalties for worshipping ancient 'idols' or not attending church. Just like Australia's brutal history of colonisation, where Christians displaced Indigenous people into missions and outlawed old customs. And just as I'd seen in Tlatelolco square, the old way was destroyed, the new way built using pieces of the old.

My eyes widened as I read the documented history of a pre-Hispanic mother goddess appearing to Nahuatl people on Tepeyac. On this same hill, sacrifices were made to honour Tonantzin, whose name means 'Our Mother'.

Before colonisation, Tepeyac was already a sacred site.

I looked up from my desk. Footsteps tapped on the thin metal platform above. Two teenagers whispered in armchairs by three-storey windows, which looked out to a garden where green palm trees waved in the wind. Was it true? Just like in Ireland? Despite a separation of 1,000 years and 8,000 kilometres, the same tactics were implemented to remove old religious practices and implant the new. The church was built from temple stones. My head spun. The conquest was not just physical, but psychological, and spiritual. Intertwining new religion with old was a policy of colonisation: the imported European Mother of God was syncretised with the mother goddess Tonantzin.

I moved to an Airbnb in the north, a second-storey apartment above a yapping Chihuahua forty-five minutes' walk from La Virgen's basilica. Nearby, a collection of mechanics took up an entire block, where streets of men idled cars, and greasy jeans and sneakers protruded from beneath rusted navy bonnets. Closer to home was my local tortilleria, where I bought ten pesos of corn tortillas sold by weight. A feminist guide claimed CDMX was one of the world's best cities for female-owned small businesses and galleries. But I made sure to be home by dusk.

Femicide is the killing of a woman or girl because she is female. This gender-based hate crime exists in every country on earth: an epidemic of violence against women in workplaces, the streets, and homes. A few weeks ago, a woman was kidnapped on the Metro here in CDMX. The journalists Frida Guerrera and María Salguero conducted a national count: 8,904 women killed between 2014 and 2017. Caution kept me home most nights.

At 9.00 am, I walked across the patterned ceramic floor to the breakfast table, where Juana, the Airbnb host, had laid out plates of chilli scrambled eggs. She sold clothes at a night market, returning home between 1.00 am and 3.00 am. Her partner, Miguel, was a big-shouldered, slow-moving man with a broad nose and dark spiky hair, and as I sat at their table with another Airbnb guest, I tried to follow their conversation in Spanish. Miguel asked me if I would visit anywhere beyond Mexico City.

I replied with terrible grammar. 'No — I am travel alone. I am woman.'

Miguel sighed, placed his fork down, and shook his head. 'It is not dangerous. All the world is dangerous. All humans are dangerous. Not any more here.'

Clearly, he was tired of Western media conflating Mexico with drug cartels. I managed to make a joke in Spanish, and the easy rhythm of Miguel and Juana's laughter together was like music.

Miguel looked me in the eye. His thick hair stuck up at odd angles. '*No vivas con miedo.*'

I pulled on black skinny jeans, jumping to pull them over my hips, and laced my boots. It was easy for Miguel to tell me not to live in fear. I hadn't mentioned femicide counts — in Mexico, in Australia, or elsewhere. Nor the self-defence taught by our mothers, aunties, friends. The vulnerability to violence simply by existing in a female body. And I didn't even experience the worst of it — transwomen, women of colour, and indigenous women face violence in higher numbers around the world.

I pushed into the bustle of morning. In the dog-grooming shop, two men in backwards baseball caps chuckled while trimming a bewildered Jack Russell; beside a six-laned highway, a blind woman blew a whistle and a teenage girl took her elbow to guide her through traffic. At a *comida corrida* stand near the Metro station, a big-bellied cook in an oil-stained T-shirt poured buckets of soapy water on concrete and scrubbed with a heavy broom. Beside him, a long plastic-coated table held two-litre buckets of guacamole, lime wedges, cilantro, and onion, glistening in the sun.

I got off a couple of Metro stops early and climbed above ground to a river of cyclists streaming along Paseo de la Reforma. Inside the gates of Chapultepec Park were chaotic dog walkers clutching four leads in each hand, teenagers on electric scooters, and vendor stands with popcorn and balloon animals. Dance groups practised hip-hop routines in rotundas. Rollerbladers crisscrossed legs over concrete in smooth waves, and muscled performers in feathered headdresses danced to a mesmeric drum, all sheltered by Mexican cypress trees. Known as the city's lungs, some of these enormous trees were planted by the Aztecs. At 1,695 acres, Chapultepec Park contained a castle, a zoo, a lake, nine museums, and, today, it seemed, all the families of Mexico City. I entered El Museo de Historia y Antropología.

Inside dim, high-ceilinged rooms, an old man in a grey blazer and fedora squatted to whisper in a pigtailed girl's ear, his hand gentle on her shoulder as they peered at the map of the Valley of Mexico. I darted through the crowd and gravitated towards sculptures from the Preclassic Era, where I found female figures with voluptuous breasts, buttocks, and tummies. Often called Venus of Willendorf figures, historians theorised the emphasis on sexual attributes denoted the importance of fertility, idealised in women.

Mexican indigenous culture was not the only historical source of female effigies: in fact, archaeologists had found them in different parts of the world. In the 2012 BBC documentary *Divine Women: When God Was a Girl*, Oxford scholar Bettany Hughes said, 'Of all the images of the human form found in sacred spots between 30,000 BC and 1000 BC, over 90 per cent are of the female form.'

Using evidence found mostly in Mesopotamia, many historians agreed that humans evolved from nomadic communities to agrarian around 7000–5000 BC when we discovered how to farm. Survival was vulnerable to food's availability; humans were dependent upon the earth's provision. Before scientific knowledge of conception, the ability to give birth and bring forth new life was seen as a uniquely female power. A supernatural mystery of creation. Women were the source of life.

Informed by this existing knowledge base, people prayed to goddesses. The Valley of Mexico was once home to numerous holy mothers. Teteoinnan, whose name meant 'Mother of the Gods'; Toci, 'Our Grandmother' — and many more, including Tonantzin. As I peered at engorged bellies and rounded breasts, I felt thrilled that the figure of God, the ultimate creator, the image of power and perfection, had been a woman.

Heart pounding, I searched for the exit. Realisation after realisation rolled in like furious waves pounding a cliff. *Boom* — God wasn't always a man. *Boom* — the image of God evolved through history.

God was constructed. *Boom.*

Into bright sunshine, blinking at the blur of families, roller-bladers, dancers. By the park's wrought-iron gates, I bought a cup of sliced mango, pawpaw, and watermelon for twelve pesos and watched a cheery, thick-moustached street seller squeeze lime and chilli powder over my snack. Chewing spicy, acidic fruit as I walked, I realised that, like Dolores Whelan said, I'd thought Christianity 'fell out of the sky'. That it had been ordained and delivered by the Supreme Being, pure from human influence. It was baffling to consider that religions might be a response to a people's environment and social conditions.

Chilli made me hiccup. Ancient mother goddesses existed across the world. Yemaja in the Nigerian Yoruba tradition. Cybele, the Anatolian mother goddess. Kunapipi in the Roper and Rose River areas of Australia's Northern Territory. And in some Australian Indigenous cultures, the Rainbow Serpent creator spirit was female. But Christian patriarchy had done its best to erase them and secure the Father's place.

Skipping down subway stairs to the sound of squealing brakes, I threw the sticky cup into a bin as hot wind blew curls from my face. I wondered, as I pushed into the packed women's carriage, what would happen if there was an earthquake while I was underground. Earthquakes took things you thought were solid, and shook them fiercely. They made them fragile. And what was once set in stone crumbled.

I woke, sensing a presence in the dark room. I switched on the lamp — nobody. I could have sworn my Husband had leant on the door with crossed arms, watching me.

It was 3.00 am, December 10. Two days until pilgrimage. Rolling onto my stomach, I yanked my backpack on the floor towards me and pulled out a plastic bag of half-crushed *gorditas*, sweet floury cakes from a roadside stall. I leant back on my pillow and chewed as I squinted at my phone screen to re-read yesterday's messages. Laura, my contact, confirmed: it was happening. I would join a group from Santa Rosa, a town in the mountains. I searched on Google Maps. We would walk twenty-seven kilometres.

I pulled another biscuit from the bag. Even though I'd been hoping I could pray to La Virgen, I didn't identify with her. Maybe I was just another white girl trying to impose my ideals on a culture that didn't belong to me. But the whole Mother thing put me off. I wasn't maternal; I could barely take care of myself, much less other people. Dolores Whelan had told me that the qualities of the divine feminine were compassion, nurture, generosity, and trust. Some Mexican women looked up to La Virgen as a role model. While other cultures revered a she-wolf or mother-bear, this focus on kindness and patience seemed an ideal of obedient womanhood, designed to divorce women from potency and rage.

I was reminded of the Irish American feminist theologian Mary Daly, whose book *Beyond God the Father* critiqued Catholicism's patriarchal values. She wrote that the Mother Mary was a 'remnant of the ancient image of the Mother Goddess, enchained'.

Like Brigit, La Virgen de Guadalupe had been dethroned from ultimate power. This did not sit well. This whole yonder-shining-light thing wasn't providing any easy answers.

Still, I was looking forward to witnessing the devotion of Mexican believers, and being a part of their adventure. I opened a magazine I'd bought at the museum gift shop to an article on *la peregrinación*. Pilgrimage was a journey made on foot from home to a sacred place. Leaving home — like *The Pilgrim's Progress*, like my trip — was meant to move a believer beyond the known, to open herself to the unfamiliar and therefore new insight. The December 12 pilgrimage to La Virgen de Guadalupe and her basilica, wrote anthropologist María J. Rodríguez-Shadow, was specifically in search of atonement, redemption, and miracles. By nature, it was supposed to take many hours or days, and to incorporate deprivation and suffering as penance.

'These severe conditions are viewed with joy,' Rodríguez-Shadow wrote. 'Because they are considered to be part of the sacrifice … it is an event that must express devotion, humility and commitment so that the pilgrims can be deserving of the benevolence of the holy image that intercedes on their behalf before God.'

A rite of passage that proved the strength of the *peregrino*'s faith, the task was often motivated by pragmatic requests: a promotion, a harvest, the health or recovery of a loved one. In buses or in vans, on bicycles or on foot, pilgrims travelled in groups.

In two days, I would walk the longest distance I'd ever gone with strangers through a dark city. My 'training' had been wandering along CDMX's traffic-fumed footpaths and highway overpasses. What the hell was I doing? I wiped crumbs from my sheet, turned out the lamp, and stared into black, trying to ignore the scrape of fear at my ribs.

The city rested in cool shadow before sunlight pushed through milky smog. After an afternoon nap, I walked to the Metro, my backpack filled with a water bottle, dried fruit, and a jacket. The women's carriage was a beauty salon: a teenager curled her eyelashes; another applied thick pink lipstick in a hand mirror. The train sped up, subterranean wind pushing through half-open windows. I placed my hand protectively over my phone in my pocket as the crowd tightened, then alighted at my station and hurried up the steep stairwell to ground level. Laura, the friend of the friend of the friend, met me at the entrance with a tight hug. Together, we would go into the mountains.

She hailed a lurching, packed bus, and turned her round cheeks and gold-tipped curls towards me. Over the two-hour trip, Laura prepped me on my fellow pilgrims. Santa Rosa Xochiac was at the south-western edge of CDMX, she said, near a national park called Desert of the Lions.

'The people of Santa Rosa are proud of being from this town,' she said, raising her voice above the bus' grunting motor. I gripped the metal bar of the seat in front to steady myself against abrupt braking. 'A family, the Mendozas, maintains the shrine of La Virgen in the town, so it is important they have representatives on tonight's pilgrimage.'

I followed Laura out the side door. The bus belched into dusk's dark haze, and I sucked in clean, silent air. Below, city lights twinkled. We marched higher into the mountains, the temperature dropping with each step. Santa Rosa's main street was decorated with green, red, and white bunting, lanterns were strung between two-storey buildings, and shops burst with Christmas tinsel and La Virgen prints. Every thirty seconds, fireworks exploded with an invisible *crack-boom* and smoke dispersed in the sky. *No vivas con miedo*, I whispered.

Laura turned a corner into a church car park. Thirteen men and women in their early twenties were waiting beside an empty shrine: the statue of La Virgen was strapped to a young man's back, golden rays spiking around his broad chest. Laura introduced me to the group — I thought she was coming, too, but it appeared I had misunderstood: she was not; she would take the bus back to the city; I was on my own. Everybody looked at me, the *guera*, the white girl, and I was asked to speak, but I couldn't remember my Spanish, so stuttered, '*Gracias!*'

A grey-haired woman made a speech, and the elders and Laura waved us off. We began. I followed the group through shadows. Townspeople gathered on street corners to watch our procession; children ran beside us, yelling; a pastor preached from a makeshift pavement pulpit; a man burnt a fire at the end of his driveway, arms crossed. A red Volkswagen bug trundled past, and confetti erupted from its window. The descending road twisted towards a vista that revealed the lights of twenty-one million people, glittering in dark.

Fireworks in the inky sky. Two nights ago, a green comet had flown over Mexico City, and tonight a yellow crescent moon hid behind the clouds — the same shape as La Virgen's moon. A fluttery lightness in my chest, my limbs afloat. Despite my fear, joining the path of millions of believers felt shrouded in cosmic significance.

The Santa Rosa crew chattered and joked. Couples walked in tandem; three men carried a towel-sized sheet imprinted with La Virgen on their backs. The young man carrying her statue led us all, and we followed her down a rocky, uneven road, the men pointing phone torches at the ground for the women to find the way. Lupita, long dark hair, pulled me by my backpack from the path of a car. I looked back at her with a sheepish smile. She rolled her eyes.

I had planned to conduct interviews on this eight-hour journey, but my language proficiency was a delusion. I asked a question and received a polite answer, and I nodded, too proud to say I didn't understand. I walked through the darkness, following the feet of the person in front. Idiot, idiot. Why was I always so unprepared?

A tall man in a black jumper, Horacio, played *ranchera* music from a speaker in his backpack. Playful horns echoed into the still night.

'*Quieres un cigarro?*' Ricardo dashed through the group with puppy enthusiasm, offering cigarettes to everyone. I stopped walking so he could cup his thin hand against the wind, flick the lighter close to my lips. I leant my head back and blew strawberry-flavoured smoke into the violet sky.

We climbed a steep, rocky path between two roads, ferns brushing at our calves, and then hopped over a barricade to

Autopista México-Marquesa, a freeway with an 80 km/h speed limit. Stretching out into single file to pass through a tunnel, we pressed tight to the concrete wall and emerged to Santa Fe's modern skyscrapers and neon global brands. Trucks, vans, semi-trailers roared past. Horacio told us to cross the road, communicating with whistles that cut through traffic noise — long for stop, short for go.

'I have fear of the automobiles,' I told Ricardo in Spanish. He replied that everything would be all right, the eighteen-year-old thereby establishing himself as my ally and confidant on this trip. Pilgrimage-mobiles roared past, elaborate flower or balloon wreaths bursting high from bonnets, back windows scrawled with pueblo names: Palos Altos, Acatitlán … Some buses crawled, flashing multicoloured fairy lights, passengers sprawled on metal roofs.

Pilgrimage on foot was a rhythmic, physical meditation. Long distances gained by small steps. A rosary hung from La Virgen's neck, swinging with the cadence of the leader's walk, *clack, clack, clack*. She held a small white globe, and someone had tucked into her arm a fibreglass rose that faded from blue to green to red. The entire world was reduced to that sound, *clack, clack, clack*, and her glowing rose.

As soon as we hit the edge of the city, Carlos unstrapped La Virgen from his back, and rested her against the closed shutter of a burger store. Everyone squatted on the curb. Only two hours in, my legs ached. Ricardo ducked into a *tienda* to buy tequila and a lemon soft drink, Squirt, and doled it out like a priest.

'*Salud!*' We drank from plastic cups and shared a bag of spicy potato chips. Mexican communion.

'*Te quieres llevar la virgen?*' Ricardo asked, and the effigy was strapped to my back. María, in pink tracksuit pants and a fuchsia beanie, held out her hand for my backpack. We returned to the freeway, and Ricardo walked in front, holding a torch out so incoming cars could see us.

'*Vamos!*' he said. 'Let's go,' grinning, beckoning, wild.

The 1.5-metre sculpture was nailed to a wooden rectangle. I bent forward so it didn't knock the backs of my knees, holding the straps at my shoulders with the posture of an old man.

Ricardo checked in: '*Todo bien?*'

Yes, everything was fine, I replied, refusing to admit weakness, convinced this was a test. Luckily a strap broke, and Ricardo lowered La Virgen onto the road beside a forest, where the men gathered to fix it. A few people sneaked away to pee in darkness, and Horacio pulled on the newly tied strap. We began again. Half an hour later, I regretted not joining the forest pissers. My bladder pushed against the belt of my jeans. Why did I let Ricardo pour me that third tequila?

Fireworks *crack-boomed* nearby. Festivities began at 10.00 pm at the basilica with mariachi bands and dancing. But we were hours away.

We passed our first support team at hour four on Avenida Paseo de la Reforma. Volunteers at a trestle table pushed sandwiches and water bottles into plastic bags with practised swiftness. While pilgrimage was an act of devotion, for others, handing drinks and food to pilgrims was a faithful act of service. I remembered my third rule of pilgrimage (*Never steal, even if you have no money*) and thanked La Virgen for the food from strangers.

Near a Chapultepec Park stadium, we sat on concrete benches, chewing baguettes stuffed with frijoles and queso. Couples leant against each other's shoulders. The forest-lungs chilled the air, and María pulled on pink mittens. I buttoned my coat, recognising the shadowy trees I'd passed days ago in bright sunlight. When we rose, my back was leaden, my calves tight.

But bladder pain was the biggest threat. The need to pee was so exquisite, so all-encompassing, that it summoned my attention to my lower torso with a fiery urgency. I could think of nothing else, and breathed long and slow. Our path through the centre of Mexico City yielded no bathrooms, only eerie, quiet streets. I couldn't bring myself to falter in Spanish, too embarrassed and uncomfortable with the group, who saw me as a burden. Instead, I remembered suffering was sacrifice that illustrated my commitment and faith. Could this extreme need to pee be my road of trials?

We passed a sign for Librería Porrúa, the bookshop on the lake. I summoned all the words I knew for lake, hypnotising myself away from bladder-press, and whispered in steady rhythm: *lago, lough, lake, lago, lough, lake.* The street before us was dream's dark soup, orange lights floated in black. *Lago, lough, lake.* Nothing else. Only this holy passage. *Lago lough lake.*

The *crack-boom* of a firework. My attention snapped back to sore feet, and I watched the effigy in front of me, *clack-clack-clack*, left and right with the cadence of Ricardo's steps. She knew about my feet, my bladder. My search.

At 2.30 am, I experienced La Virgen's miracle. An apartment-complex guard was generously providing his private bathroom for pilgrims, and we joined the queue of strangers dozily leaning against a wall. After thirty minutes' wait, I thanked the guard and entered the tiny cubicle, and then I thanked La Virgen that there was only a small smear of shit on the seat, and prayed to her for strength, that my ruined legs would hold my arse above the seat for the entire duration of this marathon piss.

The flush, the zip of my fly — I strode into the night with supernatural renewal. My whole torso was light. Two kilometres left? Ha! I could fly.

Ricardo was lying against Lupita on the pavement, snoring. María roused them, and we found ourselves on Calzado de los Misterios, yellow streetlights shining ethereally in fog. A man in a grey jumpsuit stood on a dump truck full of rubbish, dancing to music from the cabin's radio. A river of people emerged from black mist: endless shuffling feet and backpacks draped with textiles of La Virgen; teenage boys carrying cardboard signs and red and blue tinsel. Some people were in groups and some on their own, some joking boisterously, some hunched and bedraggled, each carrying hometown banners and rolled sleeping bags atop backpacks. A woman with dark hair and wide shoulders moved forward on her knees, back bent, shoulders shifting with each shuffle. Two men took turns laying blankets beneath her. This was the practice of prostration, of approaching La Virgen *de rodillas*, on the knees. Furrowed brow, lips tight, she whimpered with each step. Her heightened suffering would curry extra favour for her requests to be granted. Images I'd seen from previous years depicted proud pilgrims displaying blackened, filthy knees, pink where the skin had been rubbed raw by hours scraping over asphalt, concrete, dirt.

More volunteers — pastries, tequila, saccharine Nescafé from silver vats. We accepted them all, threw them into our mouths, but never stopped. Police watched the endless flow, moustaches curled in contempt; cleaners in yellow jackets swept styrofoam cups and food wrappers into piles as high as my chest.

Everyone checked in. *Como vas? Estas cansado?* How are you? Are you tired? I stumbled, María took my arm. At 3.30 am, we came to an abrupt stop 500 metres from the basilica, the thick crowd scraping forward several metres every ten minutes. Tepeyac rose above thousands of heads, its 300-year-old cathedral sparkling in velvet black. We were almost there, oh God, almost there.

A man with a long moustache and lined forehead appeared to be asleep standing up. Leant against roadside shopfronts, hundreds and hundreds of tents and blankets covered lumpen bodies. Horacio's speaker battery died, and a silence settled over the tight crowd. A sign on a metal pole — *Peregrinación de Cholula*. Shit, that was over 100 kilometres away.

We entered the gates at 4.20 am into a square the size of three football fields, breathing air thick from vendors' frying oil. Souvenir stands sold prints of La Virgen beside red-cheeked baby dolls and emaciated figures on crosses, Jesus' naughty bits hidden by tiny purple-sequined cloth. The sea of *peregrinos* lit candles, sat on folding chairs, or nestled in sleeping bags on the hard ground.

We entered the basilica. I suppressed the urge to clutch at Ricardo's hand. Families snored in pews; warm, soporific air settled like a blanket. We limped down the centre. There, at the back of the massive church, above a Mexican flag: there she was.

La Virgen de Guadalupe. The tilma. The vision of the Mother of God, allegedly imprinted on Juan Diego's robe almost 500 years ago. I followed the back of Ricardo's head, past the front of the altar, where grim nuns in grey habits held out bowls for tithes. The push of the crowd streamed around the altar to the left, and twisted to an underground passageway onto a tourist conveyor belt.

The travelator inched from left to right, bodies pressed on all sides. An ensemble of hands holding camera-phones. I squinted at her face, metres above, trying to summon a sense of significance, frantically searching in my exhausted body for a flash of ecstasy. La Virgen de Guadalupe, in whom lived the ancient practice of the Aztecs, who held remnants of the indigenous Mother Goddess Tonantzin.

'Thank you,' I said to her in my heart.

A spike of panic as I looked for my group. Sweet Ricardo waved his sky-blue beanie, arm high above the crowd. All of us reunited, we spilled from the basilica's hot womb into the cool black dawn.

before

The Awakening

It happened in the winter of my fifteenth year.

Religion didn't come from family tradition, though certain things prepared me for teenage revelation. Mum fostered a compassion that supported her work nursing at a rehabilitation hospital, reading Dalai Lama and *Chicken Soup for the Soul* books. Auntie Liz introduced my brother and I to angels, an afterlife, and a sense of the infinite at backyard fire circles and camping trips. She taught us to read mystical significance from encounters with kangaroos, koalas, and kookaburras, inspired by stories she'd learnt from First Nations wise women.

My childhood was blessed with a spirituality of fables and fairytales. The fantastic lived in the everyday. In early primary school, I chewed through Enid Blyton novels where worlds hovered on clouds, chairs flew, animals spoke. Mum invented bedtime tales. Nan convinced me tiny people called 'the borrowers' stole her crochet needles and balls of wool, only to return them when she no longer needed them. Dad chomped carrots my brother and I left out for Christmas reindeer and drank Santa's milk. I piled my arms high with library books.

The world was full of magic: you only needed eyes to see. Stuffed toys came alive after midnight. I nurtured a distrust of furniture, who were mischievous, sometimes malevolent spirits (a wheeled chair at my grandparents' house featured in several nightmares). Mum and Auntie Liz encouraged my fairy obsession with picture books and films, and taught me to make a ring of stones in our creekside garden with gifts of cake inside. When morning came, the circle held only crumbs.

I knew nocturnal possums could have gobbled the snacks, but I *hoped* it was the fairies. These outcomes existed in parallel, unified realities: the seen and the unseen. The possible and the impossible. This childhood magical thinking gave me two things: a powerful identification with the mythic, and an active imagination. Both would bolster my later spiritual experiences.

Early adolescence saw me retreat into the sanctuary of books. The first two years of high school were especially torturous: first of all, my twin brother separated from me. Together, we grew in the womb, suckled at our mother's teat; as toddlers, we slept in the same room; at kindergarten, he followed in my wake. There was a dualism to being a twin. Like Plato's halved souls, we appeared as two complementary elements of a whole. Yin and yang, male and female. His thin white limbs, my plump tanned legs. His loose brown curls, my blonde-white frizz. The naughty boy, tree climber, class clown; the good girl, quiet reader, obedient student. I unfurled like a petal in response to teachers' praise, while Ben became boisterous and antagonistic. We became defined in opposition to the other.

As we bumbled into adolescence, he withdrew. I wasn't invited. He slammed his door and turned Limp Bizkit tapes up so loud the bookshelves in the lounge room shook. An argument over the family computer descended into a ferocious battle: he whacked my back with solid fists, and my only weapon was to bite, leaving teeth marks in his shoulder. Mum sent us to our rooms howling. It was our last physical fight, and I realised he was no longer a weedy child, but stronger than me. In my defeat, and in line with socialised gender, I externalised strength and aggression as male.

As my companionship with my twin brother faded, I was also distressed by my changing relationship with my parents, the nurse and the butcher. They both came from families with strict patriarchs, and thus refused to pass down hard laws, preferring to be subtle moral guides. When I was small, Dad would arrive home with his bootcut Levi's stiff with the aroma of fat and blood. Sometimes, his left hand was stitched, and he let me touch the black curls of his forearm, asking me to be gentle as I turned his wrist to examine sutures stained dark. He warned me to take care with sharp blades. And throughout my primary-school years, Mum and I visited the library together. She browsed shelves, dark curly hair pinned with decorative chopsticks, milk-chocolate lipstick above her nurse uniform: striped white-and-green shirt and sensible black pants. She showed me books about my body, puberty, the world. When I started menstruating, she took me out for dinner and wrote me a letter in her special calligraphy. The most important words were not spoken; instead, they became elegant marks on a page.

But as we entered adolescence, Mum and Dad slowly stepped back as authorities in our lives. The year before I started going to church, they sat Ben and I down: it was time, they said, to tell us they smoked dope to relax.

I'd always half-known. After bedtime, I heard a bubbling over the TV's ad-blare, punctuated by forceful coughs. In search of the hidden chocolate stash when nobody was home, I'd stood on a chair to open a high cupboard, and spotted a black bong peeking from behind neon packets of lollies. Once, I found dried green herbs in a small silver tin, and smelt that herbaceous musk. I jumped off the chair, heart thudding, nausea clutching my throat.

I'd half-known, but after Mum and Dad confessed, I *knew*. In Health class, Mrs Kennedy showed pictures of brains after twenty years of daily marijuana use. They were cloudy grey like overcooked vegetables. Some kids smoked joints at the school gates, but they were Trouble.

Mum and Dad kept me warm and safe. They gave us everything we needed to be healthy, strong, and loved; braces and sports uniforms and guitar lessons. But by acknowledging their drug use, they revealed their transgression of what seemed good and right. I no longer trusted their authority.

Amid adolescent rites of passage — first period, first job, first hand job in the bushes at a party — I harboured a distinct terror of being ordinary. I began to believe my parents had surrendered to Suburban Life. Tea Tree Gully's safe streets and shopping centres were eerily dull, like the pastel homes of Tim Burton's *Edward Scissorhands*, and its mediocre landscape fostered a robotic apathy in the hearts of its inhabitants.

Whereas I was undeniably alive. Each day, I felt my skin would burst from all I felt. I was too old for fairies, but still yearned for magic. Where was the poetry, excitement, hope? I wished someone would spot me in the crowd, like the model scouts I read about in *Dolly* magazine. Someone who knew I was special, who could tell I was destined to be extraordinary.

I no longer felt a sense of belonging to my family, and felt like an outsider in friendships. School was ruled by social currency. My best friend, Becky, and I leafed through magazines, examining Pink and Christina Aguilera's flat bellies and hypnotic breasts. In the second year of high school, Becky grew tall and sprouted double Ds, and discovered how to get boys' phone numbers. Popularity depended on girls' body shapes, our navy skirts as short as the principal allowed. The imperative was to construct ourselves into something a boy might want. Teenage desire was male approval, which conferred personal value. The boys in my classes were fallen angels who emanated dirt scent and dark heat. They incited such wanting and fear that I fell silent whenever one spoke to me. Which wasn't often.

Make-up, and the transformation from girlhood to beauty, was a humiliating ritual I never got right. Cheap orange foundation line at my jaw, clumped mascara, black kohl ringed around blue eyes — a costume that never fit. When no one was home, I took off my bralette in the bathroom mirror and examined puffy caramel nipples. Boobs, could you even call them that? They were *wrong*. I was exiled from womanhood. No matter how much sweet perfume I sprayed on my light-blue polo shirt, boys didn't want me. In sexuality's economy, I was poor.

At fifteen, I entered the apex of my despair. Floating between social groups, I felt rejected and victimised, contemptuous of everyone — yet still wanted to be invited to their parties. My brother, on the other hand, was having a great time.

During the holidays, a car with a broken muffler belched down our street to whisk him away. Ben told me of cheering crowds, powerful worship music, American preachers. Two thousand young people in a megachurch called Paradise, lifting their hands and yelling for Jesus. The mosh pit, the jumping, the sweat. He handed me flyers promoting special events. After a while, I stopped throwing them in the bin.

It was all because of a man called the Pastor. He put on lunch-time games — couch races and soccer with giant blow-up balls — or invited musician friends to play indie rock on the assembly stage. Covers of The Vines and The Strokes reverberated between two-storey buildings while the Pastor cooked a free sausage sizzle. He ran the local Uniting Church's youth group, and was employed as our school's chaplain. (Now called 'pastoral-support workers', chaplains were employed by the school to give counselling and spiritual guidance to the students. Government funding for this religious service has been contested in recent years.)

Attracted by the smell of barbecued snags, loud music, and the promise of adventure, my brother and his friends had started attending the Pastor's youth group. Ben came home close to midnight on Friday nights, grunting goodnight as he passed Mum, Dad, and I in front of the TV. He became the Pastor's protégé — in Christian language, his 'disciple' — which meant special attention. The Pastor picked him up early before school for Friday morning prayer group, on Tuesday nights for Bible study, and on weekends for special adventures for just the two of them, climbing hillsides in Morialta Falls conservation park. The Pastor resented rules and courted recklessness, preferring the electricity of danger: once, my brother came home with a burst eardrum after rock climbing then jumping three metres into a pool and landing sideways.

I felt betrayed, by my parents, my brother, my body. But the day I met Ben's mysterious mentor, everything changed.

My English teacher recruited me as an extra for a rehearsal of *The Glass Menagerie*. At lunchtime, I pushed open the auditorium door, sending a beam of harsh sunlight into the dark, and there he was: shaggy black hair, sharp cheekbones, a close-shorn beard, hazel eyes. Leaning back on his chair, ankles crossed, resting a pair of black Converses on a cafe table. Hands clasped behind his head as if he'd been waiting for me. The Pastor.

The door slammed, and I blinked in the dim, high room. The teacher brought me to his table and turned back to the stage. With an enthusiasm I'd never received from a handsome grown-up *man*, the Pastor jumped up to greet me.

'Hi! What's your name?'

Something within me stood to attention. He looked inside me, and with his eyes he showed me he had a soul, and he knew I had a soul, too; he knew that I was extraordinary.

I didn't know then, but I would follow this feeling for the next thirteen years.

After our first meeting, I spotted the Pastor at school assemblies wearing patterned vintage shirts and a beard of varying length. He exuded positivity and glowed with a metaphysical spark. There was a rumour he was a spoken-word poet in a jazz band that played at a bar in Hindley St, Adelaide's dirty downtown.

A few weeks later, I had another opportunity to speak to him. Resigned to failure in the social ecosystem, I sought solace in the library at mornings and lunchtimes. One Thursday after the home-time bell, I lurked between shelves, running fingertips along books' spines. Afterwards, pulling myself up a concrete stairwell with a new novel, a classroom door slammed above. The Pastor shot down like a lightning bolt, clutching a stack of flyers and packaging tape against his White Stripes T-shirt. He jerked to a stop when he saw me, my eyes level with sky-blue flares.

'Lou!' His face opened into a smile above me. 'We're having a shindig at youth group tomorrow.' He bent to hand me a flyer, and as I took it, he stepped down, towards me, and put a hand on my shoulder. 'You should come!'

—

Lights dimmed; everything went black. The bass was so loud it reverberated in my chest. A guitar wail burning with distortion sang out; fog-machine smoke filtered through the rows of chairs, flashing beneath purple and blue lights.

Becky raised her eyebrow at me and leant in close to shout, 'Better than Mum's fusty old church, hey?'

Older kids filed to the front, pushing, throwing their hands in the air, a single writhing mass. The shrill electronic wail became pure and high, before a tall, thin guitarist with scruffy hair launched into a dirty riff, and the drummer, black T-shirt tight on his biceps, beat out a furious rhythm.

'Yo!' The Pastor ran onstage. 'We come here to praise God for what he has done. Now, let's party!'

'*Everybody jump around in the house of God*,' the guitarist yelled. The mass exploded. A gravity pulled; I wanted to enter the throng, to lose myself, but I lingered in the seats. Reading the words on the screen, we sang: *We need you, Jesus, you are everything*. I'd heard similar words at Becky's family church. I'd also heard the Pastor say God's name at lunchtimes. But the message had always seemed to be for somebody else.

Here, now, I shaped my lips around the words, felt the weight of them on my tongue, and sang under my breath: 'I want you, Lord.'

In group ceremonial settings, actions and language have a collectively agreed significance. I mimicked movements without understanding their meaning. Bathed in green light, I began to sway and held my forearms straight before me, tilted my palms to the ceiling.

The Pastor returned to the stage, telling us we could sit. The audience settled into darkness, watching his illuminated body. Beard dark and rugged, he prayed into the microphone, voice deep.

'Holy God, we thank you for everyone here in this place. Thank you for blessing us with your presence. We need you so much, God, we need you so much. I pray you'll speak through me tonight.'

The air changed. Everyone's energy was directed towards the Pastor.

The name of this youth group took its inspiration from the Bible, he said, opening his own little book. 'Romans 12:2. Do not conform to the patterns of this world, but be transformed by the renewing of your mind!'

God wasn't an old man in the sky, a booming voice of condemnation! His presence was here.

'Many of you know I'm also a chaplain at the local high school.'

In the third row, my brother and his friends whooped.

'Yeah!' The Pastor pumped his arm. 'And look, a couple of years ago, I was in a bad place. A really bad place. I was an alcoholic. I don't drink now, but I was using alcohol to deal with my problems. And I was so low that one night, ah,' his voice grew taut, 'I was in the kitchen, after midnight. And I found the knife. I slumped down on the floor, and held the sharp edge against my wrist.' His words shook. 'But I heard a voice. The voice of God. He told me to stop. That he had a *plan* for me.

'Later that week, one of the students felt like he could no longer live. The poor guy was struggling with depression and didn't know where to turn. Somehow, he found a shotgun. And as the final bell rang, and everyone left their classes …' He swallowed; the darkness throbbed. 'He shot himself.'

A girl gasped.

'In front of 500 students. Teenagers were lined outside my door. All day long. I'm the only counsellor in that school, and it was my job to support them.'

All fifty of us were silent, captivated by the sob that threatened each sentence.

'And I knew, I *knew*, that God had called me to *this life*. He created me for *this time*. I knew I had a *purpose*. Friends, the only thing that got me up each morning was the love of God. And the knowledge that he has a purpose for my life, a *plan* for my life.'

Jesus died so we could live and have eternal life. He took on the sins of the world so we could have a relationship with the Father. He *saved* us. But we must accept his invitation!

The Pastor was seductive. He told us what we wanted, and promised to provide it. He pointed us to God. All we had to do was surrender to the Father.

The hairs on the back of my neck stood up.

'If you have a hunger. If you feel lost. If you feel alone. If you feel like you are missing something in your life. If you, like me, tried to fill it with alcohol, or maybe with drugs, or sex. You! Have! A God-shaped hole in your heart!' A crescendo. 'God is here with us now! And he is calling your name! And he wants to wrap his arms around *you*!'

The band returned, a wall of noise that wrapped around my body.

The Pastor shouted, punching the air with each holy declaration. 'And God wants to say to you, you are loved! You are loved! You are loved! He has a plan for your life! He wants to wrap his arms around you and immerse you in the love of the Father! He will fill the hole in your heart! He will make you whole again! And all you have to do is open! Your! Arms!

'If your heart is beating fast …' The Pastor's voice lowered again; the music slowed. 'God is speaking to you right now.' A pause. 'Come up to the altar. Give your heart to Jesus. Accept the love of God.'

Becky elbowed me, giggled. It wasn't a big deal; we'd responded at her church before, even if we hadn't really meant it. Maybe we could go up? But we couldn't be the first. Some brave soul rose and walked down the aisle, eyes on the floor, sniffing. Becky stood; I followed. We emerged from the shadows into coloured lights. She was beside me as I knelt before the cross.

'Jesus, I want you,' I whispered, and to my surprise, I started crying. The band was loud, the group behind me stood again, a chorus, *You're all that I want, You're all that I need, You're all that I live for in this world*, pushing fists into the air, I needed him, I needed him to be whole, I needed him to save me from loneliness, from failure, from my stupid body, I didn't want to be empty anymore, I didn't want to be alone anymore, I didn't want to be alone, the Pastor rested an open palm on my shoulder, shouting, 'Jesus! Jesus!'

As the band quietened, the ten of us who had responded to the altar call were ushered into a side room. I blinked in fluoro lights, wiping tears in a panic. My heart pounding, my limbs light. I felt propelled by exhilaration and hope and longing with no idea of my direction, like taking a waterslide in pitch black. I relinquished myself into their hands.

A twenty-five-year-old youth leader with large breasts and a dark-brown bob met me. Together, Jane and I prayed the Sinner's Prayer and declared Jesus Christ as Lord and Saviour of my life.

Words as prayer as invocation. Now, God would fill my emptiness. Jane wrapped her arms around my shoulders, holding me, her breath on my neck. My salvation declared out loud, I became a daughter of God and entered into his family.

Learning to Be Holy

I fell in love with the Heavenly Father. Who painted the stars in the night sky? He did. Who designed me before I was born, who could count every hair on my head, who said I was wonderfully made? He did. And he laid out everything according to his marvellous, mystical will.

Finally, somebody loved me and would never abandon me. One essence, split into three: I praised the Lord, listened to the Holy Spirit, but my relationship with the beloved was personified in Jesus Christ. Prayer was a conversation; he sat beside me in my empty car, or perched on the end of my bed as I wept.

Jesus also gave me eyes to see. He fed 5,000 from five loaves of bread and two fish. He healed the sick and resurrected the dead. He walked on water. Nothing was impossible, because he held God's miraculous power in his hands, and I could, too.

This lined up with my conviction that the world was inherently magic. The seen and the unseen; the possible and impossible. There was a parallel, invisible reality that existed beneath the surface, and now, through prayer, scripture, and song, I could transcend the material. I could touch the spiritual realm.

My social life shifted. A few months after I was saved, I followed my brother to Sunday-night church. Soon, I went every week — not knowing I was beginning a rhythm that would anchor my life for over a decade. Mum came, too. She told us it was because she liked the singing; later, I learnt she was wary of priests, and wanted to meet the people who had rapidly altered my and Ben's priorities. After a year, she preferred to just drop us off in the church car park. The pastors seemed nice enough.

With constant exposure to this new doctrine, I memorised phrases verbatim and allowed them to integrate into my speech. 'Jesus came into my heart', 'the Holy Spirit spoke to me', 'I surrendered to the love of the Father'. At first, I didn't quite know what they meant, but as I heard them repeated in particular contexts, I began to understand my new community's language. It allowed me to verbalise deep inner experience, and became a common tongue. As I reproduced the terminology, I cemented my connection with others in the group.

There were always opportunities for advancement: fortnightly Bible studies with girls at Jane's house, an after-school course to which the Pastor invited a select few. Diversion from group social norms wasn't punished vocally; instead, obedience was rewarded. When leaders decided a teenager was ready to 'handle the responsibility' (code for they could be trusted to regurgitate the ideology), they were given a platform: share a testimony on Friday night or perform a ten-minute sermon on Sunday mornings. To speak from a raised platform, to broadcast your words to a silent audience of thirty or fifty people — maybe even 200 at Sunday church — was a taste of the Pastor's privilege. We were expected to desire hierarchical significance. Comply, and the stage is yours. Obey, and maybe one day you'll be like the Pastor.

Another reward was special access to him. When I signed up to his after-school course, he let us rest our feet on chairs and chew snacks as he taught from the whiteboard. It was a hot summer month, and he wore a navy singlet, removed from the formal context of Friday nights or chaplain responsibilities. My new friends and I scribbled on photocopied handouts as we looked up New Testament verses from the chapel's rubber-covered Bibles. The Pastor taught us the religion's fundamentals, explaining spiritual paradoxes that I thought poetic in their mystic impossibility. God the Father was always present. Jesus was the Son of God, fully divine and fully man. Sin was a selfish act, where we chose to follow our own desires instead of God's. This separated us relationally from God, and caused pain and damage in our lives. But Jesus' sacrifice — his death on the cross — meant he was a stand-in for the punishment for our sins. And because he was resurrected, death had no power and the power of sin was destroyed. Therefore, through Jesus we were saved, and could have a relationship with God. The Pastor said this was the greatest desire of our heart.

The devil was responsible for all the bad in the world. He haunted our consciousness and tempted us to sin by making it taste sweet. But we must stand strong, the Pastor said, for we were called to a life of holiness; we should follow the laws of God. We were unworthy, weak, and easily swayed by Satan, the thief in the night, yet God loved us still. The best response to this grace was to become Jesus' disciple. To be holy, then, was to be separate to and distinguished from sinners, by our Christ-like actions.

In stained school uniforms, we stood and sang. Without the pageantry of a full band, just a singer and his acoustic guitar, I couldn't hide my out-of-tune voice. I told God he was wonderful, that I loved him, that I was grateful he sacrificed his only son so I could live. So I could learn to be holy.

The Christian bookstore-cum-cafe smelt of reheated lasagne. Children screamed from a coloured playground. Today was a new Christian's rite of passage: Jane had invited three of us from my Bible study group to choose our first Bibles. We passed the Christian Living section; then Spiritual Growth; Heaven, Hell, and the Supernatural; Prayer and Prophecy; Men and Women. Bible college resources, too, books of history and etymology and theology. Though the bookstore's American-esque sentimentality chafed, with its pastel magnets and saccharine catchphrases in frames, I was thrilled to enter a network of knowledge. The family of God came with an inheritance of mythology, a suite of parables and story, and a framework to understand the world. It promised a shared meaning and collective identity that would unite me with my brothers and sisters in Christ.

We stood before four tall wooden shelves with holy books in varied colours and sizes. Different translations, from old-fashioned *thou*'s and *thee*'s (King James Version) to colloquial paraphrases from common parlance (The Message). Bibles were the word of God, Jane explained, which was delivered from the Father to man in ancient times. His wisdom belonged to us and was there whenever we needed. We could study it to encounter God and understand his will for our lives. I scoffed at a pink girl's edition with dangling silver love hearts, choosing instead a NLV (New Living Version) with a distinguished crimson leather cover. Katie found one that highlighted Jesus' speech in red. Sally — whose Dad was a pastor, so she'd been around church forever — picked *Jesus Freaks*, a book everyone in youth group was reading about people who obeyed God in the face of persecution. Like the Apostle Paul, Sally said, one of Jesus' closest disciples: he was arrested and jailed and beaten for his faith.

'God never asks anything of us that we can't handle,' she smiled.

I flicked through a copy, and skimmed a story of a nun being raped. In the midst of the act, she told her violator that God loved him.

As we waited in line, Jane advised us to start by reading the gospels, the four chapters at the beginning of the New Testament that told the story of Jesus' life. She paid for our books, and I bought a purple cotton bracelet embroidered with WWJD. The white letters stood for What Would Jesus Do, designed to remind us to allow actions and thoughts to become holy, and to thereby internalise God's commands.

I tied the bracelet on my wrist as we left the store. To follow the will of the Lord would bring him glory. It would bring approval from my peers, my pastors, my God. I would be worthy.

That night, I read my Bible before I fell asleep.

While my school friends snuck in vodka to underage nightclubs, my new friends and I went to booze-free band nights. Adelaide's evangelical Pentecostal culture in the early 2000s was punk-adjacent and intertwined with skate culture; Bouncing Souls, NOFX, and Antiskeptic blared on Friday nights. Inter-church gatherings of suburban youth groups always saw multiple Che Guevara T-shirts. Utilising cultural symbols of rebellion, and painting Jesus as a humble yet righteous warrior, Christian culture became a stand for integrity against secular hypocrisy. Perfect for an adolescent aggrieved by losing trust in authorities. I wore my friends' band T-shirts tucked into studded belts.

Our revolution was fun. The music, the mosh pits were catharsis; we sang and danced in darkness, pushing against heaving, sweating bodies as the lead singer yelled, 'Something amazing is going to happen tonight!' We were trained to associate youth group with anticipation of magic. Anything could happen: healing, prophecy, revelation. Miracles!

Sure, there were doubts. Were there kiddy fiddlers in my

church, like kids at school joked? If God made us, why did he make us want to sin? Why couldn't he just have kept us in the Garden of Eden? And, most importantly, as a boy with a pierced tongue asked me one school lunchtime, if Jesus were to microwave a burrito so volcanically hot that it was too hot to eat, could Jesus then eat that burrito?

I learnt to accept. The paradox was the mystery; herein lay the poetry. In fact, our definition of faith was belief without proof. And my privileged life meant I'd never personally witnessed, in my family or community, acts of injustice or terror. So the biggest question — 'Why do bad things happen to good people?' — was removed from my protected, suburban existence and didn't herald enough anguish to tear down tentative belief.

Besides, any questions were sublimated in consistent messaging. Friday nights, Sunday nights, Wednesday nights. Attendance at church was imperative for indoctrination. We danced into a frenzy, then sang of longing and repentance, swaying and opening our hearts. The embodied ritual, encoded with collectively agreed meaning, made it possible to express the inexplicable and make emotional contact with God. After months of nervously studying people in church, the actions emerged spontaneously. I raised my palms to the ceiling and felt soft electricity whip up my spine, span out to every capillary and nerve. It was pleasant, almost pleasurable. I felt closest to God when swaying in blue light, hands out in supplication. Once I had a taste, I wanted more.

And then the band quietened, the lights changed, and a leader invited the emotionally pliable audience to sit. Movement and sight and sound led us into a receptive state. The Pastor — or a youth leader, or one of the senior pastors, 75 per cent of whom were men — would step onstage. And speak.

But these were the formal services. Fridays were also adventures. The Pastor hired coaches and took us to beach nights, to city-side hills where we rode large blocks of ice down dark descents, to huge bonfires in the Adelaide Hills. There was a lawsuit, I heard years later, after someone soaked a ball in methylated spirits for a game of fire soccer and it was kicked into someone else's face. The hint of danger made these nights appealing. And every one contained the spiritual imperative: a youth testimony, or a short sermon about how Jesus chose us to change the world.

The Pastor was a poet revolutionary. He hated traditional churches' hypocrisy, those Pharisees, those tax collectors, who focused on accumulation of wealth rather than Christ-like solidarity with the poor. His faith was informal — we all called Jesus by his first name — and emotionally intimate. By telling us stories of his own life, he showed us we could reveal our complete, broken selves to God and still be listened to, accepted, and loved. The Pastor's talent for validating teenagers through charismatic attention was bolstered by his position. He stood onstage, three steps above the crowd, an admired, handsome leader certain of himself and the order of the universe. The symbolic power of the microphone, the amplification of his voice, his right to tell us to 'shush': this social dynamic conferred power. And yet he knew each of us individually, and treated us with kindness. He asked me about school, discovered my love for reading, and recommended I listen to Belle and Sebastian, Arcade Fire, Muse — he was the source of my music taste for years. One Sunday, he picked Ben and I up in his battered hatchback, and when we arrived at church, he handed me old copies of *Nineteen Eighty-Four* and *The Great Gatsby*. Another time, when it was just me and him, he gave me a folder of poetry he'd written as a teenager. This was typical of the Pastor, making himself vulnerable in a way that transcended boundaries. I was never quite sure of the limits of our relationship.

Of course, I did whatever I could to receive his praise, and evangelised. Six months after I accepted Jesus into my heart, my two closest school friends, Jessica and Cherie, came to a big event. The Battle of the Bands night altered the direction of my life: I demonstrated to the Pastor that I was a star recruiter. And I saw my future husband for the first time.

My friends and I sat on a handrail next to the chapel's double doors, swinging our legs and watching punk boys on skateboards wearing low, loose pants and black-and-white checked belts, before entering the chapel.

'Hey, Jessica! Hey, Cherie!' The Pastor's exuberant face opened in delight. He stretched an arm around Cherie's shoulders — a church-appropriate side hug — and my friend complied, surprised he knew her name. 'Come in, come in!'

We sat, watching two long-haired musicians unpack acoustic guitars, a Rage Against the Machine song hammering through the sound system. Then the back doors of the church flew open. Three tall boys entered, anointed by shining light.

In black private-school blazers decorated with red insignia, they were bored and elegant. The first, with dark curly hair, five o'clock shadow, and a popped collar, twirled a drumstick in his long fingers. The second flicked a long, blond emo fringe to the side, his bass guitar slung over his shoulder on a strap. And the last: tousled dark hair, white shirt half-unbuttoned, and a hard guitar case in his left hand. Round blue eyes ablaze with fiery sorrow.

We watched them stride towards the spotlight. And one by one, these man-boy-gods and their instruments entered the stage door and disappeared.

—

Youth group became an opportunity to talk to the private-school boys. On Saturday nights, Katie and Sally and I went to their parties. On Sundays after church, we all went to McDonald's and sat on tables, throwing burger wrappers, and the drummer dropped us home in a Hondamatic held together with duct tape. I crushed on one, then another, delighting when they turned their teasing humour to me. They played in the kids' church band, so when the Sunday School pastor, a determined woman with tight ringlets, rang up my parents to ask, 'Would Louise like to teach children?', I was happy to be chosen.

Jacinta, a university student with straight silver-blonde hair, picked me up each week at 9.00 am. The first Sunday I climbed into her banged-up red Toyota, she raised an eyebrow behind large sunglasses.

'Morning,' she croaked. 'I may have had a few too many Vodka Cruisers last night.'

Despite her hangover, we set up trestle tables in the church hall, laying out coloured pencils and print-outs of shepherds, burning bushes, and stable animals. When the private-schoolboy band played, I demonstrated dance moves with exuberant arms, yelling *Jesus you're my super hero*. After song time, I balanced on a child-sized chair as Jacinta and I followed the morning's teaching. Lessons meant twisting coloured pipe-cleaners, or gluing cotton wool to loose paper that kids handed proudly to parents when church finished. Relief flooded me when adults appeared at the hall's door to release me from the prison of entertaining their children.

I disliked every child, their sticky fingers, their nostrils ringed with dried snot. Jacinta and I taught them the rudiments of Christianity: when we die, our spirits go to live with God in heaven (small hands colouring pictures of clouds, smiling angels, a throne). God made Eve from Adam's rib (a man and a woman in a forest, holding hands, leaves on their bits). And the Teaspoon Prayer, which stood for Thank you, Sorry, Please.

I began to use the Teaspoon Prayer myself. It set out a basic structure of talking to God that began with thanksgiving, had an apology in the middle, and ended with requests. I didn't question the Sorry, the idea that we must confess mistakes or failures, because I already knew that asking forgiveness for sins was a fundamental tenet of the Christian faith. Using the Teaspoon Prayer, I told Jesus all my secrets. He rested his hand on my shoulder and forgave me.

There is a shadow to all things. When I asked God to clean my heart, I believed my heart was by nature unclean. In the morning I told nine-year-olds they were born sinners and at night I told myself I had to try harder to be good. A conviction grew like a vine in my subconscious, nurtured by the soil of poor self-esteem: I was wrong. Nothing I could do was enough.

But I wanted so bad to be a good girl.

I Want the Cross

One year into Christian life, belonging was everything. I packed my new Bible for Easter Camp. Dad dropped Ben and I off at the church car park, and I spotted the blue-eyed guitarist I had a crush on. We'd been texting and meeting after school at the park. One Saturday at Katie's house, all of us were watching the footy, and He found her dad's acoustic guitar, tuned it, and plucked a Led Zeppelin tune. I watched the way His fingers dashed across the fretboard. He was full of certainty; unlike me, He didn't feel the need to please anybody. He was intense, recalcitrant, and aloof. He was irresistible.

I waved before finding Jane's car. During the hour's car ride squashed between pillows, eating lollies Katie passed from the front seat, I thought of the *Jesus Freak* nun. What would I do if someone raped me? I'd tell him God loves him, I thought, playing with my WWJD bracelet. I wasn't sure if Jesus could be raped, but that's what he would do.

When we arrived at the River Murray campsite, the girls and I reserved seats in the chapel with red spiral notebooks before rolling out sleeping bags in our dorm room. At 6.00 pm, the Pastor clanged the bell at the eating hall, summoning us to run past gum trees and the toilet block and into the meeting hall. Sally picked up her Bible, fat with fluoro-pink post-it notes and dog-eared pages, and placed it on her lap.

'All right, folks.' The Pastor was wearing a casual T-shirt and jeans, but he was quivering. His excitement was contagious, the atmosphere electric. And behind him, in the band onstage, *He* was there, long tousled hair, large palm curled around the neck of a navy electric guitar, meaty fingers shaping chords as he strummed the opening to Hillsong's song 'Awesome God'.

'Tonight! God! Is! Going! To! Show Up!'

We whooped, we yelled. My limbs felt light and floaty.

The Pastor went on: 'The Bible says that whenever two or more are gathered in his name, God is present with us. And here we are!' Cheers.

He turned and nodded to the band. 'So let's! Get! Started!'

A wall of sound. Sally and Katie and I rushed to the front.

You ask me why

Why I'm so different

Why I'm not the same as everybody else
Well something changed
It just happened
When I opened up my heart and let him in
Jesus came in
He came into my life
And I know
It never felt so good

We sang, cementing our identity with performative declarations of faith. We were not the same as the world outside — but special. After two high-energy tunes (*praise* songs), the band began a slower, contemplative song (*worship*). I shut my eyes, my breathing slowed, and I opened my arms wide with palms upturned.

'You are the universe,' we sang, repeating, repeating, repeating, tunnelling into the words, the band got louder, the sound expanded, there was nothing else but me and God, my eyes squeezed tight, I felt goosebumps on my arms. Swaying, I knocked my hand against Katie's forearm, which woke me from my inner focus. I cracked an eyelid, and could just see the Pastor, on his knees, the shaggy black of his head tilted up. The stage lights flashed blue. He glowed.

When we returned to our seats, his face was wet. He allowed tears to rest on his cheeks as he spoke with a shaking voice. Welcome, he said, to four glorious days a hundred kilometres away from school and family. Then he began the sermon.

'Take up your cross and follow me, Jesus said, and you will become fishers of men. The path of Jesus, which means acting in selfless love, is not easy, and we must be ready to sacrifice.'

To follow God's command was sacrifice. Any ensuing suffering was noble and godly. The question that came next was so gentle we could barely hear. My back arched towards him.

'Do you want the cross?' The Pastor pulled his shoulders back, lifted his chin, became fierce. 'Do you? Want? The cross?'

After what seemed like minutes of terrible quiet, a shy boy from school stood. His face ugly-red with tears, he declared with clenched fists, 'I want the cross!'

Across the room, teens moved from the comfort of their seats to follow. I felt faint as I stood into God's light.

Over the four-day weekend, friendships flowered. Gone were my days of lingering by the edge of the oval, feeling excruciatingly inadequate. Like my brother, I'd found my tribe. Camp was Christian utopia, away from the world that corrupted our souls. We were cradled in a daily schedule of worship, sermons, Bible study, and mass-produced meals: morning service (most people rolled straight out of bed at 9.00 am in pyjama pants, chewing toast), then Bible study with muffins and biscuits, a salad roll for lunch cross-legged beneath eucalyptus trees, then free time all the way until lasagne dinner at six, canned peaches for dessert.

Day Three. Tonight was the dance party, I thought before I opened my eyes. Would He sneak a kiss? I pulled on faded jeans, slid feet into thongs, and shuffled out the dorm door, careful not to disturb sleeping bodies. In the shower block, Katie was blow-drying her hair, her make-up scattered. She waved then turned back to the mirror, focused.

Mist lingered over the river, fading in weak sunshine. A cacophony of black cockatoos shrieked and tore at branches high in the eucalyptus trees that lined the water's edge. Wrapping my arms around myself, I trudged to the dining hall and pushed open a door to the lingering scent of detergent and old plastic, the camp parents serving bowls of cereal from the kitchen window.

I spotted Him, bleary-eyed with sleep, head on hand, talking to Sally over an empty plate. Clutching a plate of Vegemite toast, I swung a leg over the bench and sat across from Him.

'Hey, Lou!' Sally smiled, and wrapped a warm arm around me.

'I'm off — band this morning. See ya.' His 8.00 am–deep voice. A thrill ran through me as we locked eyes.

As soon as He was out of earshot, I made a face at Sally as if in pain. 'Doesn't He have dreamy eyes?'

We chatted for a while, friends joining us with cups of hot Milo. The bell clanged and we followed the stream of teenagers into the meeting hall. I rubbed my neck nervously before stepping over the threshold. A new preacher had been flown in from Melbourne. He was known for unleashing the power of the Holy Spirit. There were stories of demons being exorcised, miraculous healing, people falling to the ground.

Together, we stood, we sang; my spine tingled, ecstasy sparkled in my limbs. Jay, a twenty-one-year-old leader in sunglasses, jeans, and thongs, held the black lens of a camcorder to his eye. He'd film all day, and cut together a clip for the next day's service.

The band quietened. The guest pastor gripped the microphone. Tight white polo shirt, shaved head, biceps marked with risen veins. A man of discipline. He strode back and forth like a caged leopard, beginning soft. 'We're going to be reading from Acts 2 today.'

I picked up my Bible, hoping he'd ask someone to read out loud.

'Do you know why I am so familiar with the Bible? Why I can recite the word of God from memory?' He paused. Sun reached through the windows onto worn, brown carpet. Somebody sneezed. 'I get up at 5.00 am. Five in the morning! So I can worship the

Lord, and spend time with him.'

He told us about Jesus' miracles. The healing of the sick. The raising of the dead. The casting out of demons. I floated in and out of listening, appreciating his chest's curve, the hint of nipple.

'When Jesus left — the last time before he returns to us, as prophesied in the Book of Revelations — he sent the Holy Spirit to stay with his disciples. On the day of Pentecost, the followers of Jesus gathered together, and a mighty and violent wind came upon them and anointed their heads with tongues of fire. This was the supernatural power of the Holy Spirit.

'Now, I hadn't planned this.' Silence. The room spiked, alert. 'But God has been speaking to me. And he is telling me things about you. The Word says your sons and daughters will prophesy, your young men will see visions, your old men will dream dreams.' He closed his eyes, breathed into the mike. 'Hey — John. You picked me up from the airport. Thanks, brother.'

John sat up, ran a hand through long greasy hair.

'God wants you to know that the big choice you have to make? He's gonna hold you. Jesus says what father, if his son asks for a fish, will give his son a snake? God's gonna hold you and give you what you need, okay? He looks after the sparrows of the field. They don't need to worry about what they're going to eat tomorrow. If you leap, God's gonna catch you, okay?'

Who would he speak to next? Did God have a special message for me? He prophesied for twenty minutes, then finally his gaze landed beside me. 'Hey, darling, in the blue dress.'

A thrill of adrenaline before I remembered my black jeans.

'What's your name?'

'Katie,' she said, raising her chin.

'Hey, Katie,' his voice a caress. 'Look, God wants you to know that he sees you. He sees you. When you feel on top of the world, he sees you. And in your darkest moments, he is also beside you. He never leaves, okay? In Romans 8, it is written that neither death nor life, neither angels nor demons, not our fears or worries, no power in the sky or on the earth, not even *hell* can separate us from the love of God. He is with you, Katie.'

She sniffed. Red-rimmed eyes.

'And hey, look, I'm feeling, I'm getting a sense of an eating disorder here. God wants you to address that. You are so loved. And nothing you can do to your own body will change how much he loves you. He wants to heal you. He wants to heal you.'

Following his discreet gesture, Jane pressed on the synth keys and pulled the volume up. The sound was a pulsing light, and his voice rose with it.

'God wants to heal every one of you! Whether your physical body, or your heart, he is *here* to *heal you* with his love.'

The guitar pulled in, bass and drums, too, and the song grew, and grew, and the guest pastor began to shout.

'If you want to be healed to-DAY! If you want Christ's supernatural love to come into your heart and give you breakthrough, breakthrough, breakthrough, then I want you to come to the altar. Show God you are committed to HIM, that you need HIM. Open your arms! And I will pray, and the Spirit will come upon you and do! his! work!'

Jane sang the repetitive chorus, *You're all I need*, her body rolling from hips to shoulders, eyes closed. Katie stood as if in a trance, floated to the front, knelt. Three boys went down to the altar together, then two girls. The guest pastor's hand was over the forehead of one of the boys, he was speaking in tongues, shouting, a vein visible in his brow, a warrior, a disciplined warrior, a vessel

God used for glory, and he curled his hand into a gentle fist, then flicked it open, as if releasing a spark onto the boy's pink forehead, and even though the boy's eyes were closed, he fell back, his knees buckled, his friends grabbed his arms and floated him to the floor. A mass of bodies, my brother, too, crying, I tried not to look, I wanted the spirit, I knelt, I hoped I would be changed.

Sally's breath tickled my cheek as she leant close to draw a thick Egyptian flick. Katie and I had planned our costumes for the Saturday dance party weeks ago; the theme was power.

I pulled the straight black wig with plastic golden jewels over my curls, tucked in stray frizz, and stepped into a second-hand gold dress. The meeting hall was transformed, the preacher's stage now the Pastor's DJ deck. He looked like a cross between Jack White and Jesus. Under green-and-blue lights, the bass line throbbed, and bodies on the floor jerked and swayed. The guest pastor danced stiffly, sans costume, punching fists into the air. I spotted my dreamy-eyed guitarist in the throng, His shaggy curls, His five o'clock shadow, and danced towards Him.

'Wow, you look great,' He shouted in my ear, and drew back to reveal the white teeth of His smile.

'I'm Cleopatra,' I yelled back. He was wearing a navy singlet, a heavy, twenty-metre length of orange extension cord wrapped around his shoulder. I leant in, 'What are you?'

'An electrician.' He grabbed the plug, tapped it on my nose ('boop!'), then danced away. An hour later, I slipped from the mass and stumbled to the dining hall for water. The Pastor was right, my friends at school didn't understand, who needs alcohol? When I drew the empty cup from my mouth, still panting, He was beside me.

'Hey, Lou,' He said, voice soft. I abandoned my cup and followed Him into the dark.

We climbed onto the riverside gum's smooth branch. His sweat a thick, heavy scent mixed with sweet deodorant. When He took my hand, lightning shot up my arm. The Milky Way hung over the black river, silent, silky, elegant.

'Hey, guys,' a leader called, voice equivalent to a raised eyebrow. 'Curfew in ten minutes, okay?'

''Kay,' He and I replied together. I was spinning, I could say no more. He had the beard of a grown man and He smelt so good, I wanted to push my nose into His hollows, I wanted to breathe Him in, lap Him up, swallow Him whole.

He cleared His throat. Looked at my fingers between his two large hands, ran a thumb up and down my palm. I shivered.

'Y'know, the Pastor said to me, damn! Why don't you ask her already?'

My heart drummed, my body glowed.

'So — d'you wanna go out with me?'

'Um, I — sure, if you want?' I nodded, cheeks red.

We slid off the branch, and held each other in a standing embrace. Boyfriend-Girlfriend. A couple. A single noun. We held hands and walked back to the lights, before splitting off to our gendered dorms.

At next day's service, the video of the day played. I spotted my brother's hair bouncing before the stage, wakeboarders doing jumps on the speedboat's wake, last night's costumes; at the end, a close-up of He and I, sitting on soft grass. Pulling up grass tufts, talking in the sunshine. Our knees touched.

'What?!' I yelled. Behind the sound desk, Jay grinned. The all-seeing eye of the camera, of the group. Our names flashed on the screen in red. It became a chant; fifty teenagers and twenty adults joined voices and punched fists in the air. If marriage was a relationship approved by the state, this was a relationship approved of by my Pastor and my tribe. Out the door of the meeting hall, our names rang across the water, to the ochre cliffs, up into the bright sky.

after

Sweden

'C'mon, church,' the man on the stage shouted, striding lengthways in a black-and-white flannel shirt, slicked hair, polished boots.

The audience answered, 'Thank you, thank you, we love you, Lord God.'

I was in a nightclub, though it was still light outside. Hillsong Gothenburg hired the space only hours after Saturday's sins were mopped up. All was shadow except the stage, where *Welcome Home* was projected onto two screens above the nine musicians. This same phrase lit screens in every Hillsong campus worldwide. I once worked for a hotel chain that placed identical armchairs and shampoo tubes in every room from Johannesburg to Hong Kong. Hillsong had a similar branding strategy.

It worked for me. I didn't know Swedish, but we spoke the same language. Teenagers jumping before the band. The progression from praise songs to worship. A 100-strong audience with arms stretched to heaven, eyes squeezed tight. Brian and Bobbie Houston founded Hillsong in Sydney in 1983; now global, the church had campuses across twenty-one countries. According to a 2017 official press release, 40,000 people attended the church across Australia every week, and over 100,000 worldwide. The doctrine had a neoliberal, individualist bent, fixated on Jesus Christ as personal saviour.

This was modern-day Pentecostalism, birthed from Protestantism in nineteenth-century America. Think revival tents in rural fields. Charismatic preachers and water baptisms. Falling over backwards, speaking in tongues, casting demons out *in the name of Jesus*.

Speaking of the supernatural, I was in Gothenburg myself thanks to yonder shining light. I'd read an article claiming that the Swedish Church gave a non-binary pronoun to God: *hen*. Whenever this intriguing linguistic approach came to mind, a zing of excitement flew from my belly button to my shoulders, which I interpreted as the Holy Spirit's electric touch. So I looked up cheap flights. I'd been running on empty — still waiting on some invoices to be paid — and had to ask for a loan from Mum. Hunched shoulders relaxed when I saw her money arrive in my account. Just in time to buy a ticket to Stockholm.

I'd followed the goddess trail, as Sister Margie Abbott had advised, but my encounter with the saint and the mother of God had been a disappointment. In their histories, I saw female power usurped, symbols twisted, and goddesses enchained. They'd been divorced from sovereignty to fit under the Father God. If I couldn't find a solution within Christianity's female figures, the logical next step was to consider a genderless divine. Many believers said God had no gender, that the bearded white man in the sky was an incomplete paradigm. All humans were made in God's image, which meant he was unlimited by gender or biology.

Theologically, this was correct, but cultural practices adhered to the masculine. Linguistic philosopher Wittgenstein wrote that the limits of our language are the limits of our world. Could I liberate myself from the boundaries inherent in the male pronoun, Him? Could I meet a non-binary God? Perhaps interacting with a supreme being that queered gender could present a more expansive encounter with the divine and nullify patriarchy's sins.

Now that I was here, part of me believed that the Holy Spirit had guided me to Hillsong Gothenburg. Another part believed it was a mix of coincidence, wile, and luck. Before I'd arrived in Sweden, I emailed churches and convents with the subject *Accommodation Request* or *Help for a Fellow Christian*. The nuns said I had to pay, and the churches didn't know anyone to host me. I changed my strategy. Being a church leader had taught me to demonstrate godliness *when other people were watching*. To act as 'a light in the darkness' was an act of evangelism, meant to inspire unbelievers to Christ. I knew this performance-based morality. So I went public.

The only Hillsong Sisterhood Facebook group in Sweden was in Gothenburg, with a header image of four white women laughing in sunshine. I posted in the group, asking for a host, using deferential, saccharine language, conforming to the familiar, pandering model of femininity. True to form, the leader's admin, Annie, got in touch. She knew someone. Why didn't I meet her at church? I clicked my fingers in victory when I saw her public comment, recognising its dual purpose: a generous offer of hospitality, and an opportunity to heighten church attendance.

And it worked — here I was. When I'd entered, Annie, who grew up in the Philippines, threw her arms around me and told me her life story in a breathless rush. She had shining wavy hair and rose-apple cheeks. In the crush of people milling in the foyer, she introduced me to Ingrid, my host. Annie dashed off — she was about to sing onstage, she was *so grateful* to serve God with her gifts — and I pulled my red suitcase to sit beside my new friend. Ingrid was not so bubbly or exuberant. With no make-up, unfashionable glasses, and bad skin, she didn't fit the cultural mandate of cherry-lipped girl-womanhood. I pitied her. She scored far less in the Hillsong social milieu than Annie.

Everyone lifted their hands, closed their eyes, and sang *Helig Andes eld / Brinn här i min själ*, which translated to 'Holy Spirit fire / burn within my soul'. I knew the tune. But ten months since

I'd left, worship felt different. Not because of the country, but due to my evolving relationship with the church. It was easier, now, to see Hillsong as spirituality under capitalism. The megachurch was a slick machine that released a new studio album each year. My ex-Husband had listened to them as they came out (topping ARIA charts); then, our church paid for the rights to play their music on Sundays. It's hard to overemphasise their importance in Australian church music culture. Talented young musicians in any denomination were often supported by their congregations to spend a year studying in Hillsong's music college. And no wonder: they were the best in the business.

The music facilitated an experience that felt incredible — if you opened yourself to it — and was invoked by a series of finely tuned signals, cues, and conventions. Now, my emotional distance gave me eyes to see, and I observed the rise and fall of energy. The French sociologist Émile Durkheim described this as 'collective effervescence', where individuals in a group participate in a ritual, and, in this process, electricity is created and released, often leading to excitement or delirium. It serves to solidify the identity of the group, transport believers into a different realm, and allow them to feel connected to something greater than themselves. The only time I'd felt anything close was at a Muse concert when I was eighteen.

The sermon began, a different pastor beneath the lights. In his late forties, balding and overweight. Not cool, dude. Where I came from, we knew the importance of image.

'There's nothing more attractive than seeing someone flourish and grow,' the balding pastor said, all confidence and grin, nailing the Hillsong brand of Jesus-soaked self-help. As he quoted Bible verses, they popped up on screens, framed by the vertical words: *God is on your side God is on your side God is on your side.*

—

Ingrid's studio apartment was a few minutes' walk away, in the city's outskirts. I slept on her couch with two cats. During my week-long stay, she gave me coffee vouchers, her bus card, and as many homemade saffron buns as I could eat. We watched movies together and commiserated about boys, and her tech-savvy friend fixed my laptop for free. I had manipulated her social circle into providing me with free accommodation, and she trusted me because she thought we both loved Jesus.

It wasn't the first time I'd enjoyed the hospitality of brothers and sisters in Christ: I'd once travelled with YWAM, a global network of 'missionaries', to the south of India. When our eight-strong group landed, we waited for our host in the hot chaos of Chennai Airport at midnight. Our leader, a blonde woman in her fifties with a high-pitched voice, told us to look for a man with the Holy Spirit sparkle in his eyes. She was adamant we'd recognise him by a physical manifestation of his faith. By miracle or by magic, we found him, and he took us to YWAM's communal living quarters. An international tribe came with benefits.

I spent most of my time in Gothenburg at Ingrid's kitchen table, priming myself on Christianity in Sweden, reaching out to interviewees, drinking percolated coffee, and eating pastries. At lunchtimes, I stretched my legs under icy white skies. My favourite path was besides Gullbergsån river, covered by tangled dark branches and hidden, croaking blackbirds. Sometimes, I was startled by a presence at my shoulder, and looked back in alarm. Nobody was there. But it felt as if my Husband lurked, and He would grab my arm, and cry, 'Lou! What do you think you're doing?'

Swallowing this unease, I returned to my research until the sky darkened. The Swedish Church, or *Svenska kyrkan*, valued gender equality. Female priests were approved in 1960, and now 45 per cent of priests were women; Reverend Antje Jackelén became, in 2014, the first female Archbishop of Uppsala, the highest representative of the Church of Sweden. All the priests I'd read about using *hen* were women, and many lived near the capital. I decided to go east.

I took a rattling, blue-and-white tram to the city centre, and left Gothenburg at 11.55 pm. Rocked into half-sleep by the rhythm of the night coach, my forehead resting on cold glass, my eyelids cracking whenever the bus hit a bump. The moving roadside evolved from black dirt to glowing snow, weaving through my half-dreams.

At Stockholm Central Station, I splurged on a 7.00 am coffee and pastry and waited for my midday train beneath a golden clock. The only Airbnb in my price range was a village almost two hours from Stockholm. My host Fredrik was waiting at Skutskär train station, his mountainous frame topped by shoulder-length straight hair and a sandy beard. As he leant to pick up my red suitcase from ankle-deep snow, I noticed he was wearing shorts. Was this the mark of a sociopath?

His street was a row of wooden houses blanketed in white, puffing radiator steam, like a row of pipe-smoking grandmothers. I settled into my upstairs room, where a tabby cat was curled on my bed. Fredrik and his partner invited me to join them for a dinner of Swedish meatballs, vegetarian especially for me. In the middle of the night, I woke sweating, and rose to turn down the radiator. When I drew back thick curtains, cool air pulsed onto my naked torso, and I watched snowflakes drift like white whispers in violet. Wonder and fear slashed through my body in one brilliant, single stab.

———

Snowdrifts sparkled under dawn's luminescent clouds. Teenagers stalked on the train platform in black puffer jackets, their boisterous chatter silenced by a thundering express locomotive that roused furious, blinding clouds of white powder.

The train carriage was overheated, and at each station more passengers hung thick coats on pegs by the windows. Dark forests whipped past, and fir trees gathered in secretive clusters. I disembarked at the university town Uppsala, and wandered slowly between people hurriedly disembarking. Feathery ice floated onto running school children in orange, red, and lime snow jackets. *Swish swish*, the efficient walk of office workers in snow pants. Students biked on ploughed roads, bodies leaning left and right with each arduous pedal — the Swedish used gravel, not salt, to clear snow, resulting in a rocky surface. Piano scales drifted from a *musikskola's* cracked window, and I could almost see the sound, slipping out the window, floating to the sky like a prayer.

In a mercifully warm cafe, I slid into a red leather booth opposite retired priest Reverend Anna Karin Hammar, and pulled off my gloves. She came from a long line of priests: her father, grandfather, and great-grandfather were all men of the cloth, and one of her brothers was an archbishop. She had been called a 'controversial priest' by one of Sweden's most prominent news outlets for her outspokenness, and served on Geneva's Church Council from 1986 to 1990, as the director for Women in Church and Society. She'd subverted gendered language since she was a child.

Her voice was gravelly between thick lips. 'When my father would describe that all the children had been with him somewhere, he would say, "my three sons" — but I was not mentioned! So I tried when I was a young child to call myself a male's name: Tommy.' She laughed.

In a rural village of 586 inhabitants, her Sunday School teacher became an 'extra grandmother', who five-year-old Anna would walk two kilometres to see whenever she felt lonely. 'I found my way to her. And it was my mother who was always praying with me in the evenings. I think I've always felt God *was* feminine.'

Rev. Anna pushed a fork into a *semla*, a cardamom bun filled with cream. She married priest and theologian Professor Ninna Edgardh in 2001, eight years before same-sex marriage was legalised in Sweden. Perhaps being gay in the church — a historically homophobic institution whose doctrine had been used as justification for exclusion, violence, and murder — had radicalised her. Androcentric religious language, she said, can have a huge impact on our psyche.

'It's devastating to women's self-image. Devastating.' Her voice quiet, she shook her head. 'It makes women feel less than the higher good. In fact, I think it is violence towards women — and everything that is female — that God is solely connected to male.'

'Cultural violence' was a term coined by Norwegian peace researcher Johan Galtung. It referred to aspects of culture that were used to justify or legitimise direct or structural violence. Religious symbolism was one such example.

'For myself,' Rev. Anna's voice trembled, 'I have needed a female version of God.' As a student chaplain at Lund University in the early 1970s, she prayed to God the Mother, in addition to God the Father. 'The language is so strong within us. So we need to destabilise this image.'

Now retired, she found herself using alternative words to address God. 'I say You, Source of my Life, Love of my Being. I *never* say Father.'

She tapped the back of my hand with a smile and told me she

would pay for my shrimp salad. I tried to keep the relief from my face, gave thanks for Rev. Anna's time, and exited the cafe's warmth.

In this alien snowscape, I felt like a little koala far from home. The grind-slide of each step unbalanced me as I strode to Fyris River's icicled edge. I thought again of Carol P. Christ's essay 'Why Women Need the Goddess'. Praying solely to a male God, she wrote, affirmed the male-gendered body as valid. The absence of the feminine demeaned the female body as unworthy of praise. Rev. Anna had articulated something I'd tried to say in Auntie Liz's kitchen. If the image of perfection was male, then I was imperfect. Men were holy. Women were not. Even more — what would it mean to live in a trans body, exiled from any traditionally holy image?

My guts twisted — and it wasn't the shrimp. Could I ever worship a male God again? Could I keep following this path? The next interviewees might help me understand how to interact with a non-gendered God.

Further into the snowscape, away from other walkers. Black pine cones littered untouched white. Frost dusted trees' spindly limbs. Dark water rushed between riverbanks and their spikes of broken ice. Alone, the old habit of praising God in response to beauty rose in my chest.

'Oh Lord, you are —' My tongue followed old paths, then stopped. In the silence, crows cawed.

Further north, Gävle's Holy Trinity Church sloped to a dome beneath stark blue sky, clear before a forecast snowstorm. A smiling greeter handed me a *svenska psalmboken* — Swedish psalm book — and a red cushion. The church walls were painted with colourful scenes. I had a pew to myself, and kept my heavy coat on in the cold. This morning's congregation were only fifty people in a church that could fit 800.

An enormous bell pealed high above, golden resonance shimmering in the air, and everyone stood to sing. A procession moved down the aisle, the priest swinging incense, a volunteer holding an ornate cross; then came the hymns, the sermon. After, I ate homemade biscuits as a woman explained to me in English that the sermon was about Jesus being within our reach.

The priest, she said, used the metaphor of a telephone. 'When you call an office, they give instructions — dial one for this, dial two for this. But we do not need instructions. We have a direct line to God!'

I stepped into the snow, wiping shortbread crumbs from my lips, and imagined fingering a pastel-blue vintage telephone, the rotary dial's scrape-drag-spin. Shimmering in my mind like the cathedral bell was a line from theologian Marcella Althaus-Reid's book, *The Queer God*: 'The search for love and truth is a bodily one.' The sermon had used a physical action as metaphor for divine encounter. Movement as thought: we think with our bodies. Our bodies inspire the way we think.

Watching black boots on white-frosted cobblestones, I wondered about emotional intimacy with something nameless, whose face I couldn't imagine. Was dialling the number of someone beyond the gender binary really an option? Could I learn from those non-binary and trans people who radically deconstruct and do away with masculine and feminine norms altogether? Could I queer God, could *hen* exist in between the shape of man or woman?

I strode towards Gävle County Museum, slipping on half-melted snow. Chris Smedbakken's hand was chilled when they shook mine; it was -8 and they'd forgotten their gloves. A journalist and short story writer, Chris was meeting me to give me the lowdown on using Sweden's *hen*. They identified as *icke-binär*, non-binary, and have used *hen* as a pronoun for three years.

Cheery and animated, they led me through the town under gloomy clouds. With short peroxide hair, a black jewel dangling from one ear, and a dark-grey blazer over a pink shirt, Chris presented as playfully androgynous. Round pink cheeks made them seem younger than thirty years. We found our way to their favourite cafe, and warmed up over coffee at a candlelit table.

Hen was introduced in 1966 by linguists, inspired by the Finnish word *hän* — Finland's third-person pronoun doesn't distinguish between gender. The Swedish word resurfaced in the 1990s, and began to be used by newspapers, academics, and authors in the 2000s, before exploding into national debate after Jesper Lundqvist used it in his children's book *Kivi & Monsterhund* ('Kivi & Monster Dog'). In 2014, it was incorporated into the national glossary by the Swedish Academy (which also administered the Nobel Prize in Literature). In speech, *hen* was most often used to refer to situations where someone's gender was unknown. Despite these cultural changes, some people here were still uncomfortable with folks who didn't fit cisgendered norms. To be honest, I understood, as I still struggled to use correct pronouns.

We talked for several hours, our hands gripping coffee mugs, as they told me about resistance within their family, and having to 'come out' again every time they moved newspaper jobs (twice in the last three years) or when they saw an old friend in the street. At 4.00 pm, evening blue sank heavy outside. The street disappeared into inky shadow.

Chris' English danced with the singsong cadence of Swedish as they described gendered expectations' oppression. 'People often say to me, if you don't like being a girl, why don't you just not wear heels. But I cannot always feel second rate because I do not meet these obligations of gender. This is not good for me.

'If there are only two pronouns, then those put labels on people.' Chris shrugged, face lit by dancing candlelight. 'We have all these social constructs telling us what is a guy and what is a girl. Pronouns are not just words — you force all these concepts on a person.'

A word contains images and associations. And approaching people with gendered language enforces a limiting binary of socially scripted characteristics.

'If there is a third way of doing it, which there is now,' said Chris, 'that would change the way we think about one another entirely.'

They left to catch a train, and I lingered, procrastinating going out into the cold. Marcella Althaus-Reid in my head again. The queer theologian, she wrote, has a 'corporeal and intimate spirituality' whose sexual desire is transcendent, intermixed with desire for God. How we see and touch and hear the Almighty is ultimately defined by our bodies and sexualities. Queer people, who move between and beyond fixed notions of gender and sexuality, are much wiser as to the reality of God, who is liberated from fixed personhood in his three-in-one identity of Father-Spirit-Son. This fluidity, then, embodies an expansive understanding of divine nature.

The cafe emptied, the sky purple-black. A woman studying at a nearby table was joined by her windswept boyfriend, shaking snow from his hair, who sat beside her and placed a mandarin wrapped in a napkin on the table. They were tall, icy, Nordic elegance. She peeled the orange fruit with delicate fingers, placing thin segments in her mouth. I smelt citrus in the air. Though I tilted my head down towards my notebook, my gaze kept returning. He pulled a laptop from his satchel in the pretence of work, but kept glancing at her neck.

Lamplight glowed yellow. Windswept boyfriend slid his lips along his girlfriend's cheek, and she relented, turned, and nudged his face to her slender neck. They opened their mouths to each other. My loneliness was so firm, so visceral, it had a colour: snow reflecting violet twilight. I could hear their tongues, their breath. I was condemned to walk this earth alone.

Finally, he helped her arms through jacket sleeves, and they left the cafe, which now seemed bare and dim. Mandarin peel rested on the table. Snowflakes whirled beyond the windows.

Before I turned out the light each evening, I dragged my suitcase across the bedroom door. One of the reasons this place was so cheap was that it was Fredrik's first Airbnb booking — but this meant there were no previous reviews, which went against my rules. I was a cat with an arched back, shooting under the bed at any loud noise. One morning, Fredrik knocked. I cracked the door.

'You said you needed the washing machine?'

I nodded up at his towering figure.

'I will show you.'

Clutching a bag of dirty clothes against my stomach, I followed down the wooden steps into the basement. A rake, a broom hanging from a nail on the wall: I made a mental note of possible weapons.

Fredrik pulled open the front-loader's door, white T-shirt riding up his enormous back as he bent to spoon in powder and adjust the setting. His partner was at work. I threw my clothes into the machine, noting, as I rose, that my head came only to Fredrik's chest.

Bang! He shut the door. 'Takes about an hour.'

'Okaythanksbye!' I yelled over my shoulder, scampering up the stairs.

I'm never sure, I thought on the train, when I'm being careful and when I'm a scaredy cat. *No vivas con miedo*, Miguel said, but it was hard to feel safe when you lived in strangers' houses.

Arriving in Uppsala again, I walked past electric cars plugged into charging points, a row of bicycles laden with snow, and students with arms outstretched, heads thrown back, tongues catching falling snowflakes.

At *Kyrkokansliet*, the Church of Sweden's national office, a secretary ushered me into a featureless meeting room to wait for Rev. Dr Cristina Grenholm, a systematic theologian, feminist author, and Secretary of the Church.

'No, we don't use *hen*.' Rev. Cristina's dog collar was tight and official above a patterned cardigan. 'There is not one gender-neutral pronoun in the whole Book of Worship. This is fake news.'

Huh. I came to Sweden because of 'fake news'. But language, she added, was updated to current social contexts. Liturgy was a church-mandated script that priests followed in ceremonies, and was infrequently adapted. For example, she had conducted a morning communion service just this week where liturgy used the word 'brothers' to address the congregation. There were no men present. In the heat of the moment, she said 'sisters'.

The language of how Rev. Cristina spoke about this issue, too, was important: she saw 'traditional' texts as 'outdated'. Whereas I might've said that androcentric texts erased women's experience. This illustrated how language within church politics shaped debate, denied realities, and presented a harsh truth in palatable light.

Her crystal-blue eyes sparkled with intelligence as she gave another example of how progressive the church was. 'We accepted same-sex marriage within the church in 2009. At that time, we had one liturgy for heterosexual couples and one that was applying to same-sex couples. But now we have one liturgy. You don't say "you are now man and wife" — in Swedish, we use the word *make* (pronounced *mock-e*): spouse. Of course, that can be gender neutral.'

'But what about God?' I asked, my mouth dry from black coffee. I wanted to grab her tidy cardigan and shake her.

'The male language is very strong,' she admitted. '"The Lord" is a male term. Jesus said we should call God "our Father". So when wrestling with not always addressing God as *He*, we address God as *God*, as *You*.

'Every human being is created in the image of God. So if we want to acknowledge that we are all images of God, we must be able to address God in feminine terms.' She listed the biblical examples: 'How often I have longed to gather your children together, as a hen gathers her chicks under her wings,' Jesus said. And in Isaiah 42, where God is described as having the pain of a woman in childbirth.

I knew the verses; I'd clung to them for years. But at this point, four or five metaphors in the 783,000-word book were no longer enough.

I exited the heated building, icy air a sharp relief on my hot face. Tiny snowflakes settled on my eyelashes like petals. Rev. Cristina's refusal to budge on the pronoun issue reminded me of the Catholic Church's catechism: 'God is neither man nor woman: he is God', which simultaneously refutes the maleness of God and confirms it. It was denial. Whether we use a pronoun or not, the name 'God' is as gendered as the title 'king'.

I was disappointed. The institutional church, in one of the most progressive countries in the world, was still using male language for God. The status quo was protected. And a woman, a feminist theologian high up in their ranks, was making small admissions yet still perpetuating patriarchal ideas. Her dismissal of the topic rankled: language, symbol, and metaphor are the ways we access abstract thinking. Therefore, it was imperative to interrogate their construction, to ask what ideology they propped up.

I shaded my eyes from sunlight glittering on snow piles. Despite the party line, *hen* was happening with individuals in small communities. Perhaps this was the true path to change.

In 2017, priest Susann Senter advertised Christmas services with a birth announcement in the local newspaper, *Västerås Tidning*.

'*Hen* was born', Susann's ad said in Swedish, 'while the parents were on a journey.' Describing Baby Jesus with the gender-neutral pronoun. The advertisement, printed in the classifieds section, didn't get much attention until after Christmas, when a national radio station reported it and 'all hell broke loose'.

She spoke to me on the phone from Västerås, 100 kilometres west of Stockholm. I sat on a wooden bench in Stockholm Central Station's cavernous waiting hall. Beside me, tired travellers dumped enormous ski bags on the shining floor, and above were golden art-deco lamps and fashion ads featuring smiling, grey-haired women.

Västerås' *kyrkan* Facebook page was inundated with abuse, the priest said, some using violent language or accusing blasphemy.

'I may be naive, but I didn't expect reactions to that extent.'

Susann was ordained in 1975, and was the first female priest in the province of Västmanland. Which meant she'd been challenging churchgoers' gender norms for her entire career. However, she believed we couldn't completely abandon the current masculine words for God — Father, Lord — because of Christianity's emphasis on personal relationship.

'We all say God is not He or She. God is *more*. But to come to the deep sense of God, we need to use words that put us in relation: me and you. Instead, I have *widened* my thoughts by using other words. As a basic theory, words do not only describe reality, they create reality.'

Susann didn't see her position as radical.

'Challenging the gender of God, and not speaking of God as male all the time, that I believe to be common ground.' In fact, women were leaving the church. The gender of God was an urgent and necessary topic.

'I have discussed with the former bishop, and the bishop before, topics on women in church and another language for God. And one of our bishops said, "Why haven't I heard about this?" And I said, "To you, it isn't a question. For me, it is a task of survival in the church."'

The next day, I made footprints in the snow wandering the village around Fredrik's house. Smoke from a nearby paper mill rose on the horizon, diffusing a creamy, bitter smell. The cold on my cheeks and wrists was brutal and astonishing. Needles of orange sunlight reached through thin, dark pines; when I got to the water, two swans floated on a black sea, a slushy tide lapping at frozen sand. Then, on a deserted road, lying on smooth asphalt where tyres had worn away snow, was a penis.

Lo and behold. I looked up to white clouds.

The thing on the ground was pink flesh–coloured with large taut balls, and a curved, not-quite-erect shaft. Should I pick it up? Could this be a phallic gift from God? Why was it here — mistakenly dropped from a car window? A joke discarded in disgust? And what could God be telling me through this divine dildo? A penis maketh not the man; however, this could be a way to empathise with an aspect of a masculine body. Did God want me to pack heat? Was this a holy cock? Maybe it was celestial aid to wretched loneliness. If I were to use it, how does one disinfect a roadside dick? I supposed I could leave it soaking in Fredrik's bathroom sink.

I walked on, debating the logistics of heavenly sex, and when I looped back, the sacred phallus had vanished.

A gravel path weaved between uniform apartment buildings, with treacherous puddles of slippery ice. A strangled frustration rose up my throat, as if I were trying to break a straitjacket's hold. I'd been using 'work' and intellectual enquiry as a front for a search that was actually about emotional and psychological integrity. But every possible doorway led to a brick wall, not the valley of freedom I'd imagined.

But I kept following what called. I'd spoken to priests; now I wanted to hear how a regular believer evolved God-language. I was staying in a suburban Stockholm apartment for two days before I flew out, and my married hosts happened to be churchgoers. They introduced me to Elin Lundell, a postgraduate student in gender studies. She opened her third-floor door with a shy grin; the warmly lit apartment she shared with her girlfriend personified *hygge*, cosiness, with a blue-tartan couch beneath the wide window, houseplants hanging from macramé cords, and a bookshelf partitioning the kitchen from the lounge room. I spotted Dorothy Day and Sarah Waters printed on the books' spines.

Elin poured mango tea. 'Sweden is not as progressive as people would like to think. It's not the perfect society.'

Only yesterday, she'd presented a paper outlining Sweden's growing conservatism: sure, same-sex marriage was legalised, but this merely enforced the expectations of monogamy and family life on what was previously seen as errant sexuality.

She untied her ponytail, pushed fingers through auburn hair. She had grown up in a country village near Sundsvall in the mid-north; rural churches made it clear marriage was between a man and a woman. When she moved to Stockholm, she found a Facebook group of LGBT-friendly Christians, which is where she found a nearby home-church.

'On Thursday evenings, we sing and pray together, and on Sundays we read a text, talk about it, celebrate mass. Everything we would do in church, but now we do it in someone's home.'

This small, private group gave her the opportunity to try out alternative expressions of faith, like playing with the gender of God.

'I am in a process of trying to wash away the picture of God as a man. I got this picture when I was a child, and it's really hard to get rid of.' She poured herself another cup. Steam rose. 'It comes up all the time, the songs we sing together, in prayers we read.'

Although she'd heard of *hen*, Elin alternated between using the name 'God', and 'Mother', a 'more accurate picture'. But she didn't hear anyone else in the group changing pronouns.

'All of them have heterosexual families. They live another kind of life than I do. Which makes, I think, our relationship to God different. I guess they have never felt the same way as I have: that they don't belong in church.'

——

I retraced my steps along the gravel path. As Susann's spirituality was inspired by her experience as a woman, Elin's queer identity informed her faith. I'd followed my community's heteronormative expectations and had the privilege of ignoring homophobia. When you fit in, you don't question the dominant paradigm. Conformity is invisible until it chokes.

Fifteen thousand kilometres from home, I'd met Christian women and trans people for whom the gender of God was urgently relevant. Adapting the method of relating to the divine was a 'task of survival'. This was clearly a global issue for women and gender-diverse people. Could we abandon the church in droves? Could we strike from all attendance, duties, and tithes to propel institutional change, so that Rev. Cristina Grenholm and the official church institutions would change the party line?

The apartment building was warm as I climbed to the fourth floor, considering my next move. I unlaced my weather-beaten Doc Martens at the door beside tiny snow jackets. The subversive priests I spoke to used modes of address like 'Source of my Life' and 'You'. To me, this stripped God of personhood, which was confusing. It was not a simple task to 'widen' my thoughts. It was difficult to direct attention to a humming light rather than an embodied character, a Jesus of flesh and blood who sat with me. I didn't want to admit it — I was attached to the Father God.

And anyway, using *hen* didn't do enough to disrupt masculine hegemony. Despite the subversive act of stripping God of gender, the pronoun didn't provoke necessary reparations. Women weren't given what every man and boy took for granted: a body, identity, and will affirmed by the image of God. An adjustment in pronoun was not enough to dismantle this psychological association.

I laid my suitcase upon the double bed, where the large window projected shadows of falling snow. I'd packed a box of journals to post home on my way to the airport — inside was my Bible, too. I hadn't picked it up in months. In the same way, I no longer whispered goodnight to Jesus with my head on a pillow. He was the sun that slipped below the ocean's surface; his light had dimmed and dimmed and dimmed until nothing remained.

I threw a pair of torn jeans and some flyers in the bin. Tomorrow's cheap flight only allowed fifteen kilograms of baggage, and there was no money to pay airport fines. I was getting tired of my pilgrimage. My bodily search for love and truth and all this moving meant I felt more fatigued each day. Maybe there was no clear answer to my question of belonging.

The goddess trail had left me heartbroken. Ancient symbols were coopted to legitimise the Father, instate male-centred power structures, and naturalise imperialist authority. I could no longer ignore that patriarchy had historically dismantled images of female power.

My next line of enquiry would be to seek a feminine element *within* the existing Christian God, by digging through an alternative tradition. Reading articles on feminismandreligion. com, I'd discovered that Eastern Orthodox Christianity had a female element of God: Holy Wisdom.

Chokhmah in Hebrew, *Sophia* in Greek, she was personified as feminine and found most frequently in the Old Testament's book of Proverbs. The first-century Jewish philosopher Philo of Alexandria taught that the 'Divine Origin' — Yahweh — created first Sophia then Logos, the Word, each equal paths God used to communicate with us. In Jewish scripture, Sophia was a feminine voice. And the Gnostics — religious groups beginning in the first century AD across both Christian and Jewish sects — believed

Sophia was the Mother of God. Tomorrow, I would chase after her. I hoped somebody — La Virgen de Guadalupe, the Light of my Being, *Hen* — would guide me.

It was almost dinnertime by the time I'd packed. In the warm light of the kitchen, Karl — red-flecked beard and soft voice — was chopping onions and carrots for lentil soup, and invited me to join the family for dinner. I sat at the wooden table, beneath the yellow glow, beside his three-year-old daughter. Unsure of Airbnb boundaries, of the intimacy of watching Karl cook, I rubbed my neck.

'What did you do today?'

'I took the kids down to the water — if they stay inside all day, they go crazy. And Alice? What did you see? Al-Al-Alice?'

I'd overheard that he stuttered when speaking with enthusiasm or anger.

Alice slid a wooden toy in a figure eight across the table. She grinned. 'A fox!'

Karl's small eyes twinkled above his beard, and he stopped chopping, leant on the kitchen counter. 'And Albin, he zonked out in the pram. So I had to stay on the path. And Alice went for a little wander by herself, didn't you, Alice? And when it was time to come back, how did you find out where to go?'

She giggled and climbed onto my lap.

'How did you find how to go b-b-back, Alice? You followed …'

'I followed … I followed the water! I found you.'

'Yeah! You turned around and stayed by the water. You found your way back to Papa.'

Bulgaria & Istanbul

Bending to the mirror, I examined the greasy skin around my nostrils, brown frizz fanning out like a wretched mane, dark bags beneath sea-blue eyes. 4.00 am, not quite the middle of the night, not yet morning. Basel Mulhouse Freiburg airport was the tripoint of France, Germany, and Switzerland. The word *stopover* both moving and still: I was in-between, liminal in time and space, in the borderlands of nation and state.

Thinking back on my trip, I realised that I had left Australia as soon as possible and run as far as I could. Now, four months into my journey, peering at a face puffy with exhaustion, it was clear I'd escaped. But what exactly was I running from?

I pulled myself up to sit on the sink, and took selfies in the mirror, reflecting in front and behind, thousands of echoes curving into oblivion. In every country, I turned my head before mirrors, searching for the inner shift.

Exiting into the shadowy entrance hall, I settled in an empty cafe's orange armchair. An elderly couple chewed sandwiches nearby, lit only by a green exit sign. I wasn't the only one staying the night.

I curled up, head on my hand. Maybe it was time to admit that throwing myself into situations that 'felt right' wasn't working out so well. I'd envisioned myself as a kind of investigative journalist, sniffing out stories on the ground, but the uncertainty of booking accommodation a week at a time and the spike of fear at supermarket check-outs as I wondered if I had enough to pay was taking all my energy.

And in my pilgrimage, I'd left the familiar, I'd tried to follow the light, I'd knocked and knocked and knocked. But each question led to a greater question and a greater question, and like a stormy ocean eroding a cliff, every thunderous wave tore a little more land from beneath my feet.

My eyelids began to droop in the silence. Taps and bangs echoed from the dark. Two cleaners, trolleys bulging with spray bottles and bin bags, emerged from an elevator in a cloud of hushed laughter. They disappeared somewhere and the airport became again impersonal glass and steel.

Returning home was impossible. I had enough cash to last me four weeks. But how much longer could I keep going, not knowing where I'd be next month?

Fluorescent lights flashed on at 4.30 am. Staff positioned themselves straight-backed and impassive behind ticketing desks. At the cafe counter, a red-cheeked baker arranged croissants in neat lines.

Stretched out on the carpet floor near my boarding gate, I nursed a paper cup of black coffee and fantasised somebody would meet me when I landed. A loved one searching arrivals with hopeful eyes. The exclamation of recognition. The tight embrace.

Sofia Airport's bus stop had no shelter. A young Malaysian woman from my flight and I were soon soaked by freezing rain. We sat together on the bus then took the subway — she was hitchhiking across Eastern Europe, and using Couchsurfing to find accommodation. It was totally safe, she assured me, except for when she had to leave a house at 2.00 am because the male host kept trying to get into her bed. We exchanged numbers when we parted ways, but I didn't plan on texting her. I hated her recklessness, and didn't want to be infected by her stupidity.

As I yanked my suitcase along cracked and broken concrete,

I remembered my view as the plane had descended into Bulgaria over patchwork fields. A fire burnt, orange flames shooting from dull brown. I couldn't shake the sense I was moving towards inevitable destruction.

After a nap in my Airbnb room, I stalked twilight streets, withdrew a few thousand leva from an ATM. Women here moved in couples and alone, while men laughed in packs. A stocky, zebra-printed woman in her fifties leant from a sex-shop doorway to light her cigarette, and drew smoke with a lipsticked scowl.

I wandered to the golden statue of Sofia, Holy Wisdom, overlooking a busy intersection on a pole fifteen metres high. When she was installed, people complained that her breasts were too large. Her statue had replaced one of Lenin. She gleamed in the night sky. Surely, there was a linguistic connection between Sofia, the capital of Bulgaria, and Holy Wisdom. I would make enquiries here, then visit the Hagia Sophia in nearby Istanbul.

I followed Vitosha Blvd's sparse spindly trees, hands thrust into pockets, cheeks raw from frozen air. By a United Colors of Benetton store, a man in a charcoal suit held his grandmother's hand. She was the size of a child in a faded red coat with a rounded back and a green shawl over her hair, a cartoon transplant from the old Soviet Bloc into today's hip burger joints and fetish sex clubs. Outdoor restaurants were encased in clear plastic where people sipped tall glasses of beer and gesticulated, cigarettes tucked between fingers. It looked warm.

At a church in a side street, I stepped into an Orthodox mass. Men and women entered through different doors into a dimly lit room, heavy with incense. A priest in embellished golden robes sang beside an altar with grim, hypnotic chants. Thick white candles flickered on tall golden stands. The light and sound and smell were enough for me to fall into a somnolent trance. Seven women and three men stood on patterned tiles, then at the priest's behest lined up before him. He painted a flick of oil on their foreheads in the shape of the cross. They bent to kiss his hand.

I returned to the cold, still night. Perhaps God could be both man *and* woman. By embracing a gender dualism within the singular divine, I would resurrect femininity within the Father God's masculine. There was no other way forward. I turned back to my apartment, sigh visible in the air.

From the seventh-floor window, I glanced at a ghostly Mt Vitosha standing over the city like a watching judge. At its peak, the mountain was 2,200 metres high; it was also seventeen kilometres wide, surrounding the city.

I spent the day cross-legged on my double bed, reading about how Eastern Orthodox Christianity related to twenty-first-century Pentecostalism. After Jesus died, stories were told about him orally for hundreds of years. Then in AD 325, the Roman emperor Constantine I brought together the Council of Nicaea in what is now Bursa Province, Turkey — only a few hundred kilometres from here. The Church Fathers (influential theologians and bishops) codified Christian belief into dogma. This resulted in the Nicene Creed, oral teaching cemented in text. In AD 367, the Church Father Athanasius listed the sixty-six books that made up the Bible, consolidating scripture, the official collection of holy texts. When Jane bought my first Bible, she didn't mention that a council of men in the fourth century chose which stories to keep. And which to discard.

Pots clanged outside my bedroom door. Sometimes, my New Zealander host, Marianne, made enough lunch to share, and I could smell garlic cooking in the kitchen. In ten minutes, I would put on pants and inspect my chances of a free meal.

The gospels are written records of the life of Jesus Christ, and four exist in the Bible: Matthew, Mark, Luke, and John. But it seems there were alternative gospels, including one from Mary Magdalene, a disciple of Jesus who most Christians believe was an ancient-day sex worker. Around the time of the Nicene Creed, many other gospels were collected and burnt. The discovery of the Dead Sea Scrolls in the 1940s — ancient texts found in Palestine — illustrated the existence of alternative scripture, and a multiplicity of quashed perspectives. The Book of Wisdom (Sophia) was considered 'deuterocanonical' by the Roman Catholic Church and the Eastern Orthodox Church: it was important, but not important enough to be included in the Bible I knew.

I threw back the thick duvet, stood, and stretched in my undies, gazing at the bluish snow-capped triangle of Mt Vitosha. There was a hollowness in my torso louder than hunger. I'd been eyeing a truth in my peripheral vision that went hand in hand with my discoveries in Mexico, and I was almost too scared to look at it.

Scripture didn't come direct from the divine. It was man-made!

Which led to the question of authorship: who told the stories? What were their biases? I began to panic. What stories were excluded? What did they burn?

Over a chickpea stew, Marianne invited me to an art exhibition that evening with her friend Daniela. As we prepared to leave, I looked in the mirror, noting the eternal problems of small breasts, a plump stomach. I wrinkled my nose and applied bright lipstick to distract from my failings.

Daniela entered the gallery foyer in an enormous velvet coat, clutching a black faux-fur hat. 'Sorry, sorry, sorry,' she panted, 'I hope you have not been waiting.'

An arty auntie with an exuberant face and clanking golden bracelets, she kissed me, and I pulled away after the right cheek, almost colliding with her mouth as she leant for my left.

'Two cheeks here,' she said, hand grasping my forearm.

We paced around the warehouse, watching pink smoke erupt from a tiny bottle, examining a twisted, four-metre-tall skeleton. At dinner, I noticed a red ribbon on Daniela's wrist, which dangled a silver cross.

'Do you go to church?'

She looked embarrassed. 'The Russian Orthodox Church,' she said, pushing glasses up her nose. 'I buy from there. I fall, many time, and my friends they say this one protect me from the fall.'

She was more comfortable in Bulgarian or French; her eyes widened with a worried expression when I spoke, and I cursed myself for only being able to speak English. Church here, she said, was a superstitious exchange. Christianity was adopted as the Bulgarian Empire's state religion in 865, intermingling with existing folklore and ritual.

On the triannual Days of the Dead, for example — the next one was only a few days away — people visited cemeteries with plates of bread and corn. For many Balkans, the dead were part of the everyday. Loved ones needed things in the afterlife — clothes so they wouldn't grow cold, food so they wouldn't feel hunger. Daniela's friend went to her mother's grave and lit two cigarettes. She rested one on the headstone, and the other she smoked herself, while her mother's slowly burnt to ash.

———

On February 10, three-day-old brown snow was piled on street corners. I entered St Sophia Church, stepping into shadow. Hundreds of thin red candles sputtered and stole the air. The faithful in thick black coats clinked coins in palms to buy candles, watched by cracked paintings of Christ's haunted gaze.

In the high chapel, four people sat before a priest's baritone moans. Visitors crossed themselves before ancient paintings of saints. Trestle tables lined the sides where families poured wine into paper cups, pushed bread into their mouths. An old woman in black sat on a white garden chair and chewed, her feet not touching the ground. Thick incense smoke hung over her like a ghoul.

Stairs led underground to the fourth-century crypt, where rounded stones and broken mosaics were unevenly lit. Bodies once lay in these burial chambers. The air was heavy and wet.

Two days ago, it had been the third anniversary of my Nan's passing. I hadn't had time to follow her family trail in Ireland, yet I still regularly felt her presence: the smell of her perfume, a sense of benevolence. When she'd died, I comforted myself knowing I'd meet her again in heaven. But now this certainty was falling away. Land plunged into sea. *Had* she gone to a better place? *Would* I see her again?

Down, down, further into the earth. Damp air, the smell of soil. Fingertips touched smooth stone that masons chiselled 1,700 years ago. Where were they now? Where?

My jeans were tight; my T-shirt choked. I had to get above ground.

I gulped icy air as birds on ragged branches trilled like an unwelcome alarm. People stood at Sofia Cemetery's overgrown graves and crossed themselves, walking in groups of two or three down endless, crisscrossing grey paths. Hundreds of offerings cluttered tombstones: cups of wine, sliced apples, buns, and quarter-full bottles of Johnnie Walker.

In one allotment, three middle-aged people smoked beside a graveside picnic on a white tablecloth. Next door, a priest with black robes and a heavy brow read from a book; two women and two men stood behind, hands clasped. The priest upended a bottle of red wine, pouring crimson onto the grave in the shape of a cross.

A crow cawed. Laminated portraits decorated trunks of ragged trees like neighbourhood posters of lost pets. I squinted at Cyrillic words, willing them to transform into letters I knew. Soft rain drifted as a woman with blue-framed glasses stepped into my path and handed me a plastic box. I thanked her in Bulgarian, but she strode on, her task completed. Tradition said if you gave food to strangers, they would eat and pass nourishment to loved ones in the supernatural realm.

On the trolley home, I thought about clinging to religious beliefs during hardship, how it kept you sane, gave you hope. In 1944, the Bulgarian Communist Party collaborated with the Bolshevik totalitarian regime and overthrew the government by force, ruling until 1989. Remnants of the regime and paranoid surveillance were still evident in the shoddy concrete apartment buildings, in the corrupt, struggling economy, and in the distrust of strangers. The country was dominated by violence for so long; early in the regime, the bourgeois were arrested then executed, with over 26,000 dead before the end of 1944. Enemies were purged in waves of terror and, over forty years, almost 90,000 people were sent to labour camps. Human-rights leaders, writers, and activists were murdered. I could understand why folklore and superstition had lived on. Faced with life's brutality, it was solace to believe things were ordered and arranged. Suffering was resurrected by meaning.

On the seventh floor, heating fogged the window. I made a cup of tea and tasted what the blue-glasses woman had given me, chewing *koliva*, boiled wheat mixed with honey and nuts.

'Here you go, Nan,' I whispered. 'I hope you like it.'

Vitosha loomed through the mist. I envied the priests, the graveside boozers. At least they knew what they were doing. Where they were going.

A travel writer once told me he ate two meals a day to stretch money further. I tried very late breakfasts and early dinners, porridge then beans and rice. But I gobbled Pringles at bus stations, furtive and quick as if keeping a secret from myself. I was unwilling to accept my appetite because with hunger came shame.

My desperation was apparent: Marianne let me stay longer for free, and kept sharing meals. Her Swiss husband even made a vat of vodka-laced cheese fondue one snowy Friday night. Was I depending on God's providence, or just entitled? One night, I stole a block of Lindt chocolate from their kitchen pantry, making sure to dispose of the rubbish at the local park. My pilgrimage was unravelling, and so were my rules.

I'd sent emails in English to local scholars, and nobody replied. But after two weeks, something fell into my lap: a friend of Daniela was an academic, and she agreed to meet.

The Institute of Ethnology and Folklore Studies was housed in a former royal palace, an ornate lemon-coloured building that also held the National Art Gallery. The building was bright and pristine in contrast to Sofia's rundown shops and pragmatic Soviet concrete.

Katya, Daniela's friend, was the head of the Balkan Ethnology department. On a bright but blustery morning, I knocked on her office door and was faced with a woman in her late forties, with shoulder-length dirty-blonde hair, golden wire glasses, a sharp beak of a nose, and thin limbs ensconced in an olive wrap dress. The room had folk art on the walls, framed pictures of religious iconography, and a meeting table with a half-full bottle of Johnnie Walker Red, surrounded by eight students.

Katya rapidly listed everyone's names and research backgrounds in a heavy Bulgarian accent. I turned down a cup of whisky but said yes to coffee; a student spooned instant powder into a thin plastic cup, and poured boiling water.

'Now, your project is very, very interesting,' Katya said, cheeks hollowing as she sucked on a Marlboro. 'Why don't you tell everyone.' She swept a large palm around the table. The only man here had white hair and seemed to match Katya for seniority: they alone smoked and sipped from plastic cups of whisky.

With my sequined jumper and long curls whipped wild by arctic wind, I didn't feel very respectable, and tried to remember to slow my Australian accent. I told them about my search for the female counterpart of God. 'I am wondering if you could please tell me how Sophia — Holy Wisdom — is important to Sofia, the capital.'

Maryana, who recorded Bulgarian folklore tales in the nineties, shook her head. 'No — the city is named after *Saint* Sophia.'

That gleaming dame above the intersection did represent Holy Wisdom, apparently, but the story embedded in the city's mythology was about the saint, and confusingly, the statue was also named for that saint: a mother with three daughters, Faith, Hope, and Love. After Christianity became Bulgaria's national religion, an invading army demanded the family kneel to foreign gods. But the mother and her daughters pledged faith to God and allegiance to the state, and were beheaded.

'No one prays to St Sophia here,' Maryana said. 'She is just a statue.'

Oh. I nodded, forced grin frozen, the too-hot plastic cup softening in my hand. I had (a) come here with an incorrect assumption, and (b) no idea how to conduct myself in this situation.

Expectant faces around the table. I sipped black coffee from the melting cup, and spluttered when it burnt my lip. Katya, then, took over, and began what might have been a staff meeting, or perhaps a tutorial, in Bulgarian; she talked for forty minutes. She used body language to include me, and I tried to follow the rolling rhythm of z's and *sh*, breathing long and slow, digging nails into my palms. Finally, the students pulled on coats and scarves; the man rifled through a bookshelf — he was the department's director, it seemed — and selected several university journals, printed, mercifully, in English. When I read them later, I would find recordings of folklore, which I then posted home with other books I didn't need.

Cold wind blew as the ornate building's thin door slammed shut. The horror of my public ineptitude was, at this moment, greater than the actual fact of my ineptitude. Humiliation throbbed. I trudged back to my apartment and slid into bed despite the early hour. Oh God. I turned to Mt Vitosha, the sky streaked pink. St Sophia was just a statue. Her martyr tale saw violence as reward for devotion. Another story of female submission.

Rubbing legs back and forth in cold sheets, the depth of my mistake sank into my belly. I had come here on an assumption. I had failed in my investigation. God had not led me to the right place.

—

Feather snow fell. On the bus to Veliko Tarnovo, two TVs that were screwed into the ceiling played a film where a sexy woman tried to escape a male attacker. I tried to look at the white-dusted landscape, but movement attracted my eye to the screen: a man prowled outside a house as the female protagonist dashed from room to room, shutting doors, pulling curtains. The man eventually forced his way in. He had a gun.

Luckily, it was my stop. I pulled my suitcase up a slender, steep street to Rooster Guesthouse. Niki, a stocky man with short limbs, a gruff voice, and kind eyes, checked me into the eclectic two-storey affair with patterned wallpaper and mismatched furniture. Veliko Tarnovo was once a religious centre, the capital of the Second Bulgarian Empire from the twelfth to the fourteenth century. There were at least twelve monasteries within fifty kilometres, some with active convents. The nuns sold real estate, Niki said, and the monks made rakia. A translucent liquor distilled from grapes, plums, or apricots, the holy men's booze was known for its purity. In a last-ditch, flailing attempt at purpose, I hoped to visit the nuns to see if they might have any insight into my quest. Niki called nearby convents as I unpacked. But when I came down the rickety wooden stairs, he placed the telephone down and shook his head. None of the convents were open for visitors until after winter.

Not even the nuns wanted me. *God is on your side*, said the screens at Hillsong. I could spit.

I pulled on my coat, threw up my hood, and stamped out into Veliko Tarnovo. The town balanced on three hills surrounding the creamy green river Yantra, which curved like a snake below thin wooden houses, red roofs dusted with snow.

My research methods were haphazard and arrogant: I grabbed onto the ghost of an idea and bought plane tickets, then chased it through a country where I didn't belong. Magical thinking created an entitlement to celestial provision; I assumed the power that ordered the universe would meet my needs. This foolish practice had led me to a town in the middle of Bulgaria with absolutely no leads. What stupidity to expect otherwise. All my searching for mothers or a feminine divine or belonging gave me nothing nothing nothing.

I shuffled past the fruit market and its fragrant bakery to the supermarket, comforted by neat aisles and bright packaging. I didn't need to speak and declare my ignorance, only count coins onto a waiting palm. I returned to an empty kitchen to cook a joyless meal. For days, I was the only guest, lying in bed until noon with an Italo Calvino novel, then wandering town until dark. I fell into the habit of following men in the streets, trailing silhouettes in blue twilight and hooded figures down alleyways. But always, with a whip of a black jacket, they vanished.

I extended my stay. Niki invited me to exhibitions, lunch with musician friends, but I preferred my room. Bereft of a linear path, I floated in space. Wine in empty Italian restaurants that balanced on the river's cliff. Gin in a bohemian bar, lit by fringed lampshades. Night closed in. Mist hung over the river, glowing streetlight-orange. Walking home, I realised this petulant, resentful solitude was both imprisonment and refuge. I thrust my key into the guesthouse door.

Somebody was in the kitchen. Tall and lithe with a shaved head, Frankie assumed I would like to join him for dinner. I drifted in the wake of his decision. At the market, I mumbled and looked down as I bought butternut squash, while he had no qualms about speaking English. He fretted about recycling, snatching a jar of coconut oil from a market woman before she could summon a plastic bag.

We rummaged in the fridge and found a half-full bottle of wine. Frankie made salad as I cooked pumpkin soup, and he told stories about parties in Berlin. I laughed for the first time in weeks.

In the fuzz of dawn, a church bell clanged. As I woke, I saw the bell in my mind, unpolished brass swinging in a wooden tower, its rope pulled by a man in black. I should go, I thought, I should go and see the church, do what I'm supposed to do, but I rolled onto my back, opened my eyes, and watched snowflakes hit the skylight with soft thuds, for minutes, hours, thud, thud.

Lying in the single bed, I thought of the aftermath of the Nicene Creed. The writer and restaurateur Durkhanai Ayubi wrote in an article about the Australian media's response to war crimes: 'Controlling narratives arises through a dual function of both having the power to create myths, while simultaneously blocking the narratives of others from emerging.'

Isn't this what happened in Ireland? In Mexico? Brigit was altered in the hagiographies. Tonantzin became the Mother who sat below God. The Church Fathers created myths they liked, and blocked others. Those in power tell stories that justify, legitimise, and protect their power. Throughout history, men promoted stories that made male figures powerful, and erased female sovereignty. To gain psychological control, the church was built from temple stone; colonisers blocked old religions, adapted myths, and conquered spirituality.

The symbolism, language, and theology of Christianity were created by men, in patriarchal times. And perpetuated patriarchal arrangements.

A confident knock. I threw back the orange blanket. Frankie had made porridge with a pinch of cinnamon and turmeric, 'good for the health'. He handed me a bowl sprinkled with cashews and pumpkin seeds and turned down the stairs, his shaved head shining with coconut oil. I hated him for invading my solitude. I loved him for interrupting my loneliness.

But then he left, to travel west. Alone again, I trudged through crispy snow. Each step was like pushing through sludge. My search for truth was corporeal, and I felt its failure in my body.

I passed a cracked painting of a blue cat, then stepped down winding streets so steep I could see broken tiles on roofs below. Someone threw liquid from a second-storey window, the dirty water expanding in the air and slapping cobblestones; when I looked up, an arm slammed an ochre shutter. I took the thin bridge across green water, passed the art gallery with monuments to old wars, and climbed the hill Sveta Gora slowly, careful not to slip. Early-twilight gloom sank about my shoulders. The brooding river glowed.

I was without anchor or harbour, stunned by what I'd lost, but also what I'd found: Christianity wasn't God-breathed, but constructed by men. The religion that was once so precious to me was shaped to reinforce patriarchy. Attitudes, customs, and arrangements bloomed from this ideology.

The symbology of womanhood became associated not with action, will, or might, but submission and devotion. The book of Sophia — slashed from holy texts. Women's gospels forgotten, stolen, burnt. The Father God murdered the Mother, ate the goddesses, and sat on their throne.

If only I could return. If only I could be enfolded in the arms of a loving God. Go back to dancing on floorboards with bare feet, singing songs week after week after week. If only I could look up and see my Husband on stage, and know that He was mine and I was His.

Snow weighed heavy on fir branches. Behind me, a single set of black footprints on white. There was no going back. The belief system I'd clung to since I was fifteen had betrayed me. I could no longer trust the God who was once my saviour. My entire body ached.

I moved higher, panting, and turned onto a forest trail. I hadn't seen the sun for days; perhaps it had been extinguished. I didn't know which way was up or down; I was plunging in all directions. At a wrought-iron fence covered with snow, I pressed my hips against cold bars. Before me was a terrible drop.

The old self that loved the Father had to go. I threw her from the cliff of Sveta Gora and she fell among the snow, spinning down into the river below. The self that remained was shapeless, viscous, black; a self of transitions, of train stations, of stopovers; as changeable as the line where land meets sea.

Snowfall thickened and swirled above my head.

My ticket to Istanbul was already bought. In a deserted corner on Sofia train station's second floor, I leant my back against cold glass, chewing a lukewarm triangle of rubbery pizza and trying to ignore the chill seeping through my thick jacket. A lost sparrow thwacked into the window — *inside* — and fell to the ground fifty centimetres from where I sat. Its wings fluttered, then stilled. I poked it with a pen.

'Is this a goddamn joke?' I whispered, looking up.

At 9.00 pm, I wandered through the silent, vacant station, up escalators and down, squinting at my ticket. A long platform was covered with ankle-deep snow: far away, red carriage lights glowed. Outlines of figures moved like dark ghosts, and I hefted my suitcase towards them.

I squeezed through the first open door, and an apple-shaped conductor directed me to my compartment. He checked my ticket and drew from a thin cigarette beneath a grey moustache. A whistle peeped twice before the train hauled itself forward with a deep iron groan. I pressed my fingers to the cold glass window — imprinted with a star and crescent moon — watching the landscape ease by, the phosphorescent snow clouds. My research had stalled. This pilgrim had lost faith. But at least she was moving.

The conductor stamped back and forth down the half-empty train's narrow corridor, distributing a tartan blanket, a pillow, biscuits. He asked my name and kissed my hand, his moustache tickling my skin. (In Turkey, I would later meet an American woman who'd accepted a glass of milk on this same train and awoken to find she'd been drugged, her wallet stolen.) At 11.00 pm, the last heavy compartment door rolled shut, and I closed my eyes.

An abrupt knock. The moustache peeked in.

'Passport office. Yes?'

I checked my phone. 2.28 am. Outside, eerie light glinted on barbed wire. I pulled on my Docs and coat and followed two blonde Swiss women past a circle of men smoking in the snow, guns at their hips, a German shepherd standing to attention.

The floor was ripped lino, the cream walls cracked plaster. The train had gone back in time, to a world where I and my two Western passports had to line up at a border. Two bored, handsome men in the immigration office commanded in English nouns only. 'You. Visa. Here. Now.' The bearded one sat at a computer, typing, his eyes dead, smoke from the cigarette between his fingers rising in an unbroken line. The other, who had the same hooded eyelids and prominent nose as my brother, sat in the office behind. They yelled through the doorway to each other in Turkish, replying with short barks of laughter.

I was sent to the office, where a Dutch man punched numbers into a phone, trying to book a hostel in English, voice nervy and high. The border guard who looked like my brother pointed to a green armchair, and I followed his instruction while he leant back, crossed his arms, and watched the Dutch man fret.

Other passengers filled the room; time fell away in the middle of the night, halfway between countries. I looked up and realised they'd collected a crowd of young women. The air was tense. The man who looked like my brother asked me where I was staying, how long, the phone number of my host. The bearded man turned up the radio and sang in Turkish, strode slowly around in heavy boots, a hand on his weapon belt. He rested his large palm on a German woman's cheek.

And then he turned to me. Standing, he held out his hand for my phone. He scrolled through my photos, stopping on a selfie I'd taken on my bed in Veliko Tarnovo: arm over my head, mouth open in simulation of desire. Armpit black with hair. He chuckled and wrinkled his nose, drawing on his cigarette. I laughed, embarrassed.

'Can I show?' he said, and pointed the screen at his colleague. They asked if I had leg hair; I nodded and they giggled. I couldn't tell if we were laughing together or if the atmosphere could snap; all the other women were doing the same, laughing and smiling, laughing and smiling and watching. The guards told me I could leave.

We got into Istanbul at 5.00 am. At the Eminönü Metro station exit, I parked my red suitcase away from the pedestrian surge and leant my head back in bright, bleak sunlight. Diesel fumes, salt water, traffic noise, seabird squawk. The erotic thrill of the unknown zapped from my pelvis to my collarbone. The midnight train ride and the visa office filled with dread washed away like a dream. I gazed into a clear sky full of looping birds.

Istanbul is the only city in the world that straddles two continents. I trundled my suitcase along crowded docks to the ferry that would take me across the Bosphorus Strait to Kadıköy, the Asian side. I slid into a wooden bench and ordered tea in a tulip-shaped glass, watching the endless city and its icons glide past through a window streaked with seagull shit. The Blue Mosque and its six minarets. Hagia Sophia, once a Byzantine cathedral, then a mosque, now a museum (and since 2018, a mosque again). Ever since the conquest by the Ottoman Turks in the fourteenth and fifteenth centuries, mosques had dotted the city, and now the call to prayer echoed five times a day. The ferry twisted; the sun danced in the fullness of a blue sky then fell behind a cumulus cloud, painting the rounded edge gold. I rocked with the cadence of the waves.

Kadıköy's four-storey apartment buildings rose high above the docks. My suitcase gained weight with each step up this arduous hill. My new roommates were Kubra, a social worker, Buket, an environmental activist, and their tortoiseshell cat. Bed at 7.00 pm. I was haggard after the journey, the overwhelming city, the way my world was falling apart bit by bit. I dreamt of my father, my mother, my brother and I, our childhood home destroyed by flood.

At 2.00 am, tremendous thuds shook the building. I sidled up to the window. A bellowing bear of a man was throwing pot plants at steel bars on the ground floor. A woman inside screamed. It was my fifth country in as many months — I didn't know the number for police. Luckily, the bear ambled down the steep street in the direction of the water, or perhaps another bar.

I pushed in earbuds, played a meditation app.

'Please,' I prayed, though I didn't know who to, or what I needed.

Yellow streetlight filtered through the blinds, casting shadow-stripes on the wall. I closed my eyes and imagined myself as pure spirit, a long, glowing creature who slipped out of her skin like a robe. The meditation guided me to feel my heartbeat. Spinning decades into the past, I was curled up on Mum's lap, she was rocking us both. *BUD-um. BUD-um.* Her palm on my back. Tapping out the rhythm. *BUD-um. BUD-um.* Her heart, my heart, our hearts beating as one.

I watched *Gilmore Girls* in bed until afternoon, then ambled listlessly through Kadıköy's alleys. Istanbul was red, aquamarine, coral apartment buildings, storefronts lined with arabesque tiles, windows guarded by curling iron bars. My neighbourhood held stationery shops and creative studios; vintage stores and wagons piled with *erik*, sour green plums; dim cafes with lamps glowing on walls with shelves of old books. Some were filled with wrinkled, hunched men and backgammon boards, some served americanos alongside Turkish coffee and stylish beards conferred with solemn faces while couples whispered in booths. A svelte man leant his face into purple curls, her hand on his black jeans. Speaking in Turkish but as lovers, too, thoughts whispered from mouth to ear, touch throbbing with desire. I was exiled from both tongues.

Carpet sellers idled, hands in pockets, under patterned rugs draped over branches. Starved-looking men pulled wooden carts laden with tremendous piles of cardboard and plastic, their hips twisting in ragged jeans. A walnut-faced woman tried to push a pack of tissues into my hand for one lira, and I refused. Cats yowled, crunching kitty kibble left on doorsteps, and groomed themselves on motorbike seats.

Public space in Istanbul was male space. There were simply more men on the street than women. They didn't just look me up and down; they locked eyes as I passed, demanding. Eros shimmered like summer haze.

Each day, I dangled my feet from the dock, watching ferries. Under my boots, the soft, undulating bodies of jellyfish expanded and tightened beneath a shimmering, polluted surface. An eerie fog settled. Sounds became muted. Passenger-laden ferries faded into a dream. Minarets disappeared. There was no distance, just a void. An endless, directionless nothing. I peered into white.

On International Women's Day, I wanted to walk in solidarity with local feminists. Last year, the police had arrested protestors. This year, the march in the capital, Ankara, was being shut down by authorities. My traveller app said to avoid protests in Turkey. Buket found a friend, Selma, to accompany me.

'If it gets violent,' said Buket, 'you can just go into a side street, and like, pretend to be watching.' She was bent over a bowl of lentils and noodles in the kitchen. 'It probably won't happen, but just remember with tear gas the best thing is not to breathe it. So yes, bring your scarf, so you can hold it like this.' She pressed a tea towel over her pierced nose.

'I'm not scared or anything,' I said, 'but what are the signs of it, like, escalating?'

She gave a nonchalant shrug. 'Police, they are a bad sign. But you will be able to tell. The air changes. Just keep watching.'

I waited for a ferry, the afternoon call to prayer echoing nasally from a minaret. I'd never imagined feeling unsafe at a protest back home. As much as I desired to escape Australia, it was a very safe place. For me, at least — a white, middle-class woman, I was never a target for police brutality.

The sky darkened as we crossed the water. An old lady in a floral headscarf who was sitting nearby spoke to me in Turkish. I asked her to use Google Translate, and passed her my phone. She typed slowly, before handing it back. Her words appeared on the screen: 'Are you a pilgrim?'

The ferry docked and I didn't have to answer. On İstiklal Caddesi, the shopping strip that led to Taksim Square, men and women with POLİS emblazoned in white on blue jackets stood in alleys. Some held large guns. Water cannons were parked at either end of the strip. Thunder rolled and broke across the sky. I realised the police were positioned to block all exits.

I spotted Selma, sitting at Urban Cafe, distinguished by her red lips and black blunt fringe. We ordered pizza and beer, and she updated me on activists' campaigns. The Istanbul Convention, she said, was a charter that guided EU countries to provide legal consequences for gender-based violence. The government here was refusing to implement its recommendations.

Selma wrapped strings of mozzarella around a triangle slice. Women's groups in Turkey, she told me, were still fighting for domestic violence to be taken seriously.

The street was packed. Women with hijabs and shaylas had Venus symbols painted on their cheeks in crimson glitter, and marched with drummers, Persian dancers, and Kurdish singers. Older women with long grey plaits, middle-aged ladies with flowing black hair. A thousand shrill whistles, a hundred rainbow flags. For an hour, we followed the paved tramline from Taksim Square to the east end of the mall.

Selma shouted in my ear. 'There used to be rocks under the tramline. But during the coup in 2015, protesters threw them at police.'

The beating of drums. Voices together, fury as celebration. Police didn't move, but stood stock-still by bright department stores. The might of the state, this year, was just a threat.

Selma translated a slogan: 'If women are free, the earth will shake.' And another: 'We rise from the ashes you burnt.' She pulled a blue-and-white packet of Winstons from her pocket, lit up. 'Do you know the book *Women Who Run with the Wolves*?' she yelled, exhaling smoke high into the air.

I nodded — Auntie Liz had given me a copy years ago. It was about women reclaiming wildness, learning from myths and stories all over the world. I'd never got past the first chapter.

Selma's eyes were wide. 'Women read it together in groups. It's very big here.'

On the ferry home, the black sky opened. I was soaked and unafraid, despite being out after dark: the streets were full of women.

The year after I attended, police attacked the annual march with tear gas.

Days later, I answered a call from Gemma during a storm. Cancer, she said. The man I was still legally married to was very sick. It was a scare, He had an operation, He's better now. It happened months ago. He didn't want me to know.

I laughed. It poured out like tar.

Her voice was soft. 'I was worried about telling you,' she said. 'Because you're alone.'

At the supermarket, my heart throbbed in my ears as I requested a pack of Winstons and a lighter. I looked over my shoulder as I exited, but nobody commanded me to stop. Was it really that easy? Down the hill to the ferry dock, the streets washed clean by rain. Beneath a clearing sky, I dangled my legs over the water, flicking the lighter, cupping my hand in the wind until I could finally get the first damn cigarette to light. I sucked it in, my throat raw.

I'd not wanted to think of Him for so long, and now here He was, a stubborn cow in the middle of the road. My pilgrim road, mine! There were so many things I hadn't done because He thought I shouldn't, couldn't. Cut my hair short. Wear a nose ring. Study abroad. Smoke like the cool kids at uni. How much of my life had been dictated by His judgement?

Ferries twisted, docked, and hundreds of passengers dispersed into the crowd. Flocks of carnivorous seagulls cackled in their wake.

Religion had given me a system of law, had ordered the universe into clear, straight lines. But I didn't want it anymore. If patriarchy killed the Mother, it was time for me to kill the Father God. I drove a knife into his heart. Colour drained from his unholy face. I watched the oil-slicked water and imagined the lifeless body of the king descending past jellyfish down into the deep.

Everything felt toxic. I'd laughed when I discovered my Husband had cancer. Was I evil? I'd always thought of myself as good, innocent, sweet. But today I was glad for His suffering. And I had betrayed Him at the end of our marriage, too. Why? Did I hate Him? What else was buried deep? What else would rise up unbidden? Everything certain about myself and the world was breaking, was dissolving, was slipping into black.

I flicked the cigarette butt into the water, watched it float on lapping waves. I wanted to be, I wanted to speak, I wanted to act separate from Him. The desire to destroy, yes, to cut away. I jumped from wooden planks, marched up steep streets painted gold-red in sunset's sharp light, and found a hairdresser. A man in track pants and a silver-blue beard rose from his chair as I entered. Without Turkish, I mimed what I wanted. He guided me to a mirror, shrouded me in black. Cold ceramic sink on the back of my neck, warm water spray, shampoo head scrub, his rough stubby fingertips working at my scalp the first touch in months. Upright, I watched my reflection with burning eyes. Wet curls dropped to the ground. The man with the silver-blue beard believed he was finished, but I pointed to his scissors, shook my head, and said, 'More.'

I used to love Him. Metallic click, sharp slice. Dark new moons fell on the tiled floor. When I left, it would be swept away. The Father God. And the Husband. Who told me what to do.

before

The Flesh Is Weak

Mum handed out steaming bowls of spag bol, and Ben reached into the middle of the table for a handful of grated cheese. It was unusual for us to eat at the dining table; we normally had dinner in front of the TV. It wasn't long before the special occasion became apparent: the sex talk.

'Louise,' Mum sighed. 'Your Boyfriend has been staying over a lot lately.'

I paused, fork halfway to my mouth. Dad and Ben fixated on their bowls, chewing.

Mum's voice forced lightness. 'I went shopping today, and when I saw some condoms, I put a box in my trolley.'

A pasta spiral dropped from my fork with a wet splash.

'Mu-um.' My face was red. 'We don't *need* them. I told you. We're not having sex until marriage.'

This statement seemed true because it was predicated on my intention. The reality was different: we spent a lot of time exploring each other's bodies, and hadn't yet graduated to *sex* sex — penetration. But we didn't speak about it. I'd started masturbating when I was still young enough for my parents to tuck me in. Now seventeen, I orgasmed most nights in a fantasy swirl, rubbing at my clit as if making fire from flint and stone. My 'addiction' patterned in a cycle: guilt, stopping, beginning again. Each revolution, I tunnelled further into self-loathing. If I could just rein in selfish desires, I'd obey God's will. But I was constantly coming up short.

The Pastor said God created sex to be enjoyed in the lifelong commitment of marriage. Making love was meaningful; two became *one flesh*. Sex wasn't a simple matter of bodies, but of hearts and minds, too; of souls. Seeking pleasure was simply instant gratification that would leave me feeling empty. I accepted that this heavenly logic was beyond my understanding, so tried to submit my will to God. This required great cognitive dissonance. Despite being a prolific wanker, I couldn't admit that I deeply wanted to fuck.

My struggle to be holy was concerned with appearances. Out loud, I repeated the dogma — God designed sex for marriage — and did not speak of the heat that rolled from hips to shoulders, could not describe my throbbing vulva when my Boyfriend and I kissed, was unable to voice how swiftly I got wet. I longed for the forbidden.

There were no purity rings in our youth group, just cultural norms communicated through Friday-night sermons and special nights split into boys and girls. Under Jane's guidance, Katie and Sally and I read *Every Young Woman's Battle: guarding your mind, heart, and body in a sex-saturated world* by Shannon Ethridge and Stephen Arterburn. The authors encouraged their teenage readers to 'stand strong' against pressure to give up their 'self-respect'. It was clear: good girls didn't have sex. Sexual activity was transgression and therefore disobedience to God, which had social, moral, and spiritual consequences.

The book said girls wanted love and boys wanted sex. I was confused, because I already felt loved by Him, and He was never wheedling or persuasive. There was no room in the sanctioned story for female desire. This gendered split perpetuated the myth of the active male and passive female. Boys were counselled about porn addictions, which leaders saw as one of the greatest moral challenges of our time. Girls were encouraged to dress modestly, warned against tight tops and short skirts. Whatever gender, we were warned to guard against sexual temptation. The devil lurked in every shadowed corner. *Every Young Woman's Battle* recommended leaving the bedroom door open.

Yet despite planning to 'save it', when He and I closed my cream door, when the brass knob turned and the spindle locked into its latch, all eyes died and we created our own private universe.

I was brought to rapture by the hot taste of His flesh. If He were on a throne, I would have kissed His feet. Church taught me that the object of my worship was perfect. I didn't know how dangerous it was to transfer devotion to my lover, and believe He, too, was blameless, all-knowing, and all-powerful.

We didn't sleep, but spent hours suspended in aching desire, ticking off each notch of 'everything but': kissing, groping, fingering, hand jobs. His ecstatic palm on my breast, His firm cock in navy jocks, the springing of His flesh as I lowered His waistband with shaking breath, the sparse dark pubic hairs that spread to His thighs. At first, I feared His dick, that strange and fascinating creature, that *other*; then I came to love the pink foreskin, the proud strength of the erection, the alien, soft testicles. I transformed into warm dark treacle, nothing but sensation, touch, and stifled moans. His hand lingered feathery on my hip bone, then slid beneath my underwear, soft fingertips tracing my vulva's lips. He was tender, sweet, generous. He rarely ejaculated, as the culmination of orgasm would mean we'd planned this trespass, that we chose to sin.

After the sex talk with Mum, we would finally progress to halting half-intercourse. By which I mean He'd enter and thrust several times before one of us would retract. Pregnancy was barely a risk, because neither of us ever surrendered. Jesus lingered at the edge of our momentary paradise, biting his nails, nasally whimpering, 'Guys, stop! Stop it!' until my Boyfriend pulled out.

But we weren't at that point yet. Right now, every time we went 'too far', one of us would whisper, 'We should stop.' As if we had strayed, and a leash around our necks whipped us back. Exhilaration faded, and I realised I'd betrayed God again. Those holy pairs: guilt and desire. Hunger and shame. Why was it so hard to be good?

Sex is a teenage rite of passage. But the secrecy and doublethink of the Christian approach gave sex another initiatory significance: I became intimate with the self-deception that is essential in the religious toolkit.

And here at the dinner table, I was being asked to publicly reveal that I was betraying God. Mum across from me, frazzled hair escaping her scrunchie, large empathic brown eyes. I couldn't say yes, Mum, I would like some condoms. To do so would be to admit my weakness, declare my intention to sin, and contradict my identity. I was a daughter of God. I was his obedient disciple. I was a good girl.

She raised her eyebrows at my denial. 'Well, if you ever need them,' she smiled, pretending nonchalance, 'they're in the bathroom cupboard.'

Ben huffed into his pasta. He wanted this excruciating conversation over. So did I.

'Um, thanks, Mum? I won't.'

The Interior Judge

I was on a one-way street to suburbia. After my short Sunday School career, I did not repent and love the children of God; instead, my disgust expanded. Parents, too, repulsed me. Clean-shaven, powder-blue-shirt-wearing dads whose bodies softened at thirty-five; mums in neat dresses with bulky prams who cut their hair in identical, shining bobs, whose nappy bags clattered with tiny containers of sultanas, whose homes always vaguely smelt of baby shit. In sermons, Christian family life was presented as the battleground where adults worshipped God while navigating parenthood and marriage and paying off SUVs and Thermomix parties and working a dead-end job flexible around school pick-up hours. They were all so goddamn nice, their 2.5 children displayed as trophies to moral goodness, social success, and ability to achieve heteronormative milestones. I saw motherhood as a life sentence to domestic labour.

I entered my second year of university and identified as feminist. Christian gender roles began to rub. Wise and funny women who refused conformity became my role models and taught me to take a critical eye. A community's values are visible in what it celebrates, i.e. who is onstage. Most Sunday singers wore tight skinny jeans, heels, and modest tops with make-up but never *too* much. They were thin, non-assertive, and sweet. The infrequent times women did preach, they joked about shopping, shoes, and diets. Those who were disobedient — by being overweight, or highly educated, or determined and direct — were the bottom of the dating pool. They floundered in their late twenties, attending four weddings a year, trusting God would provide them with the right man.

Men in the church excelled at performative goodness. They talked real nice to us girls, called us sweetie when we were young, and expected women to be pretty and incompetent. In closed circles, just the boys, they could talk as dirty as any non-Christian. And most of them had 'pornography addictions', which they revealed at men's breakfasts, then gave five-point sermons on handing this struggle over to God. Confession and repentance the sole method of expressing something close to an authentic sexuality.

Western evangelistic church culture is often seen as 'feminised' due to being highly emotive. The positive result was men somewhat able to express feelings; however, masculine ideals were still constructed around worldly machismo. Fathers and husbands were told to stand strong in their roles of provision and leadership, and special men's events featured fast cars, sports, or camping.

This heteronormativity, in its misogyny and sexual repression and obsession with coupling, stank of hypocrisy — but most of all it bored me. I was destined for greatness, but this road only led to a white picket fence.

Then God gave the Pastor a vision for a new church. He was in a hotel lobby on a Cambodian mission trip when the words came to him: a community of activists, modelled on the life of Jesus, empowered by the Holy Spirit. He was a visionary and needed followers. My Boyfriend and I left our teenage church to join the Pastor's core team.

Together, we stepped away from the familiar to build something new, exiting our suburb of middle-class families to drive to the other side of town, where migrants and students lived. We spent hours every Sunday setting up and packing down, and two nights a week at Bible study or strategy meetings or volunteer groups.

In sermons, the Pastor courted radical politics, diagnosing the world's ills: capitalist greed, racial prejudice, economic inequality. Sin was structural. Our answer: sacrificial service to heal this broken world. His posture sprouted from liberation theology, which followed the example of Jesus Christ as liberator of the poor and marginalised. Liberation theology was developed by Jesuits with a taste for Marxism in 1950s Latin America. They demanded economic justice through social liberation from poverty, providing a doctrinal foundation for political uprisings.

The poet revolutionary cut his hair and shaved his beard. His bachelor's degree wasn't in theology, but communications; with every role shift, he adapted his image of success. A master of rhetoric, he didn't just carry the preacher's toolbox, curating energy's rise and fall, but also used his sharp intellect to bend existing paradigms, unearth new perspectives, and present himself (and us) as unorthodox and brave. Each sermon felt like we were breaking ground, advancing towards justice like no one else on earth.

We were Pentecostal, which meant we belonged to the same denomination as Hillsong: Australian Christian Churches. At first, we merged with an existing community and inherited elderly churchgoers and two pastors in their seventies. As well as middle-class white hipsters in their twenties and thirties, our audience included young migrant families, first from countries in eastern Africa, then Iran and Afghanistan. Refugee rights became our political focus, in response to our friends' lived experience of barbaric immigration policies. The Pastor emphasised un-conditional welcome as an antidote to xenophobia, attacking racism in the Australian government and media. He preached that Christ was crucified beside thieves, condemning societal divisions as meaningless, obliterating notions of 'us versus them'. The Apostle Paul wrote that there was neither slave nor free, all are one in Jesus Christ. Yes, we cried, this was the desire of our hearts!

Sometimes people would point out holes in the Pastor's sermons, and he often listened; he had the spirit of an entrepreneur, viewing uncomfortable situations as opportunities to grow. But most who disagreed simply left. Church elders dropped away. A former administrator resigned because in a press release about a festival we organised the Pastor rounded up attendee numbers. He was always hurt by these incidents — we discussed the burden of leadership at meetings — but church seniority suited him. The Pastor was a maverick. Higher authorities got in his way.

He founded a refugee advocacy organisation, of which he was also the figurehead. Bigger and bigger community groups invited him to give speeches. In the hall beside our chapel, volunteers ran morning teas and English classes, and delivered furniture to new arrivals in the western and northern suburbs. One rainy June day, I drove my friend Emma to a politician's office. She joined a nun, a priest, and nine other activists on the floor, praying and refusing to move until all children were removed from the government's refugee detention centres. I left when they were arrested, unwilling to put my own body on the line.

God was using us to heal the world, and everyone was expected to have an activist cause. I found mine: sex-worker outreach. Funded through YWAM, an international network of missionaries, a group of young women met on Friday nights to pray and read out a passage from Ephesians, asking the Lord to protect us with the armour of God. And then we became a light in the darkness and went out into the night. My first time out, my mouth was as dry as if I'd run a mile. We sat in lounges where bored women in dressing gowns smoked or ate Thai takeaway, awkwardly chatting. Some brothels met us with hostile tolerance. Others welcomed us, recognising our clumsy intentions. And then we took to the streets, idling up Grand Junction Rd at 10.00 pm in a maroon van, all six passengers squinting with the concentration of safari hunters until someone squeaked, 'There's one!' and we pulled over and handed out not condoms but chocolate bars and Bibles. Our mission was to 'rescue' girls. I quit after two years, when a fundraising night I invited my family to hosted an anti-abortion politician.

Encouraged by the Pastor, by the time I was twenty I'd been on two mission trips, where a group of church volunteers travelled to countries in Asia. In the safe fold of familiar people, I stepped into hot, humid air, saw ecstatic visions of fireflies hovering in black night, and ate pawpaw and dragon fruit. These trips were tropical holidays, yet we also witnessed slum houses and outdoor kitchens, smelt terrible sewerage, and encountered a deep need for social welfare. My first trip was to the north of Thailand and Laos, the second to South India with the sex-worker outreach group, journeying by train from east coast to west. Though I'd never successfully wielded a shovel in my life, in Thailand I had to inexplicably dig holes. In India, we gave money to homeless outreach centres and prostitute rescue services.

These trips in my early adult life cemented two things. The first, a shocked hatred of materialism; I came to view Western greed as responsible for Third World poverty. My aversion to neoliberal thinking and the profit-before-people mentality provoked a guilty ethics of charity and alternative consumerism.

The second thing these trips solidified was my saviour complex. By name, I sought equality; but by hidden nature, I sought to enact and evidence my superiority. Evangelism consolidates believers' convictions that they have the ability to give the suffering what they need. Despite Jesus' humble character, Christianity embeds intellectual arrogance that transfers the hierarchy between God and worshipper to Christians and nonbelievers.

But I was blind to this. In my new, exciting, social justice-focused church, nothing could stop us. God's love was all-encompassing, and it was our mission to tell the world. Cognitive dissonance, a

Christian's close companion, was helpful. We threw buckets of water on hellfire. We ignored most of the Old Testament, with its warring and vengeful God. We preferred the texts that reinforced our world view.

Our community grew; weekly attendance was never more than 200, and most often between forty and seventy. We met in unused schoolrooms, then shared a dusty Baptist church, and finally found a hundred-year-old red-brick Anglican chapel in a trendy inner-west suburb. It became a hub of teachers and social workers and activists. We learnt to show 'love in action' by sharing meals, visiting the sick, signing petitions, and organising fundraisers. Everyone had important jobs. My Boyfriend served God with music; He ran the worship team, curated the weekly band, and played guitars or drums every Sunday. I was in charge of 'hospitality' and took the church's bank card to buy flour, eggs, and sugar before spending a few weekend hours baking.

For church picnics, I bought discounted sausages and steaks from Dad's shop. The men cooked the barbie while women did salads in the kitchen (to be fair, gender-balance disruptors were welcomed. Abby, a musician in sunnies and a striped T-shirt, loved to preside over sizzling meat with beer can in hand). On weekend camps I organised a roster of volunteers to cater mass pots of pasta. The work was never lonely; we served together.

I enjoyed the Pastor's praise. But voluntary labour was laced with anxiety and haunted by my inadequacy: nothing I did was enough. I knelt before the cross, singing of my brokenness, declaring I was only whole with God. Sacrificial service required us to curb the selfish true self, to model our lives on Christ. Only then could we change the world. Only then could God bring the justice for which we longed. To act, then, was not motivated from personal initiative, but a 'should' based on externally defined norms that took up lodging in my heart. I no longer needed a WWJD bracelet; I learnt to police my thoughts through the lens of an Interior Judge.

I leant close to the bathroom mirror. My curls were pinned in a fringe, a rebellion against my Boyfriend, who thought it looked silly. I yanked my backpack and flung open the door; I was going to be late.

Legs sweating in March heat, I hurried across North Tce in a lavender-red plaid pencil skirt and fuchsia leotard. Serving God was no longer limited to Sundays now that the Pastor employed me as finance administrator. I paid the bills and recorded each of his transactions, as most of his expenses could be paid by the church and therefore bypass PAYG tax. It also meant I knew where he'd been and when, as I recorded receipts by date. An intimate view as unspoken reward for my service.

I entered the air-conditioned cafe, lifted large sunglasses with practised pursed lips, and clocked him straight-backed at his laptop. A phone held to his ear, he'd let his beard grow scruffy and soft. There were dark circles under his eyes. As I swanned through the scent of basil and roasting garlic, I realised who he was talking to: a friend from a Lutheran Church. During a youth camp in the Barossa Valley, a fifteen-year-old had to be exorcised, and eight men prayed over him for hours. Now, they were on trial for assault charges and false imprisonment because they tied him up to get the demon out.

'Look, mate,' he said, raising his eyebrows to me in greeting, 'just let me know if you need anything.'

I sat down and he finished the call.

'Lou!' He grinned. 'Your hair looks cool.'

'Thanks.' I blushed. I always felt as if the Pastor was delighted to see me. I was lucky to spend time with him; the Pastor didn't do pastoral care like most church leaders, who fostered relationships with every single member. Instead, he was only close with the core team, and delegated relational care, preferring to work in strategy.

The professional line between us was blurred. For years, the Pastor had mentored me one on one, and he was intimately acquainted with my struggles and fears. Today, he was counselling me for my baptism. While some denominations baptised babies, Pentecostals followed the born-again, evangelical tradition, which saw it as an adult decision that implied lifelong dedication to the Lord. The practice sprouted from ancient times, when John the Baptist dunked new believers in the Jordan River. They symbolically died to their old selves and rose into new life. My baptism would be a public ceremony to declare to my community that my life was committed to God. A graduation of sorts, from childish belief to a mature faith that promised sacrifice and deep, spiritual reward.

I could think of no one better than the Pastor to guide me through this milestone. His life — working long hours for our community, inspiring social change, and being committed to his wife, two daughters, and disabled son — meant he was the closest person I knew to Jesus. I filed his opinions away, and when faced with a challenge, measured it with his judgement. WWJD had become What Would The Pastor Do? He encouraged us not to idolise him: he was just a man; he made mistakes. But Christian culture upheld parishioners' reliance on pastors' judgement; spiritual leaders were expected to define clear moral boundaries for others to follow. God inspired an Interior Judge, and my relationship with the Pastor meant that the internalised moral guide took on his voice.

A waiter arrived with a skinny latte and cappuccino.

'Thank you, Dave.' The Pastor threw the man a quick, dazzling smile, and I used the opportunity to steal a look at the dark chest hair at his shirt's opening. My lips tingled.

He turned back to me. 'How are you going with your anxiety, darling?'

I'd recently missed an event because I couldn't walk into a room of people I didn't know. Anxiety was the best word I knew to say I was afraid all the time. The fear of what to say, the stab in my ribs, the knowledge that nothing would ever be enough.

'Not great. But last week Emma and I prayed.' I twisted a napkin between my fingers. My best friend at church, Emma was a blonde Vicar of Dibley, all bosom, tight hugs, and dirty jokes. A social worker at the roughest school in Adelaide, she projected a nonchalant fortitude and strange power to speak into a situation's emotional truth. Highly empathic with a dry humour, she could make me burst into laughter with one sarcastic raised eyebrow. And she had supernatural gifts. She spoke in tongues on Sundays, and relayed prophecies to our congregation from the microphone with shaking breath.

'She asked the Holy Spirit to release me from it, to break the chains, you know?' I hated my weak voice. She had laid hands on me, an action designed to channel God's power. We wanted Jesus to take everything away. Our doctrine of healing meant emotional pain could be 'fixed', and psychological problems could dissolve. Because Jesus could 'break the chains that bind us'.

'And I told God how much I need him, how much I want healing. And I felt instantly better. Like he had released me.'

'Lou, I just want you to know …' He leant forward. The buzz of the cafe died. His hazel irises looked into me, unwavering, and I had to look away. Prolonged eye contact was a learnt body-language technique, intended to communicate deep acceptance.

'You can call me any time. Okay? Whenever you feel scared, or like you can't do something. I'll answer. I'm here for you.'

Two focaccias arrived, and we fell into spontaneous conversation. I was conscious of chewing, how my stupid lips closed around my fork. Our meetings always lasted a disciplined one hour. As we finished eating, I realised our time together was almost up. He paid.

'Gotta run. We'll talk about your baptism next time, okay?' He tucked his wallet into his pocket and checked his phone. 'You right to get home?'

I nodded. We stepped into dry heat and hugged before he walked away. He turned for a last goodbye and waved with an open palm. 'Love you!'

I looked at nearby strangers in Ebenezer Place, my heart beating. Did anyone else hear that?

Weeks passed and I didn't call. But we continued to meet. No matter what, he always kept his appointments. The Pastor created an inner circle. And for a time, that was where I belonged.

'In the name of the Father, and the Son, and the Holy Spirit.'

I held my breath. His palm on the back of my head guided me underwater.

'Arise! Into new life!' He pulled me back into the light. Water streamed from my face, and I wiped my eyes, beaming. We stood together onstage, in a large corrugated iron tub of warm water. Before me was a congregation of a hundred, plus Mum and Dad, Nan, Auntie Liz. They'd come to watch me die and be born again.

The Pastor took my hand and helped me step from the tub,

then got out himself, dripping on a towel.

'Thank you, Lord,' he prayed into a microphone that a helper held to his mouth, 'for Lou's commitment to you.'

I changed into a dress my Boyfriend had bought me, and took a seat beside my family. I wanted them to be proud of my transition to adulthood and to understand that I was now a woman of principle, who'd dedicated her life to obeying God and following the socialist self-sacrifice of Jesus. The baptism solidified my identity; I would cling to my commitment on hard days, when I knew I couldn't go back on my word, nor the structured, community-declared self.

Today was also our church's first birthday. That morning at 9.00 am, Maria, the Greek widow in black, had started roasting carrots and potatoes. Shane, a man in his fifties with hair growing from his ears, was once a cook, so I had delegated onion-chopping to him. Now that church was over, he carried out steaming trays of sliced lamb.

I monitored visitors serving themselves meat and roast vegetables with silver tongs. My face red, I squeezed through bodies to place hands on shoulders and enquire about the meal's edibility. Friends handed me congratulation cards with Bible verses scrawled inside.

Afterwards, I sought out my Boyfriend onstage, where He was packing guitar pedals into a neat case and ignoring my family. He limited His social engagement, thereby making it more valuable; when He finally spoke to my parents, He would be met with great appreciation. His long arms wrapped me in a tight hug.

'Great work, babe.' There was pride in His soft, deep voice.

after

Scotland

From Istanbul, I bought a cheap flight and flew to a country where I spoke the language. An Airbnb host met me in a dark alley and asked me to follow him into the shadows — the apartment entrance was at the building's rear. I scowled as I changed into pyjamas in a small, tastelessly wallpapered room. He was clueless about travelling alone as a woman, and the constant task of assessing what was safe and what was danger.

At Glasgow Station, I used a cafe's wi-fi to open my bank app, and saw the money Dad had sent. I could buy breakfast! Chewing a toasted sandwich, my red suitcase beside me, I listened to snatches of passing strangers' conversations in sweet, sweet English.

Jean picked me up from Dumfries station, near Scotland's west coast — I'd arranged through a website to housesit her renovated cottage and elderly black cat, Pudsie. Five months into my journey, I needed time to recuperate. She took me to the tidal River Nith at the end of her street. Slick sand reflected white light.

'If you feel like wild swimming, absolutely do not,' Jean warned. The wind blew with regular ferocity, icy fingers pushing through every stitch. 'The tides here are very strong, because we're so close to the river's mouth. A man fell in last December, but they couldn't find his body. We had to have Christmas while he was in the river.' She tucked strands of blonde hair behind her ear. 'Every time I put on my running shoes, I had to think, is today the day I see a dead body?'

We stopped to meet our only neighbour, Mae Clark, an elderly woman who lived riverside. Despite being almost blind, she'd stubbornly applied a full face of make-up. Her eyebrows were thick brown streaks halfway up her forehead, her lipstick defiant beyond the outlines of her mouth. She'd had two geese, she said, but someone stole the boy. 'The one left behind is grieving, ye ken?' she said, passing me a cellophane packet of clotted-cream fudge, her face an abstract Picasso.

I waved Jean and her partner off on their holiday, and in the lounge room opened the wood-oven door. For thirteen years, Jesus was with me. An eternal companion. I scrunched newspapers, laid kindling, lit a match. An orange flame flickered. Sometimes, God had spoken back: I heard words in my mind, a quiet whisper that came from outside of me. I placed a small log on the kindling, closed the oven, watched it take. But now my thoughts were sonar blips that echoed and faded into vacant darkness. Nobody was listening. Nobody could hear.

After thirty minutes, the wood oven was black. I climbed into bed on the second floor and wrapped my arms around my belly. Through the skylight, the stars and moon watched me sleep.

Mae Clark's goose honked at dawn, an ugly, two-toned squawk: *WEH-ah, WEH-ah.*

Curled up on Jean's cream couch with a coffee, I played with my hair and felt like a newborn kitten, all wayward tufts and weak squeaks. Sun pushed through the curtains, and my eyelids closed against the light. I'd killed God, now I was exhausted. I tied the laces of my Docs to greet the water.

It was bright, so very bright, the morning sun bleak, the sky tumultuous grey. I trudged to a jetty at the next town, trembling in the rowdy blow. Geese flew in a V above, a message from nature, but I no longer knew what it meant. In the quiet house, I took a hot bath with a novel, then rubbed condensation from the mirror and squinted at my tired, pink face, the short frizzy curls. Nan had a similar hairstyle in the nineties.

The next day, I ambled past Coke bottles, old boots, branches tied with coloured twine. Flocks of gulls arced over shallow water, then descended and dotted the quicksilver surface. Three miles into town, a fair flashed garish colours on the riverside. Teenagers gripped dodgem-car steering wheels; mothers rode sacks down the Superslide with toddlers on their laps; fathers rolled their eyes at the price of toffee apples. Today was my wedding anniversary. Seven years ago, we were married.

The bluster of wind was an assault upon my hollow body. I stumbled back to the fireplace, where shaky flames flared for two hours before burning out. I once thought we'd have babies, of course, like the parents at the fair. I took thick mouthfuls of clotted-cream fudge, yet still hunger gaped. I slid into crisp, cool sheets and tried to breathe deep, but there was a sharp, knife-slice pain in my ribs. I'd said goodbye a hundred times, a thousand. I still couldn't get the fire to burn through the night.

Late-winter snow whirled between Edinburgh's sombre turrets. A friend of a friend gave me a bed while I found a flat. I failed at house-guest etiquette: I never shared meals, and filched from the pantry, just enough to go unnoticed. Two crackers. One slice of cheese.

My first cafe shift returned me to the world of the living. Steam wand shrieks and a till drawer's clink, clearing plates and dishwasher heat; I found comfort in the murmur of a full house, in customers buttering scones by windows fogged with condensation. Nearby, the craggy dead volcano on the city's edge, Arthur's Seat, was capped with snow. As spring warmed tentative ground, dark basalt cliffs sprouted yellow gorse. Edinburgh softened with cherry blossoms, bluebells, creamy sunshine. On hazy days, the austere castle overlooking the city appeared as if an artist had painted medieval stone upon the sky.

I found a flat two storeys up in an 1880s building, then a week later bought a second-hand desk. It fit in the window where birds sang at dawn and seagulls cawed at dusk. The cafe chefs gave me leftover soup in takeaway cups, and I ate dinner on my bed with half-stale cheese scones.

On the other side of the world from my Husband and my history, I decided to settle in Edinburgh and began to make a home in myself. Here, I had space to examine my wounds, and in doing so was surprised to discover a deep habit of self-loathing. It flavoured every thought, and manifested loudest as disgust at my body, shame at the disobedient stomach and inadequate breasts. The dysphoria that haunted my adolescence was no more serious than most girls', but it had grown into an adult commitment to hatred. This was my mortification of the flesh. A drumbeat in my subconscious: wrong wrong wrong. I couldn't place when self-flagellation had become the norm. Internalisation is sneaky. It seeps in slow, and poisons the water.

A guy called Barry from work took his chances. We made out after a poetry event, our inhibitions loosened by cheap wine and spring's first balmy night. On Leith Walk, he pressed me against a shuttered newsagency to kiss my neck, and I ran my hands up and down his torso. He drew back, and pulled his shorts' waistband wide to privately reveal his dick standing to attention.

'Penis,' he declared like a proud child. I laughed and pushed him away. Men loved to declare their cocks, I thought, while women rarely flashed a cunt.

When Barry left the next morning, I stuck an inquisitive hand into my knickers, tracing my swollen sex. I'd once read that every feminist should take a mirror to her open legs and play peekaboo, but I cringed at the thought; my vulva was hairy and strange. Monstrous.

My pilgrimage was on hold, I didn't belong, but still I searched: this time for understanding. I thought I'd committed deicide, but my religion's thought-system was not so easy to erase. Now, I wanted to arm myself with knowledge that would help me heal.

The task was enormous. Like every time in my life I've needed answers, I began to read. Early mornings before lunch shifts, I filled a French press with coffee and sat at my desk. Grey squirrels ran through the tenement-square garden, leaping from thin limb to thin limb.

Sexism and God-Talk, by Rosemary Radford Ruether, had been in my suitcase the whole trip. I opened it again. The 1983 book was a detailed feminist critique of male-centred Catholic symbols and stories. Confirming my own discoveries, Ruether wrote that the social conditions of the era in which biblical texts were written (patriarchy) informed the imagined character of God (patriarchal). For example, Ancient Mesopotamia (a region close to where the Hebrew God was born) was a civilisation dependent upon slaves, and normalised the relationship of slave and master. This was a rigid hierarchy: people were separated into high or low. Ruler or ruled. Dominated or submissive. In this environment, men constructed a

Father God as a King, enthroning the hierarchical relationship in religious practice.

Squirrels ran along ivy-covered stone. I remembered kneeling before the altar at my church.

Christian thought was also influenced by Greek philosophy. 'The dominant white Western male rationality,' Ruether wrote, 'has been based on linear, dichotomised thought patterns that divide reality into dualisms: one is good and the other is bad, one superior and the other inferior, one should dominate and the other should be eliminated or suppressed.'

These binaries were fundamental in how we perceived the world. Master / slave; man / woman; mind / body; human / nature.

Each day at 9.30 am, I tore myself away and walked to the cafe. Ruether's words rattled in my head as I asked diners how they'd like their eggs, poured milk into espresso shots, and mopped wooden floors. And as the sun rose earlier each morning, I returned to my reading and watched the London plane tree in the garden behind my pages. Barren branches grew luscious with leaves, and in summer, they burst into flower.

I kept seeing Barry, who went to school with famous drug dealers, who lived on the same posh street all his life, who had a story for every city corner. A lying raconteur with the nose, chin, and bald head of a goblin — I assumed his hair had fallen out from grief, as he was reeling from the recent death of his mother. His humour's bitter whip encased the chaotic heart of a lost boy.

He lived in his dad's house in Stockbridge, the old-money precinct lined with dark Victorian terrace houses and private gardens reserved for the wealthy. Barry's front door was always

unlocked and the kitchen always warm. In his childhood room —
so enormous it comfortably contained a dusty pool table — he
asked me what I liked in bed, and I said it might be nice if he told
me what to do. Barry replied he'd rather I sat on his face; wouldn't
it be more feminist to have power over a man? We tried, but I
was scared I'd suffocate him, and couldn't relax as he lapped at my
clitoris like a thirsty dog. Afterwards, he smoked a bedtime spliff
out the window.

'You've got a beautiful vagina, you know,' he said, stubbing the
joint on the windowsill and wrapping his arms around me.

He showed me his city. One cold summer's day, we explored a
secret garden. We came across a cottage and opened the door to a
green-skinned ogre, a princess in a blue silk dress, and a man in a
top hat and tails with boils on his face. The actors, preparing for a
children's play, shooed us away. Barry led me through backstreets to
a dark wood-panelled pub with Scotland's oldest bowling alley, and
he bought us shandies and scampi chips. We'd expected to end our
date in bed, but something happened.

When we returned to my street, he teased me, pretending to
throw a bowling ball with a limp wrist.

'Barry. You can't, you can't do that.' The slap of humiliation.
Tears rose in my throat.

'C'mon! It was just a joke!'

Heat in my face. A choked voice. 'No. Don't! Mock! Me!'

'I think I'd better go,' he said. His car pulled away. I slithered
up the shadowy stairwell, crumpled to the floorboards, and began
to moan. Through open curtains, the sun was yellow-sharp. Animal
keens spewed from my mouth. I wiped my eyes, my nose, my
mouth; my grief was liquid and pouring and wouldn't stop.

Then I settled. Stillness. Slow breaths, precious air in my chest, my belly. The sky was fuzzy twilight, my throat ached. I crawled into bed and tucked myself around a pillow. Why did I react so severely? What *happened* to me?

I met Bri at the Broughton St tram stop.

'That's my favourite coffee shop! And there's my supermarket!'

She rolled her suitcase to my building's heavy wooden door, and we shared a bottle of wine on my couch. We'd been youth-group friends, though she'd left church when school finished. Now a photographer in Melbourne, she was visiting me on her solo Euro trip. We decided to go west.

I booked the cheapest campervan I could find, ignoring the company's reputation for sexist slurs. When we picked up the keys, our van came painted with a man's face, purple and orange psychedelic swirls, and the words *Free the Universe*. I breathed a sigh of relief. Ugly, but no sexist jokes.

Outside my house, we packed rugs, pillows, wine; I closed the boot with a bang. Oh no.

Life sucks if your girlfriend doesn't.

'Bri. Come look at this.'

'Fuck.'

I rubbed my forehead. 'I can't call myself a feminist and drive this car.' In an even worse blow, I wasn't sure it made grammatical sense.

'Do we take it back?'

'I'm itching to get on the road …'

At a service station, Bri bought a pack of garbage bags and taped one across the boot, covering the words that summoned an image of a woman on her knees. There. Now, we could drive this Ugly Van north-west with an almost-clear conscience.

Window down, bleached-blonde hair blowing in the wind, Bri wove the van along through the Trossachs, the mountain range surrounding Loch Lomond. Small mountains, or bens, anglicised from the Gaelic *beinn*, crowded around. Thick rivulets of ancient waterways eroded their sides like stretch marks on thighs.

Oban was a dark verdant hill above the harbour. We took the 6.00 pm ferry to the Isle of Mull, in the Hebrides: an archipelago of islands whose name meant 'Beyond the North Wind'. Yet the north wind haunted us still: the top-deck bluster was violent. I peered at distant mountains, clutching a cardboard cup of Earl Grey with my hood tight around my face. Distant blue rose from black turquoise as if the ferry were gliding through brushstrokes. Bri dashed around the deserted wet deck, eyes wild, switching between the cameras hanging from her neck. 'God!' she shrieked, pointing. 'There's a fucking castle on an island!'

The rain began to lash.

We docked at 7.00 pm and snaked along the coast to Calgary Beach. The sky had cleared, and we were determined to hit the western edge to see the sun sink into the sea around 10.00 pm. Along single-lane roads, I pulled into passing points to make space for cars or free-roaming sheep.

'There, there!' Bri pointed at a grassy ledge, and sprung out the door to wave me in, though her eyes were locked on her iPhone camera as she captured the view. I pulled up the park brake and threw a blanket on the ground. Bri heated chickpea curry over a gas stove. Dinner and drinks twenty metres above the soft, lapping water. We pulled on thick coats and watched sunlight glimmer then set the ocean alight. A noble osprey hung on the wind. Black-faced sheep and their lambs dotted the hill, looking to the light as if they, too, were admiring the view.

We discussed tomorrow's plan. 'How would you feel,' Bri said, raising eyebrows over a beer, 'about posing for naked photos?'

'Yesyesyesyes,' I said, throwing my head back, draining my can.

When the sun disappeared, we retreated inside, switched on fairy lights, and crawled under blankets. I woke at dawn to roll open the heavy door. The sky glowed with egg-yolk light. I squatted, my arse exposed, steam rising from hot piss splashing on grassy rocks. Sea air filled my lungs.

As Bri drove, I watched the movement of peaks, imagining their creation: tectonic plate crash, land thrusting from salt water, millions of years stroked by rain and wind. Genesis, the first book of the Bible, tells the creation myth of how the world was made. From the formless darkness God made heaven and earth, and then he said, 'Let there be light.' He made the land and plants, he made the sun, moon, and stars, he made the animals. And on the sixth day, God created man and woman and said, 'Be fruitful and increase in number; fill the earth and subdue it. Rule over the fish in the sea and the birds in the sky and over every living creature.'

This narrative proved Ruether's assertion that patriarchy inspired hierarchy. A religion's cosmology doubles as the order of the universe, and there, in the first book of the Bible, Christians were given dominion over the earth.

Bri arced onto a gravel driveway between lush, manicured grass. Dairy workers in white gumboots sat beside a flower bed with morning tea, and raised tin mugs in ruddy-cheeked greeting. I smiled back and twisted the brass doorknob of the ivy-covered cottage to buy entry tickets to Mull Dairy Farm. At the milking shed, a tabby cat curled her tail around my feet and trotted away.

We followed her into two long concrete rows with green guard rails, metal tubes, and rubber attachments. Shit smeared the floor; the place smelt sour. Cows were milked morning and night. I imagined rubber mouths, their vampiric, mechanised suck.

We trailed the tour-guide tabby out to a bristle-haired pig's wooden enclosure. Past rusting tractors, Bri pushed open a corrugated iron door. Sweet bleats filled the dim, dusty air, motes dancing on sunlight shards. Calves stood in a series of small stalls, shut in by thick iron bars. Their velvet violet eyes were wild. They were less than two months old.

In dairy farms, calves were taken from their mothers within forty-eight hours of birth, to optimally harvest milk. An animal biologist at the University of British Columbia found this had a painful impact; he monitored cows' cognitive behaviour, concluding that their diminished capacity of balance and movement were signs of grief. As for the babies: female calves were reared for milking, while males that couldn't be sold for veal were disposed of on-farm, some only days after birth. It was more financially viable for farmers to kill them. A 2018 *Guardian* investigation estimated close to 100,000 male calves were killed that year in the UK, considered industry waste.

Bri guided the Ugly Van through winding roads, slowing for sheep walking like distracted schoolchildren. 'C'mon, mate!' She beeped.

I felt ill thinking of subjugation as means of production. A family farm with flowers and a friendly cat echoed with despair. What, then, of factory farms, their mess of steel, their tiny cages? We breed animals for a life of slavery for profit. Rule over every living creature.

The road curved, and a verdant hill drew back to reveal a

desolate scene: a logging forest, recently harvested. The land was painfully naked, a wasteland of broken wood.

'It looks like a woman's shaved legs,' Bri chuckled, and slowed to the side of the road. She jerked up the handbrake and pulled her camera strap around her neck.

Feet on the dash, I leafed through my notes. As with animals, Ruether wrote, nature's domination was justified through the foundational view that the earth was subject to our control. Increasingly efficient and technological agriculture was seen as positive advancement. Fuelled by a neoliberal, exponential-growth mentality, exploitation was normal.

Bri squatted a few hundred metres away, holding her camera to her eye. Clouds swam shadows over mountains. I turned another page in my notebook as wind rocked the van.

'Women are the life-givers, the nurturers,' wrote Ruether, 'the ones in whom the seed of life grows. Women were the primary food gatherers, the inventors of agriculture. Their bodies are in mysterious tune with the cycles of the moon and the tides of the sea.' I thought this was a limited stereotype, but it informed conventional gender symbolism nonetheless.

Bri emerged from a cluster of beeches, pulling up her fly. 'Right! You ready?'

I grinned, nervous. We edged our way into the forest, and I hung my coat on a branch. One arm out of my turtleneck, I yelled, 'I gained some weight over winter … and Bri, my boobs, they —'

'Shut up!'

I peeled off frayed black knickers and half-tucked them into a shoe. Auburn sticks broke off in my hair. My bare feet sank into wet mud. Tiny flies rested on my back. She told me to stretch hands high. I leant back and watched a seabird swing above treetops.

The second time I took off my clothes was on the side of Ben More, the Inner Hebrides' second-highest mountain. We wandered the ascent until Bri spotted ferns 200 metres from the hiking trail, and I lay in their soft, green embrace, their tendrils stroking my hip. My arm above my head like a Pre-Raphaelite girl with mosquito bites and a small afro. I closed my eyes and savoured the sun's delicate kiss on my white belly.

Higher up the mountainside, ragged stones were speckled with mint-coloured moss. The incline swept down to Loch na Keal and Mull's coastline; further across the water was Ulva, a small teardrop-shaped island glowing in blue haze. In a field beside the Ugly Van, two men and a dog rounded up sheep and ushered them up a trailer's metal ramp, transporting the animals to get shorn. Or slaughtered.

One last time, I untied my Docs, pulled off skinny jeans. The wind murmured through a thousand blades of grass and slid around my waist like the arm of a dancer.

'That big rock there,' Bri pointed. 'Lean against it.'

I pressed my lips, my nipples, the fuzz of my pubic hair against the two-metre-tall basalt. It had a magnetic charisma. The calm, grating texture touched my torso, and I trailed fingertips along the line of its peak, inhaling the mingled scent of the sun-warmed rock and my own odour.

'How about you get up on top?' Bri called out.

'It's, um, very high.'

She grinned at my protest and held my gaze, camera between her hands.

I begged her not to look. Finding footholds, I grasped my rock's rough surface and pulled my body high, then swung a leg over. Suddenly, I was straddling a giant stone on the side of the mountain. I twisted to the view: indigo hills rose beyond Ulva. The water was a sparkling sea-path to the sky. I gripped my rock with upper thighs and leant forward under Bri's direction.

The lips of my vulva kissed ancient rock. Flesh pressed to earth. Boundaries blurred. The tang of warmth, the stroke of air, a hundred metres high. With each shutter click, my friend declared my worth.

Back in Edinburgh, Bri left for Paris and I returned to cafe shifts and morning research, gradually working my way through the cheese we'd bought at Mull Dairy Farm. Read, work, home.

I dreamt Edinburgh's dark buildings catapulted into the sky and fell back to earth, the castle reduced to rubble. Arthur's Seat slid into the sea. When I woke, my tall window framed a luscious, round moon glowing in deep blue. Not even this ethereal vision could bring comfort.

After six months, I felt strong enough to continue my journey. I squashed everything into my red suitcase. The last morning in my temporary home, I took one final, luxurious shower. Warm water sparkled in ecstatic morning sun. I felt tender, and yanked back the curtain, tilted my hips towards the light.

Politics — the way power is arranged in our world — lives in our bodies. My journey was self-focused, obsessed with inner experience. Deeper than navel-gazing, this was vulva-gazing: I wanted to examine the impact of misogynist ideology on my most intimate parts.

One foot on the edge of the tub, I ran my fingertips over my dark, wiry pubes, swallowing the urge to wrinkle my nose. I pushed two fingers to my lips — open sesame. Such detail in bright light. So many shades of cinnamon and pink. The petals of the labia minora, the eagerness of unfurling, the pearl of the clitoral hood. I guess — yeah, okay, maybe she did look a little like a flower.

Ireland

Six people on the flight to Dublin wore black jumpers printed with block letters: $REPEAL$. Designed by activist Anna Cosgrave, the white text referenced the fight to Repeal the Eighth Amendment.

In 1983, the country introduced an amendment to the Irish constitution that granted an unborn fetus equal right to life as a person. Abortion was made equivalent, by law, to murder, with a maximum penalty of fourteen years in prison. Tomorrow, the country was to vote on its repeal.

The abortion debate encapsulated Catholic attitudes towards female bodies and sexuality, and religion's legacy of control in Ireland. I was returning to witness history in the making, to understand the sins of the church, and hopefully, to celebrate a political moment that signified its fall from power.

Dublin Airport was rowdy with cheers, posters, and streamers to welcome returning expats. The tremendous Irish diaspora, unable to cast absentee votes, were flying home from Boston, New York, London, and Perth, a prodigal return similar in scale to that seen for the successful 2012 marriage-equality referendum.

On the bus to O'Connell St, I thought of the women who'd travelled the opposite way, flying Dublin to England. Since 1983, it was estimated that over 170,000 Irish women had travelled for abortions: twelve women a day.

After independence from British colonial rule in 1922, the Irish Republic had given responsibility for education, health, and social welfare to religious organisations. Since then, Catholic ideology informed legislation, and the state funded church activities.

At time of writing, 90 per cent of primary schools were Catholic. If hospitals were not owned outright by churches, nuns or priests sat on their boards. Contraception was illegal until 1980, and when condoms were legalised, their distribution was highly controlled. Divorce was legalised by referendum in 1995 — even then, applicants had to be separated for *four years* (in 2019, this was altered to two). The country was in the long process of rejecting the law of God.

I waited at the Luas tram stop, backpack heavy on my shoulders, and spotted a campaign poster of an in-utero fetus. Evidence showed in *every country of the world* that, no matter the legality, women sought abortions when in need. What was currently up for discussion was accessibility to safe services.

On the tram, I swayed with movement. The current shadow system of going to England or the Netherlands was a logistical minefield. Even the cost: a person experiencing a crisis-pregnancy must book time off work, take an international flight, pay for a hotel, then pay for the procedure itself. Or attempt it in twenty-four hours on the cheap, take a bus from clinic to airport, and hope she didn't bleed on the seats. Never mind the secrecy, the emotional and physical trauma, for some the expense alone made it impossible. Reproductive healthcare was an issue of class.

In Rialto, Sarah's silhouette was all bushy hair and waving arms. She pulled me into a tight hug, tickling my face with red curls. Her blue-glitter winged eyeliner glimmered under every streetlight.

'I spent, like, five hours dancing for Repeal today,' she said, unlocking the front door. I dumped my backpack on the couch, and she put the kettle on, calling from the kitchen: 'I was only gonna stay for two, but it felt like if I stopped dancing, somebody would vote No.'

Sarah and I had met last time I was in Ireland. An artist with a fondness for vibrant pink and leopard-print, she'd won a prize for her Repeal-themed short film at the Dublin Feminist Film

Festival. She passed me a mug and sat down.

'What has it been like in Dublin lately?'

'I screamed at a priest the other day. I did! It was on Henry St, huge for No canvassers. He was on his fecking soapbox, with a microphone, and he was treating it like a circus. "Give me one good reason to kill a baby!" So I took a deep breath and yelled, *Repeal the fecking Eighth!*'

Tensions in Ireland were reaching a peak. Recent public events demonstrated society's low value of female bodies.

Sarah talked fast. 'The last two months: Jesus fecking Christ. Two women have been raped and murdered. Then there's the Belfast rape trial.'

I'd read the news. A young woman accused two rugby players of rape. During the trial, the defence had displayed the victim's lacy underwear as a sign of consent. The men were acquitted.

The media was recently full of stories of women's pain, calcifying to legend as they became foundations for the fight. In 1984, fifteen-year-old Ann Lovett died giving birth at the foot of a Virgin Mary statue in County Longford. She hadn't revealed her pregnancy to her family, or asked anybody for help. The X case, in 1992, detailed a rape survivor who planned to travel for abortion. She asked the Gardaí (Irish police) if DNA from the fetus could be used as evidence; when they discovered she planned to abort, a High Court injunction was granted to stop her travelling. The Supreme Court then overturned the restriction, establishing that a woman had a legal right to travel for an abortion if there was risk to her life (in this case, suicide).

And in 2012, a thirty-one-year-old dentist, Dr Savita Halappanavar, was seventeen weeks pregnant when she presented at a Galway hospital with severe back pain. Diagnosed with a septic miscarriage, she requested a termination multiple times, but was denied because a fetal heartbeat remained. She died after contracting septicaemia, and her death in October 2012 brought the fight for reproductive healthcare to the forefront of public debate.

In the wake of this tragedy, Irish women began to break the taboo, and speak about the law's abject cost. The Termination for Medical Reasons group amplified stories of aborting due to fetal abnormality. They shared personal testimony, many leaning towards the absurd, like parents who wondered how to transport a tiny coffin and its remains home — in hand luggage or checked luggage? And the 2017 art project Not at Home, produced by Grace Dyas and Emma Fraser, published tales of travelling. No longer encased by a cultural mandate of silence, and propelled by public debate, newspapers, radio, and talk shows platformed women's lived experience and the brutality enacted upon their bodies.

Sarah offered me caramel chocolate. 'If it's a No,' she said, breaking off a square and popping it into her mouth, 'I will probably leave. I'll move. I don't want to be here.'

The hot-blooded debate crowded public space. The No side — reportedly funded by American fundamentalist groups — utilised street preaching, Sunday sermons, and placards on church buildings and telephone poles. *Your vote can kill or save babies. In England, 1 in 5 babies are aborted.* Yes volunteers canvassed; old women, young women, and men, many who'd never previously been politically engaged, knocked on doors to educate: body autonomy was the right to self-governance, without external influence.

'If it's a No vote, what does that mean?' I asked Sarah.

'It's Ireland saying we do not give a feck about women.' Her right eye winked erratically. 'Excuse me, I think I have glitter in my eye.'

—

I left Sarah's early, marching beside the River Liffey. Above me, seagulls swung through creamy blue. I sat down with an americano and a banana in a cafe near Tara St station, already spinning with adrenaline.

I'd never needed an abortion, but one of my best friends in church had, at eighteen. She completely withdrew, and stopped coming on Sundays. I was angry that she abandoned our friendship. One year later, she got in touch and told me the story: she and her boyfriend, who was my close friend, were 'doing it'. When she got into trouble, he stopped answering her phone calls. She went to the clinic alone.

Her silence infuriated me, and I was horrified she'd insisted on going by herself. I didn't understand, then, that the sexual activity of our entire youth group was wrapped in secrecy. Shame was a gag stuffed in our mouths.

Irish Times columnist and Yes campaigner Una Mullally wrote in the anthology *Repeal the 8th*, 'Like many people, I was indoctrinated by the Catholic Church in school and at mass to believe that abortion was evil … My memories of how sex and reproduction were spoken about in school are hazy; visiting nuns talking about black marks on our souls, or equating our souls with the water used to clean our classroom paintbrushes — how one dirty brush could soil the whole jar.'

I was reminded of another church friend. She lost her virginity when her boyfriend raped her, and she stayed with him for another year. She'd thought she was dirty, she told me; there was no point trying to become clean again.

Concepts of purity and filth are intertwined with judgements of good or bad. Cradling the warm ceramic cup, I opened my laptop and clicked through notes from *Dublin's Lost Heroines*. Social historian Kevin C. Kearns recorded the lives of working-class women from the 1900s to the 1970s. Women who got pregnant out of wedlock, he wrote, were young, ill-informed, and often didn't even know how it happened. To be unmarried and pregnant was to suffer 'a humiliating fall from grace … Besmirching the family's good name, bringing disgrace upon their kin'. Visible sexual sins tarnished the surrounding community. Priests instructed and protected parishes' social and moral wellbeing, and arrived at the door of unwed pregnant women, supported by community surveillance. An interviewee reported that on her street in the 1940s 'a mammy had a baby with no daddy'; the neighbouring women were so incensed that they took up a petition to have her thrown out.

So where was she sent? Perhaps to England, to a married sister's house, or if the family had money, a private institution. But if they did not, she might have been sent to a Magdalene Laundry.

Also called asylums, Magdalene Laundries historically grew from workhouses — institutional homes for the destitute, designed to tackle societal poverty — and were funded by the state. In truth, they were punishment for deviant female sexuality. Women and girls arrived pregnant, and under nuns' command, steamed and washed and pressed, often for as much as six or seven days a week — without pay. Hospitals and hotels had contracts with laundries until the 1990s, women's servitude thereby generating income for the church. They were called 'penitents'.

'Every convent,' Kearns wrote, 'emphasised rigorous scrubbing duties — cleaning laundry, floors, furniture, brass, walls. Symbolically "cleansing their souls" … to wash away the "sins of the flesh".'

Black coffee bitter in my mouth. Men encountered no such

punishment. Mothers were also sent to Mother and Baby Homes. The most famous (but by no means exceptional) was the Tuam home, which made international news headlines in October 2017. Run by the French Bon Secours Sisters between 1925 and 1961, the home was set up to take 'fallen women', brought to its doors by parents and priests. One year after birth, the mothers had to leave, while their infants remained. 'Home children' went to the local school, where they were ostracised by students and teachers alike. Otherwise, they were adopted out, often illegally, sometimes to America.

The Tuam home's records were investigated by a local amateur historian, Catherine Corless, who made a shocking discovery. During its thirty-six years of operation, the state-funded institution illegally buried 796 children's bodies.

After the home closed and the building was knocked down, evidence was unearthed. A boy found a skull, stuck a stick into its eye socket, and ran around with his grim talisman. Construction workers walked off a housing-estate build because they kept finding skeletal remains. Policemen dismissed these as 'famine bones'; priests said a prayer and turned away. Houses were built on top.

But recent investigations had discovered that the children's bodies were buried in an unused septic tank. Journalistic inquiries have since found neglect and lack of care to be the reason for the inordinate number of deaths. In 2021, a five-year government investigation into eighteen homes found at least 9,000 children died between 1922 and 1998, double that era's infant mortality rate.

The last Magdalene Laundry closed in Dublin in 1996. The government is facing serious reparations, with official governmental apologies and special welfare payments for laundry survivors.

Caelainn Hogan, the journalist who documented these human rights abuses in her book *The Republic of Shame*, wrote that the church was at the heart of a 'shame-industrial complex' that destroyed thousands of lives, and continued to impact people today.

I placed my coffee cup on its ceramic saucer, and walked out onto the street. If we did not perform purity, we were punished, condemned to prisons, slavery, torture. This was the history that hovered over today's vote.

I saw my first street preacher on Henry St. Standing on a blue stool, wearing a headset microphone, he gripped a 1.5-metre poster printed with a crying infant and the words *CHOOSE LIFE!*

'If a woman has an abortion, what is she legally? What does *the law* say?'

A short woman with a pram and shiny, black hair yelled, 'Don't you have anything better to do?'

'Oh, I am doing the Lord's work,' he replied, pushing his shoulders back. 'It's a beautiful thing, a privilege.'

I pushed through the morning rush-hour crowd parallel to the Luas tracks, on my way to meet last-minute canvassers. Mary Condren's *The Serpent and the Goddess* was in my backpack again. She wrote that Christian ideology created a 'profound dualism between the spirit and the flesh'.

This echoed Ruether's words I'd read in Scotland. But Condren explained further: in the dualism of mind / body, the body's nature needed to be overcome by will. 'Men had to separate themselves from anything representing mere instinctive sexuality.' Sex wasn't just dirty; it was shorthand for sin. Theology therefore heaped contempt on the body and its sexual potential, demanding celibacy from nuns and monks; only those who suppressed desires of the flesh could be holy.

The Luas' sharp chime snapped my attention back to the street. The tram snaked past, and I crossed the tracks to Connolly station.

Volunteer leader Mar had an unflappable, cheery vibe. Ireland was changing, she said. In her university years, she'd organised condom machines for college bathrooms, and in 1990, she was a Women's Services Officer at a university. There was a secret abortion service hotline, but it was illegal to distribute pamphlets, so activists marched through the campus chanting, '6-7-9-4-7-0-0, women have a right to know!'

A river of commuters dispersed into the financial district beside a sign offering *free hugs for Yes!* Iliana, a vivacious young woman with a warm grin, wrapped me in a tight embrace, rocking playfully. 'Oh, I'm glad I'm wearing dark glasses. I'm so emotional today.'

'Why?'

'I'm Malaysian. I *have* to be visible,' she said. Forty per cent of maternal deaths in Ireland were migrant and ethnic-minority women, even though migrants were only 17 per cent of the population. 'With every Yes vote, that's a vote for me, for migrant women.'

Savita Halappanavar's face was on Yes posters across Dublin, beside the caption *Savita Matters, Women Matter*, and a quote from her father, Andanappa Yalagi. 'I want the people to remember her ... I request that all Irish people vote Yes for this law to change.' Her husband, Praveen, also reportedly supported the Yes vote.

A woman of colour as the posthumous face of a social-justice movement — was this a picture of the new, inclusive Ireland? Or was a person of colour being exploited in the service of white aims?

Kitty Holland, the *Irish Times* journalist who broke the story about Halappanavar's death, wrote for *The Guardian*: 'The fact that Savita was not Irish has been central … We Irish like to think of ourselves as an eternally welcoming people who look after our visitors and yet it seems we let her down at her most vulnerable moment'.

But Halappanavar had become a white woman's mascot, wrote political analyst Dr Chamindra Weerawardhana in a Medium article. 'A well-educated professional with a light skin tone (which was photoshopped even lighter in much of the repealthe8th promotional material), the cis white women spearheading the abortion rights movement found in Dr Halappanavar a powerful marketing strategy.'

Her image was only used, said Weerawardhana, because it was acceptable to the white Irish public. Unlike women with darker skin who didn't have Savita's social standing, such as those in Direct Provision immigration limbo who also suffered under a misogynist and white-supremacist healthcare system.

In the city's north, Sarah's art studios had turned into a self-care retreat with homemade cakes and salads, on-duty masseuses, and soothing herbal remedies. Everyone I met was exhausted and nervous yet spoke with an assumed solidarity. The posters, the shouting, the news reports; the tales of imprisonment, punishment, powerlessness; the tears of rape, the pain of abortion, the loneliness of secrecy; it sat in all our bellies, hummed in all our limbs. History's wounds resonated in our bodies.

I poured a cup of sparkling water and sat on a bench to read. Ruether again, outlining the conflation of female bodies with sin. In the binary system, men were equated with mind or spirit, and women with the body. Ruether tracked this from Hellenistic Jewish philosopher Philo — born 25 BC — who believed women were the source of evil.

This echoes throughout Christian thought. The creation myth (which, remember, lays out the order of the universe) blamed women for humanity's expulsion from the Garden of Eden: God told Adam and Eve not to eat from the tree of knowledge, but the serpent convinced Eve to take the fruit, and she persuaded Adam to bite that sweet, juicy flesh. The archetypal woman was responsible for the Fall of Man. Female disobedience, then, was the cause of sin.

'Do you know that you are all Eve?' wrote Tertullian, a third-century theologian. He believed women were 'the devil's gateway', an entry point to sin. (I could go on about misogynist philosophers whose works were foundational in Christian philosophy — like Aquinas, the Dominican priest who believed 'a female is a misbegotten male' — but that would take up too much space.)

Our bodies symbolised the vices. The repression and punishment of women, then, represented man's successful mastery of sin, and therefore righteousness, goodness, and transcendence. We pay the price to make men holy.

I lay on a cushion in a dim room where Sarah was running a screaming workshop. With a soothing voice, she instructed us to lie on our backs and breathe deep, then 'kick your legs, just like how it felt when you were having a tantrum as a toddler, yes, that's it, pump your fists, aha, SLAM them onto the floor, that's right, keep banging, now take a deep breath and SCREEEAAAM!'

'Aaaaaaah!' the room yelled, a cacophony of high-pitched wails and grunting moans, 'Aaaaaaah!'

Bloody hell, it was time for a drink. I met a writer friend, Lauren, in Temple Bar's flashing red-and-green lights. We climbed the stairs to Project Arts Centre's upstairs bar. Drunk after one glass of wine because I hadn't eaten lunch, I didn't ask Lauren if she thought it'd be a Yes — everyone I'd spoken to was unsure; liberal Dublin would vote Yes for sure, but rural Ireland could go either way. Instead, she told dirty jokes and I snorted with laughter.

Coincidentally, the venue was hosting Dublin's Together for Yes volunteers. The air was tense and desperate. Young people arrived, threw backpacks down, and beelined for the bar. Older women took tentative sips from pints of Guinness. They'd campaigned for decades. They'd seen No's before.

At 10.00 pm, a woman in her fifties with a red shirt and cropped grey hair stood to read *The Irish Times'* exit poll (typically, the margin of error was 1.5 per cent).

'Voting is over,' she said, and everybody was quiet, no one spoke, we listened to that small, strong voice with our whole hearts, our whole bodies.

'The exit poll predicts 68 per cent Yes.'

The room exploded. A rush for the bar. The grey-haired woman remained standing, turned her back, and held her hands to her face.

The next day, beside Portobello's Bernard Shaw pub, a mural of Savita Halappanavar became an altar. Her face, painted in crimson, and that word: Yes. Then three identical posters pasted next to the mural with the promise, repeated like a prayer: *never again never again never again.*

After the exit-poll announcement, Una Mullally had left a flower to dedicate the country's victory to the woman they failed. In the hours since, people had left flowers, candles, and written dedications stuck to a wall.

Censor the voice, Hélène Cixous wrote, and you censor the body. It also worked in the opposite direction: censor the body and you censor the voice. Premarital sex had been forbidden (for women), reproductive healthcare had been withheld; language was enchained, tongues arrested by taboo. A political framework of power enacted in the body, through the body.

By the pile of flowers, a delicate-looking woman in her early twenties laid a black Repeal jumper on the ground and knelt to light incense. Her brown-speckled staffy shivered on the asphalt beside her, and she held him to her and wept. When she rose, we wrapped our arms around each other.

'This represents so much pain for Irish women,' she whispered, rocking. 'And now it's over.'

Up Aungier St, I pulled a stool between brunch tables with bloody marys at hip restaurant Drury Buildings. On the phone, writer Kathy D'Arcy, who chaired the Together for Yes campaign in Cork, apologised for her hoarse voice — she'd spent last night in the pub. I asked if she felt like things had changed.

'Personally, walking around all the posters, I felt shamed for a long time. I believe I felt in my heart that the country hated me. A lot of women felt that. And now? We *are* the country. It's our country.'

After our call, I walked up Dame St. The air sparkled. Traffic crawled. A hatchback with YES taped in red and yellow on its bonnet and side windows beeped, a passenger yelling through a megaphone. Pedestrians responded with triumphant shouts.

The final count would be announced at Dublin Castle's medieval courtyard. Media tents lined one wall, and cameras faced the growing crowd. Endless Repeal T-shirts in black, maroon, dusty blue. Queer dress-ups: angels in fluffy white, handmaids in red robes. Women, men, kids. People hugged long and tight. I found Sarah dancing, and she handed me a cup of gin and lemonade.

Attracted by her fuchsia jumpsuit and feather boa, Buzzfeed UK and HuffPost and a German reporter with a fat, fluffy microphone interviewed her.

Every so often, a cheer went up as politicians and senior campaigners — mostly women — appeared in the media tent and raised their arms to the crowd. There was no formal stage, no proper speeches; we'd gathered to celebrate. 66.4 per cent for yes, 33.6 per cent for no. A landslide victory, twice as many Yes votes.

Thousands chanted, fists pumping, voices ricocheting off sixteenth-century walls. *Yes! Yes! Yes!*

My last morning here was spent in Brother Hubbard on Harrington St, dropping chocolate babka crumbs on *The Irish Times*.

'Personal stories are precious things,' wrote Booker Prize–winning author Anne Enright. The Repeal victory belonged to those 'mighty souls' who spoke out, provoked sympathy, and prompted change. 'How did we turn ourselves from fallen women into women rising? By telling the truth.'

I remembered the chant in Istanbul. *Women will rise from the ashes you burnt.* Free the voice and you free the body. This was the un-silencing.

I borrowed Sarah's bike and pedalled along the Grand Canal in early summer's evening. It was a bank holiday; young people lined the water's edge with picnic rugs, drinking cans in the orange light of dusk. Near Portobello Harbour, I wheeled the bike onto grass and rested my elbows on my knees, peering at the glossy water's reflection: creamy sky over dark and tangled trees. At the bank, a mute swan pulled at underwater reeds. I thought of Savita Halappanavar and Ms X and Ann Lovett and my church best friend and the violence and loneliness of it all, and I wept.

When the tides of sorrow cleared, a full moon glowed in shimmering rose. And in my chest, I felt something new: rage.

Italy

Midsummer sun blazed over Rome's baroque buildings and their enormous wooden doors. I ordered a caprese salad and negroni, leant back, and enjoyed the heat whispering on my bare shoulders. Today, I would see Mum for the first time in seven months. She was on a trip with two friends for her sixtieth, and had paid for my flight to meet her in Italy.

I walked down a steep hill to Piazza Navona, gaping. This city was unthinkably *old*; traffic thundered by architectural remnants from almost 2,000 years ago. Monuments to long-dead emperors stretched into the sky. Every corner venerated the might of the state.

It was also the historical centre point of my old religion. Jesus Christ was born in what is now the West Bank, and Christianity spread from the Middle East. But after the crucifixion, it was believed his disciple St Peter became the first Bishop of Rome, thereby the first Pope. In the fourth century, Emperor Constantine made Christianity the state religion and built a basilica on Vatican Hill. Centuries rolled on, and popes plotted and murdered in pursuit of the throne. In medieval times, it was believed the Pope could grant 'indulgences' to reduce time in purgatory — as long as the sinner would confess, and more importantly, donate. The Vatican, here in Rome, had been the centre of Catholic power for 1,700 years.

Dark clouds gathered. The air cooled. A pope was the highest authority in the Roman Catholic Church, elected by council and believed to be chosen by God. In the 2,000 years since St Peter, there had been 266 popes. All men.

But a year ago, in Melbourne's brunch cafe Pope Joan, I'd seen a picture of a female pope on the back of the menu. Since then, she'd been on my mind. And when Mum had suggested we meet here, I knew what I had to do.

In my mission to understand the sins of the church, I'd learnt about the ideology that inspired the violent silencing of women's bodies. But I'd never felt physically threatened by the church — I was curious about the gentler, insipid, internalised beliefs that had kept me obedient. As I followed Pope Joan's trail, I would use these ancient streets to probe alleyways of my interior world. What psychological stance had allowed me to accept the majority-male leadership in my church, in organisations, and in my government as natural law? How had my love of the Father conditioned me to accept an unequal power balance? These questions terrified me. What else would this search for truth reveal?

Thunder shook the sky. I hurried through Piazza Navona and its tremendous Fountain of the Four Rivers, built in 1651 for Pope Innocent X, whose palace overlooked the square. Then onto thin cobblestoned streets, between five-storey buildings of rough concrete and stone, walls etched with Latin words and the Virgin Mary. Above me, terrace flower boxes burst with colour.

Heaven opened. Fat drops cleared dust, drenched streets, and seeped into my white shirt. Phone on 1%, I quickened my pace, boots slipping on Via del Governo Vecchio. Was this the right place? My screen was black. Rain became tumultuous and loud, the road a blur, the tiramisu shop across the way a yellow haze. I stabbed at a brass doorbell.

A woman in a skirt suit and immaculate lipstick cracked the

mammoth door. '*Buongiorno?*'

'Hello!' I paused, allowing her ears to attune to English. 'I'm staying with my mother. She has arrived?'

'Ah, *si.*' She turned. I closed the door to rain's cacophony and scampered behind her, past a tinkling fountain, across perfumed tiles. Golden lamps glowed. I yanked open the door. Graham and Sue were in bed, napping after their flight from Croatia. Mum, her curly hair wonky from the pillow, threw back the covers and embraced me. I felt her laughter's rhythm in her chest and inhaled her scent, unchanged since I was a girl.

I rose early for yoga in the courtyard. Swifts dove in the strip of blue sky. A cool breeze stroked my ankles.

During sun salutations, I thought of Pope Joan's mystery. She was born in the ninth century, a brilliant student at a time when education wasn't for women; she disguised herself in men's clothes to further her studies in a monastery. Then she went to Athens, took a lover, and arrived in Rome, where she set her sights on the highest position known to man.

According to monk Martinus Polonus' *Chronicle of the Popes and Emperors*, 'La Papessa' climbed the ranks of Catholic hierarchy from secretary to curia to cardinal, and was elected Pope in 855. Records of her life existed in whispers and shadow. A cathedral in Siena that housed busts of former popes supposedly contained her statue — before, wrote a seventeenth-century Vatican librarian, the name and nose were scraped off and replaced with Pope Zachary's.

I took a shower and told Mum I'd meet them later for lunch. Author Donna Woolfolk Cross, who wrote the 1996 novel *Pope Joan* (adapted into film in 2009), claimed she had 500 pieces of documentation that proved the myth. I jammed a black sun hat on short curls and went in search of Pope Joan.

Vatican City beckoned with a shadowy gravity. Chiselled into a building in morning's cool shadows was a wolf mother suckling two human infants. At street level, women in tight, elegant dresses holding thin leather briefcases expertly navigated cobblestones with stilettos. Men in tailored pants with exposed ankles kicked scooters to life under iron lampposts curling from coral walls.

In Australia, the Uniting Church was seen as progressive, and had ordained women for decades, as well as queer pastors. Women leaders were increasing in the Anglican Church, with female archbishops in several states, and women outnumbering men in ministry training. Australian Christian Churches — Pentecostals — allowed female pastors doctrinally, but in actuality they were far more common as half of a husband–wife team. Catholics had it worst — Marilyn Hatton, Associate Convenor of the Ordination of Catholic Women Incorporated, complained in a 2009 submission to the Human Rights and Equal Opportunity Commission that the discussion of female ordination was forbidden on church property; the Vatican threatened excommunication to bishops who ordained women. At time of writing, women could not be priests in the Catholic Church.

Blinding sunlight as I crossed the low, green River Tiber. Then the long stretching road to the Vatican. With a circumference of only two miles, the smallest country in the world is the only nation where women can't vote, as the Pope is elected by cardinals, who must be male.

I'd read claims my lady pope was buried beneath St Peter's Basilica. Its piazza was circled by double colonnades; inside, *polizia* with muscular buttocks guarded thousands of seats. Tomorrow was the Pope's weekly address.

I gazed up at the statues of saints ringing the piazza, some over 300 years old: martyrs, mystics, bishops, popes. Out of 140 figures, there were about thirty women, nearly all of them 'virgin-martyrs'. One of the statues was Thomas Aquinas.

I crossed the border, desperate hope clutching the back of my throat. I felt if I found proof of Pope Joan, I would find redemption: my helpless rage would be given a sense of triumph by the woman who gamed the system and succeeded.

The basilica was sacred and beautiful and full of tourists. Every surface glittered. Echoes of a thousand shuffling feet bounced from rounded fresco paintings and marble columns. Like La Virgen de Guadalupe's basilica, this was a site of religious pilgrimage, a rite of passage for the devoted. Nuns in pressed grey habits and black sandals, silver crucifixes at their breasts, took selfies in front of cherubs; a tall priest with a sweeping black robe and dusty backpack crossed himself; a gaggle of monks wandered, their brown cassocks tied with ropes. I trailed a tour group wearing identical T-shirts, their leader speaking Polish into a headset microphone and holding a plastic sunflower high in the air. We gazed at *La Pietà*, Michelangelo's sculpture: the Virgin Mary cradling the beaten body of Christ. She was depicted as younger than the Son of God — because, my €5 audio guide said, 'those who are without sin do not grow old'. Or, I thought, because male artists prefer the idealised female body.

My boot heels clacked on patterned ceramic. Bright light burst through stained glass. Rome once meant empire, and I wondered what was stolen to fund this seductive, opulent beauty.

I soon gave up counting statues and paintings of men. The only female figures were the Virgin Mother or angels and helpers.

Christianity's revered figures were male. And there certainly wasn't a statue of Pope Joan.

I dodged the gift shop and exited into glaring heat. Did any tourists question the ubiquity of men on thrones? Perhaps nobody thought it worth discussing; gender's hierarchy was invisible, or inevitable.

Stepping down endless concrete steps, I remembered that pastors were tasked with the responsibility of teaching and guiding a community. They were expected to act for the common good; I once believed that, like God, men in authority had my best interests at heart. The Pastor said he put his own needs aside to govern his church. My Husband's job was to protect and guide me.

I'd since discovered the infantilised obedience I was trained into as a teenager expected their sinless perfection. I placed leaders on a pedestal and didn't question their motives; their wisdom had eclipsed my own.

I pushed against the tourist-tide and crossed the River Tiber.

Mum poured me a chilled glass of chianti at a vegan pizza place, and I explained my failed pilgrimage over fake mozzarella. As we waited for dessert, I leant back on my chair and opened Mary Beard's *Women and Power*, which I'd found in an English bookshop by the hotel.

Classics scholar Beard claimed that ideas from the beginning of Western culture — Greek and Roman times — heavily influenced thought today. Images of power in classic texts were explicitly masculine.

Ancient playwright Aeschylus wrote *The Agamemnon* in 458 BC. During the Trojan War, Clytemnestra ruled the city while her husband fought, and murdered him on his return. She was described in humiliatingly masculine terms, depicted as heinous in her capacity to decide, to act, and to destroy.

Beard pointed to further examples of female power as an anomaly in the classics. Athena — goddess of war, dressed as a man-like warrior — was a virgin: these factors excluded her from procreation and therefore womanhood. Odysseus' wife Penelope spoke in public before being silenced by her teenage son. Aberrations of female power such as the Amazons and Medusa were both conquered by male warriors, inferring a return to patriarchal order and an end to the mythical monstrous woman.

Gender roles, Beard theorised, were defined in relation to power.

'Weakness comes with the female gender,' she wrote. 'Our mental, cultural template for a powerful person remains resolutely male.'

Mum and I took a morning alone together to explore. We charged through streets, sweating, ticking famous landmarks off our list.

'Did you hear about the Pell trial?' Mum said. Once the third-most-powerful member of the Vatican, George Pell was born in Ballarat, Victoria, in 1941, and ordained in 1966. He rose in power — bishop, archbishop, cardinal — to lead the Vatican's Secretariat for the Economy. The figurehead of Catholic power in Australia for decades, he knowingly protected some of the nation's most prolific paedophiles, and was currently in the news for being the global Catholic Church's most senior official accused of sexual abuse (Pell was found guilty in December 2018. In 2020, he appealed to the High Court and was acquitted).

Mum snorted. 'Swines.' I noticed her face was pink in the heat, and slowed my pace. We strolled through Trastevere, where graffiti crawled up cracked and stained walls, and ivy dripped from tiled roofs. At a small fountain, we sat on soft-edged concrete and pushed our hands through cool, clear water, full of light.

Inside a gargantuan baroque church, signs demanded silence in three languages. Religious architecture was designed to make you feel small, the psychological condition from which to approach a higher power. We sat on a polished pew and observed the dark wooden confession box. A red light shone when it was occupied, a green light when free.

'Like a check-out,' Mum chuckled. We watched confessors' silhouettes. She told me that Nan was taught by nuns, and that Mum herself was sent with her sisters to Sunday School; once, in school religion class, she was kicked out for asking questions. Though we had no family faith, the women before me had been educated into this system.

She suggested a midday aperitif. I could get used to this, especially if Mum kept picking up the bill. We checked our phones at a terrace covered with white tablecloths, and I returned to a video of a sermon called 'God Created Man Male and Female'. John Piper, the leader of the Complementarianism movement, was an American pastor and author of more than fifty books. He founded the Council on Biblical Manhood and Womanhood in 1987.

There are male and female souls, he believed, designed by God and whose expressions were 'written on the heart'. For the book of Ephesians said:

Wives, submit yourselves to your own husbands as you do to the Lord. For the husband is the head of the wife as Christ is the head of the church.

Piper's powdery Minnesota twang laid out his gender theory: men are leaders who initiate, provide, and protect; women's sacred role is to gladly receive and affirm that initiative, provision, and protection. He made clarifying statements: 'It's nothing to do with power, it's about responsibility … It doesn't mean women sit at home.' But a woman's role was only defined in relation to a man. Her will and action never stood alone.

I sucked my Campari down to ice. Complementarianism legitimised social hierarchy between men and women and made an unequal power dynamic seem natural. Discomfort weighed thick in my stomach. Mum paid, and we met Graham and Sue outside the Vatican Museum.

The second hour under relentless sun, I began to whine for lemon gelato. I was bored of waiting but also irritated by John Piper, who'd enshrined masculine leadership as divine design. Who could argue against God? This patriarchal order rewarded him, and so he kept writing sermons and books to perpetuate its message.

In 2017, journalist Julia Baird mounted a huge inquiry into religion and gender-based violence. She discovered that 22 per cent of domestic-violence perpetrators went to church regularly. She asked, 'can emphasis in some churches on the doctrine of headship — that man is the head of woman, and women are to voluntarily submit — create a climate where men who seek to abuse their wives are enabled?' The results were worse than she imagined. 'One woman wrote to tell me she stayed with a violent man for fifteen years because her pastor told her that as her husband, he was her leader. Another was punched and dragged about by her hair by a husband who gave her a Bible with verses on submission highlighted in it.'

Male power and female submission naturalised through

ideology — this was Anna Karin Hammar's cultural violence, and it set a theological precedent for abuse. Men's dominance was imprinted on the imagination, creating a psychological foundation for obedience and control. When I first read Baird's article, I'd thought it was about conservative churches. I adjusted my black sunglasses. The sun beat down. I would've liked to keep thinking this story was about other people.

The line shuffled closer. Mum nudged me with her elbow. 'Y'know Nan came here?'

Almost twenty years ago, after a period of mental illness in her sixties, Nan had returned to England for the first time since she'd left at twenty-seven years old with her husband and three young daughters. She took her sketchbook to Edinburgh's dark castles, Swiss mountain villages, and the Vatican Museum. An artist with a room full of watercolours, collages, and crocheted objects, Nan couldn't resist the mecca of Renaissance art. I hadn't managed to trace my maternal line in Ireland, but today we would follow Nan's footsteps.

Finally, we entered the palace. Windows were flung open to blue skies; summer wind teased the back of the neck. Through halls of maps, past frescoes of angels and kings, we edged, inevitably, towards the Sistine Chapel; down a tourist-crammed passageway, pressed on all sides by the push of sightseers' bodies, I sucked slow mouthfuls of air to quash panic. At last, the space opened to Michelangelo's masterpiece, and we craned our necks, a crowd of heads tugged on simultaneous strings. All the stories were there, Adam and Eve, Noah's boat, Jesus Christ, painted impossibly on the ceiling. Mum's moist hand slipped into mine. Nan was here. She'd taken a seat, adjusted her glasses, and looked up.

I spotted *The Creation of Adam*, where white-bearded God

reached out to touch the first man. I felt sick at their muscled bodies, and had a sudden urge to pierce these marbled corridors and the hushed awe with a violent scream. But this would be inappropriate, would disturb my mother and everybody around, would get me shushed and judged and thrown out. So I kept my mouth closed.

The next day, we diverged. Pope Joan ruled the Vatican for two and a half years, hiding her lover before becoming pregnant. I followed the path of her procession to St Clement's Basilica; it was between here and the Colosseum she is said to have given birth. I ducked into a deserted backstreet away from thundering traffic to find her path. Some stories say she died crawling on the ground, a trail of blood between her legs. Others say she was imprisoned until she starved, or she was exiled; the most brutal retelling saw Pope Joan tied to the back of a horse and dragged through the streets until she was a ragged corpse.

Like the Amazons, like Medusa, the monstrosity of a woman in power must be destroyed.

Cicadas buzzed; my back was slick with sweat. I scuffed my feet and shuffled through alleys as if I could spot a thousand-year-old splash of blood. Modern historians theorised that the legend of Pope Joan was untrue, a myth used to discredit papal authority: the worst thing a pope could be was a woman.

Between two tall ochre buildings, I opened Google Maps. My jaw dropped. A shrine, a few streets from here. To Pope Joan!

Heat haze shimmered. The din of cicadas heightened as I quickened my step. Squinting, I turned onto Via dei SS Quattro. There! At the bottom of St Clement's Basilica's steep hill was a concrete enclave, a locked green gate; between the curling iron, a plastic rose's petals were sun-bleached white. Two scooters passed, then I scuttled across the street and pressed my face to hot metal. On the decayed grotto's back wall was a faded, flaking painting, I could barely see a woman in a robe, and — oh. A baby. With a halo. Above the shrine, engraved in concrete, was a dedication that translated to: 'The smile of the mother Mary will cheer all those who greet her.'

No! The bloody Virgin Mary, again! An altar to the eternal feminine, the goddess enchained. There was no Pope Joan. There was no triumph for my rage. There was no redemption.

I trudged to the chaotic road beside the Colosseum. A red double-decker tourist bus shuddered past and dusty air whirled my curls. My throat raw, I could only be soothed by an Aperol spritz, brimming with ice.

Sipping the chilled, sparkling orange, I watched a nearby fountain, where children balanced on their knees on concrete, dancing their hands in water. I remembered the question I'd left home with: could a woman belong in Christianity? Only if she agreed she was inferior.

I swizzled the white straw, feeling nauseous. It could be all the pasta I'd eaten this week, or it could be this: I submitted before the throne of the Lord God. My next thought rose up my oesophagus like thick vomit: I transferred this posture of submission to the men in my life. It informed not just structural reality but also intimate relationships.

It wasn't conscious. I would never have agreed out loud. Such is the insidious potential of ideology; implied by symbol and story, it may never be discussed in full. Nevertheless, promoting a cosmology bereft of powerful women was a fundamental way to ensure we accepted the imbalance. My religion furtively created a psychological reality in which I saw myself as less-than: less able to decide, less qualified to act, than men. Our psyches were conquered, and it felt *normal*.

I thought back to the mossy hilltop in County Louth, Ireland. Dolores Whelan's deep voice. I'd asked her, as winter wind blew through beech trees, about the difference between worshipping a masculine or feminine God.

'The patriarchy goes outside,' she'd said. 'It's always somebody else who tells you what to do. But the feminine energy — and that's what has never been encouraged in men or women — is to really, really go inside and check out *what is true for me*.' She'd patted her chest.

I was ashamed to realise I didn't know how to do that. Somebody else always told me how to think, what to believe, how to act. And this continued even as I travelled far from home: by depending on God to show me the way, I'd undermined my own ability to listen to my wisdom and act of my own volition. I chose to sublimate my own power and project it onto an invisible authority.

I gripped the cold, wet glass as if it were my only anchor to the earth. Now I understood why Margie had suggested I follow the goddess tradition: she'd met me when I first exited my marriage, when I was uncertain, afraid, and could barely make a decision. Used to feeling small to encounter a higher power, I unconsciously minimised my own strength; I'd thought my Husband was strong, and I, in comparison, was weak. That's the sacrifice of letting someone else tell you what to do: you surrender your own decision-making capacity. It seemed there was a deeper reason I'd clung to Pope Joan as a vision of female autonomy. I needed to recover my own power.

——

A shadow-cloud of swifts twisted around Piazza Navona. The sky rumbled. Mum and I walked and walked beside relentless traffic, past men in crisp shirts and fitted blazers, searching for final-night fun. A sandwich board outside a church: *Opera Favourites*. Inside was prosecco in plastic cups, and free pasta. We waited before an empty altar.

A tuxedoed tenor with a painted goatee bellowed. And then a woman in an emerald ball gown appeared, her mezzo-soprano voice shimmering like sunlit water. A nonna in black clapped at the end of every song — *bellissima*, she whispered, *bellissima*. In the intermission, I climbed over the back of the pew to buy more prosecco, and when I returned, Mum placed a hand on my arm.

'Nan would have loved this.' She dabbed at her eyes during the last duet.

Out of the chapel and into a deluge. The dark Italian sky cascaded like my first day; we weaved through slick, empty back-streets, identical curls plastered to our cheekbones, roaring *O mio babbino caro*. The rain had eased by the time we got to the tiramisu shop's bench and ate coffee cake with tiny spoons.

'Do you ever talk to Him?' she asked, her cocoa-coloured eyes open wide.

What to say? The line of power: Husband, Pastor, God. Patriarchy was not a whip but a smile. The subtle erosion of certainty. I confessed: 'No, Mum. He was controlling.'

This is what I didn't say to my mother with her dark, wet eyes: You were there when He and I began. You loved Him, too. Why didn't you warn me?

And more, this: Mum, I kept saying yes. I kept saying yes.

before

A Husband

We married in late March. A koala watched us from the fork of a eucalyptus tree in a garden of palm trees and wisteria, dehydrated by drought. Contemptuous of Christians' identical ceremonies, we'd forsaken fancy dining, bridal bouquets, and a white gown for Indian curries, coloured balloons, and a red dress His mum made. I walked down a grass aisle to Jimi Hendrix.

We kept some traditions. My dad, moustache waxed and bowler-hat handsome, delivered me to the altar. We sang, praising God for washing away sins. And our vows, 'All that I am I give to you. All that I have I share with you,' were a public promise I'd later remember on difficult days.

How proud I was to stand before my loved ones, with an intelligent, determined man with long hair and cowboy boots, piercing blue eyes and a strong jaw. He was mine and through my ownership I rose in value. We kissed, and everyone threw streamers, colours descending like paper fireworks.

The sun went down, I wrapped a scarf around my shoulders, and we danced under stars. At midnight, my new Husband and I exited to a chorus of cheers. My brother, extended family, school friends, and church community stayed to tidy up, stacking chairs and blowing out hundreds of tea lights in glass jars.

We fell into a vintage car, and I was stiff in the leather seat. We hadn't touched for six months, as if to erase the taste. As if to reclaim a virginal veneer, as if my hymen could knit itself back together. In the hotel room, I was nervous and exhausted, dry and tight; we fucked with grim commitment.

When I woke, His arms were around me, and all anxiety melted in a luxurious shower. Sleepy and shy, we lathered soap and circled suds across shoulders and backs. In silence, we sang devotion.

Marriage was the only space I was able to imagine where I could be free to unleash my sexual self. It wasn't a conscious, logical equation: let's get married as soon as possible so we can fuck. Let us unhook the shame that rests upon our shoulders. But irrevocably, longing for freedom led us here.

I was twenty-two years, two months, and twenty-four days old.

A Husband was something holy. A Husband was a goal, then He was a gift. When His meaty hand took mine and His large thumb stroked my palm, all His strength turned to tenderness. His authority became gentle. His deep voice became soft. And in brief moments of surrender, the tall man disappeared and the little boy crawled into my lap. For six years of marriage, I clung to that small wounded one, with wide blue eyes, soft round cheeks, and wet pink lips. The vulnerable self of my Husband that nobody else saw. I alone would protect Him. I would nurture Him. I would save Him.

One year in, I pressed my lips to His warm, freckled back. The mattress creaked as He shifted in the morning sun. Before, a fantasy of our marriage bed had made me weep with longing. Bright sunlight through a large window, I saw us lit by a sacred, naked glow. But adjusting to sleeping together hadn't quite turned out so ideal. My dream-shuffles disturbed Him, so He never felt rested. I hated early mornings and spat *fuck-off*s at him if He tried to wake me.

Even on rare days off, He never slept in. I cracked my eyelids, watched Him pull on shorts and slip a wrinkled T-shirt over His head. Things had to get done. Sprinklers turned on, the metal creak of the back screen door. Then His weight on the bed. That deep voice.

'Give this a try, Lou.'

A cherry tomato's red globe at my lips, dusty with soil and warm from morning sun; I opened to His invitation and bit with sharp teeth. Sweet juice burst on my tongue. I smiled up at Him.

'We grew this.'

'Yeah.' The treat of His large-toothed smile. I stroked His shoulder. United by His surname, we were one body, building something raw, trembling: a garden, a home, a fortress. The winds would rage, but we'd take refuge in each other.

'Well — better have breakfast.' He left again. 'The car's not going to clean itself.'

A Husband was a road of trials. A Husband was the narrow gate. A Husband was a wise man, a leader, a temple. A Husband chose me and called me worthy.

My identity was the foundation on which I stood: Christian, feminist, wife. Prompted by American writer Sarah Bessey's book *Jesus Feminist*, I saw Christ as a radical liberator of social norms. He spoke to the woman at the well. He rescued the adulteress from stoning. He healed the woman who bled.

But not everyone thought Jesus was the answer. A year after I married, I received a message from Auntie Liz.

A cold wave rolled through my body when I saw her name on my phone screen. I'd only seen her a couple of times in the last year; she made me feel uncomfortable. Two weeks before my wedding, we'd picnicked by Karrawirra Parri, the River Torrens, and I'd fed sandwich crusts to a black swan.

As we watched birds on the sparkling river, she said, 'You don't have to go through with this, you know. If you have any doubt. Any doubt at all. You can say no.'

This was the first time anyone had said anything like this. But God had ordained a path for my life! My task was to accept, and follow! I burst into overwhelmed tears. Two swans grunted and snapped their ruby beaks.

'It's too late.' I shook my head, rubbing my eyes with the heel of my palm. 'Too late to even think about it.' I was ignorant to other possibilities. Not-knowing is a darkness; beyond the city limits, the streets had no light.

Auntie Liz had a habit of dropping bombs like this. I would've much preferred that she avoid difficult topics like the rest of my family. But as my mother's sister, she was my and Ben's godmother, and spiritual guide.

When we were kids, she lived alone down the road from the airport. Inside her magical home was swirling incense smoke, gentle music, and teal, indigo, and forest-green Faber-Castell pencils in a dented tin. When we slept over, we drew pictures or coloured her mandalas, bent over the kitchen table. At sunset, we walked her dog, Libby, who looked like a dingo, and Auntie Liz pulled a carrot from her pocket. Ben and I took turns feeding it to a horse in a nearby field. Homemade chips and apple juice for tea, peppermint chocolate for dessert.

In her hatchback, which had a bumper sticker 'Angels protect me', we sang our favourite song. An explosion of auburn curls, her loud voice; Auntie Liz tapped her hands on the steering wheel:

Will the circle be unbroken
By and by, Lord, by and by
There's a better home a–waiting

In the sky, Lord, in the sky

Grass grew through her concrete driveway. We slammed the car doors, and heard the drone of a Qantas plane. Auntie Liz unlocked the front door, and Ben galloped, curly brown hair bouncing, through the seventies kitchen, past the laundry painted lavender with a sponge. His screen-door slam sent the twin black cats running through the back garden forest, and Ben swung his weedy eight-year-old frame to perch on the Hills hoist. The Qantas Airbus came in to land, its white body and red tail soaring slow and lazy through late-afternoon blue. As it cast a magnanimous shadow over the house, Ben stood, thin thighs gripping the metal clothesline's peak, and reached up a hand to touch the plane's metal belly.

At teatime, we balanced plates on our knees. Ben squeezed the sauce bottle and tomato-red shot out with a farty squirt. We fell into giggles. Auntie Liz put on a movie where a man died in a car accident and his spirit returned as a spaniel. As the credits rolled, she stroked my white-blonde curls. Ben's pale legs tucked beneath him, her arm around his shoulders.

'What do you think happens after we die?' she asked.

'Um, heaven? We go to heaven?' I hoped this was the right answer.

'Some people think that. Like the song, a home in the sky. But what did Fluke do?'

Freckles scattered across Ben's pink-tipped nose. He looked up at Auntie Liz, eyelashes wet, voice croaky. 'He came back.'

'Yeah, he came back, as somebody else. Some people believe in re-in-car-nation. That our spirits never die, but are recycled. What sort of animal would you like to come back as?'

'A dolphin!' I cried, leaping into the air.

We changed into jimjams and settled in the spare room under Nan's crocheted blanket. Two bodies side by side, breath slowing. Auntie Liz turned off the lamp, then washed the dishes and slipped biscuits into her pets' bowls. As the cats crunched in the kitchen's corner, she sat at her table to draw deep into the early hours, sweet nag-champa smoke clouding the air above her head.

That was when I was a kid. But now, I was a grown-up, a wife and university graduate renting a house and building a church and life with her Husband. This first marital missive began a campaign that would last years, cement Auntie Liz as an acute antagonist in my life, and ultimately send me to the refuge of her house when everything fell apart.

I'd shared the Pastor's sermon audio on Facebook. 'Christianity came out of the flawed-woman-as-temptress story,' she responded. 'Because she led Adam into sin, we needed a father-and-son team to save everyone.'

The emails came next. They were longer, written in a voice spitting with anger. I was participating in a religion that had annihilated the goddess traditions, that had enacted centuries of violence against women.

I couldn't stop myself reading these attacks immediately, heat flooding my body. Whenever I responded, defending myself, she fired back, intending to disrupt my beliefs. In turn, I clung to them, and felt brutalised and disturbed. How could she speak to me like this? She'd come to my baptism — I thought she supported my faith. Couldn't she see I was on the side of women? And anyway, I'd never thought about God being a man before, he was just *god*, the wind the rain the stars the ever-present sea. And Jesus was my best friend. Who cared what gender they were?

Auntie Liz had had enough of my Husband, too. During our

pre-wedding picnic, she'd been disappointed that He rarely attended our family celebrations. I told her it would be different when we married. Now, she reminded me that nothing had changed; she criticised His unwillingness to engage, His sarcasm and disdain for things I loved, the way I kept the peace. When it came to intimacy, I made a banquet out of crumbs. I was a hypocrite, gullible, groomed by men. My love was a romantic tale about a good girl healing the bad boy's wounded soul.

I was furious. She'd somehow decided I was some sort of victim? How dare she!

Auntie Liz challenged the core of my identity. But I wasn't ready to accept her perspective, or even to open my eyes and examine things for myself; her criticism threatened to set the foundation of my life alight and burn everything down. So I shut her out. Closed my eyes.

Ben and his girlfriend, Nichola, were in the Women's and Children's Hospital. When I parked on Frome St, lined with tall London plane trees, I tried not to break into a run; at the entrance, I got directions before marching through labyrinthine corridors, turning corner after corner until suddenly there they were: Oliver, squishy and red, more animal than human. Nichola lay on a bed by the window, tired and proud; Ben looked young and old at the same time. His carpentry apprenticeship saw him climb house frames and carry heavy materials, and he'd become muscled and tanned. I held my little nephew for the first time, kissing his forehead with careful lips.

That night, serious health issues arose, there was emergency surgery, a colostomy bag. That precious body on a sterile operating table. Ben kept our group chat updated, and his baby's first bowel movement was celebrated with cheers. Who knew it could be so arresting to wait for news of a tiny shit? The new family moved to a house in the suburbs. They visited the hospital regularly. At six months old, the colostomy bag was removed, and with some hiccups along the way, Oliver grew strong.

When the new baby was almost a year old, my brother was in trouble. It wasn't working out, he said, he needed a place to crash for a few months. I said on the phone it should be fine, we had a spare room, it just had His guitar gear. I'd check with the Husband.

At dinner He said, 'I'll think about it.'

The next morning, I listened to Him get up for work. The rush of plumbing when He turned on the sprinkler. When the front door slammed, I rose, trod barefoot into the lounge, and got on my knees.

I bypassed buddy Jesus and bent before the Father God, thinking of my brother in primary school, high school, youth group; I thought of his baby son and how he and his girlfriend were trying to make a life and he couldn't do it but he still wanted to be a dad; I thought how Christians should give up our lives for one another, for the poor, should share our resources like the first church in the book of Acts, should sacrifice to show God's love — and the sprinklers said *chuck-chuck-chuck*, spraying vegetables — and I said please-please-please, rocking, pounding my fists, pressing my face to dull, scratchy carpet, please-please-please. Please change His mind. Please change His mind.

I called Ben a week later, stuttering.

His voice was tired. 'I already know what you're going to say. I've found another place.'

I couldn't challenge my Husband's authority, and betrayed my brother when he needed me most. Two weeks later, I met him for a parmy at a trendy pub on Gilles St. Striped wallpaper, an open fire, a tall glass of cider with ice. Ben drank beer.

My mouth was dry. 'I'm sorry.'

He scrunched his eyebrows and wrinkled his nose, as if saying this disgusted him. 'Look, Lou — just make sure He doesn't call the shots, okay?'

Love and Betrayal

It should never surprise when a man grows to dominate the ones he loves. For patriarchy teaches that masculinity means having power over others.

He didn't transform behind the closed doors of our marriage, but had already shown me who He was, and I ignored the signs. Years before, I'd driven us home from a friend's house late at night, and when I resisted his instructions, He slammed his fists on the dashboard. His arms pounded in rhythm with His bellows and broke the rear-view mirror from its casing, which spun to hit my car's windshield. As I drove at 80 km/h, a four-armed crack spidered across the glass.

This explosion was the result of months of suppressed fury. Now, in our home, it was my role to weather His darkness, as I believed He did mine. I would witness and be faithful still, inspired by Christ's all-forgiving embrace. God had called me to shine light in a world of shadows. My forgiveness, my kindness, my joy would heal Him.

His mother and father had separated when he was eleven years old, in a vitriolic divorce that incurred tens of thousands of dollars in lawyers' fees. They both came from farming families in different parts of rural South Australia, and passed down to Him groundedness, stocky legs, and a constant sense of betrayal. He inherited a soft voice when calm, a commanding presence when angry, and a Germanic sensibility that inspired harsh and blunt speech. As an adult, my Husband was a sad man who did His best while smothered by a chest-deep sense of being overwhelmed. He was convinced there was but one way to move through the world, so He demanded perfection. If He was displeased, His tongue struck sharp as a trident's fork. Of course, this judging eye turned towards me. My behaviour was policed. If I spoke too much, became excited, did something foolish, I received an offhand comment, or my name hissed like a teacher catching a child stealing a forbidden sweet. 'Louise!'

It was theologically impossible for God to not be good; the devil was responsible for evil. As I projected my God-relationship onto men, so I believed they could only be good. I didn't dream of their capacity to harm. But this harm did come; most confusingly, it arrived in disguise. Disdain and criticism were wrapped in jokes or encouragement. ('I like this dinner, Lou, but I think next time, you could do better by cooking the asparagus like I showed you.') He outlined the rules in a soft voice. My Husband was a gentle man — until He wasn't.

In the law laid out by my Pastor and my God, I thought things were either good or evil. Now I know they can be both. We laughed together, a lot. We made love. And if I took too long to leave a party, or I disagreed and didn't admit He was right, dark clouds dropped heavy and low. Thunder rumbled. That stab of alarm up my oesophagus to my trachea, when I knew I'd done wrong, been careless, or ruined something — again. Hypervigilance meant I watched, alert, for lightning's crackle, anticipating His judgement, guessing His thoughts, jumping to placate. I stuffed my needs down deep, numbed them, froze them. Anxious to please, to not be a burden.

I adored Him. I wished I could gaze upon His strong jaw, His determined, furrowed brow, His icy blue eyes all day. I wished I could spend all night stroking Him. But I couldn't — He was embarrassed by my indulgent attention — so I endeavoured to please. One method was silence. Silence when He instructed. Silence when He thought I spoke at the wrong time. Silence when He needed space. Silence silence silence.

My family taught that love was affection, not confrontation; my Pastor taught that love was self-sacrifice; my Husband taught that love was obedience. My parents rarely argued, so conflict provoked fear; I did anything to make His ire fade. I listened, pretended to agree, or apologised even if I wasn't sorry. The tension dissolved. Self-betrayal for safety.

My imagination was both saviour and executioner. Just as I escaped into magical tales as a child, my fantasy life served me as an adult. I wove my Husband a new coat, new face, new heart. Magical thinking expanded moments of grace, when we did laugh, when we did play, until they were so magnified they took up the whole sky. I wove this story and clung to it for years. But the illusion became wreathed around my neck, and I held it there, even when it began to choke.

Unwilling to acknowledge the uncomfortable truth — my Husband did not respect me — I embraced toxic positivity. A grinning nonchalance, sunshine-sweet, even if my heart was heavy. I enshrined Him in praise. I didn't speak my shadow, and justified hurtful episodes. He criticised because He wanted me to be the best possible me. His unwillingness to change was the mark of a strong man. Unbeknown to me, this was all part of my training. Despite resisting the cherry lips and maternal care of ideal womanhood, I'd still been socialised into a femininity that demurred and reassured and smiled, even when it hurt. Especially when it hurt.

Thus arose the enabler. I *understood* Him. I sympathised, always, with His plight. I assuaged His guilt and never truly called Him to account. My pain emerged only in eruptions of anger that dissolved into hot, confused tears. In His eyes, my protests were undermined by raw emotion. I didn't know how to argue my case or stand my ground; in fact, it was impossible to go into battle for myself, because my thoughts and needs were so vague and unknowable, they were incommunicable. The suppression of the true self — it was a slow and terrible erosion.

Midnight. On my feet since five. Before I started work at this steak restaurant, I'd never opened a beer. Now, I floated starched napkins onto round bellies, poured blood-coloured Barossa shiraz into elegant glasses, and remembered how scotch fillets were to be cooked. I cleared heavy plates stained with red-wine jus, navigated chefs' moods, and smiled and appeased, thank you, sir, yes, ma'am. Poked my face into refrigerator chill, stocked beers, glass clinking, and swept. Tonight, I passed on the staff ritual of wine and cigarettes out the back, where evening service was dissected. If I sat with my colleagues, I might drink too much to drive.

I slumped in my seat and turned on the ignition. Not far from home, in an unlit backstreet, a chef texted me and I squinted down. The car ground up against something — it sounded like a Coke can crumpling, but heavy.

'Fuck fuck fuck!' I slowed to a halt, swung around to look: a navy Mini, a streak up its side. Just like me to do something so stupid, I thought, I never paid attention. My behaviour was policed, then I policed myself; His voice became my Interior Judge.

I eased around the corner to my house and pulled up the handbrake, dread in my belly as I examined the red hatchback: a buckle on the front bumper and scratch on the left side. He would be livid. My key loud in the front door, I crept from the hallway into the bedroom's darkness.

'Babe,' I whispered, hand on His sleep-hot shoulder. 'There was an accident. The car is fine, but it got scraped. A taxi hit me.'

The next morning, He inspected the damage, then called me to the bathroom to question me as He showered. He wondered if there was CCTV. I should call the taxi company. We'd find out who was responsible.

I lied and lied to the silhouette behind the curtain, concocting the physics of a ghost car. Squinting into the fogged mirror, pinning my hair for a friend's birthday brunch, sweating, nauseated.

When He was dressed, I asked Him to sit, my hands shaking. 'I did it. I was so tired and sideswiped a car around the corner.'

'Fuck, Lou, this is a rich area.' His voice was low, calm. 'They probably have a super-expensive car. I don't even know if our insurance will cover it.' Any cost was a jolt, further proof the world was against us. 'You know, it's actually illegal to drive away from an accident. You better go talk to them.'

Winter sunshine, lead in my chest. I tiptoed to the street with a note in my hand and left it tucked beneath a windscreen wiper. The car was shiny and clean, its side-mirror strewn on the ground.

When I got back, He was fastening motorcycle gloves. I would weather this dark mood for days. Yet another piece of evidence in the trial against my competence.

'You know,' He said to me over His shoulder, 'you really should start taking responsibility for your actions.' I sat on the bed to tie my shoes as His motorbike roared away.

It took me years to ask why I was afraid to tell Him the truth. Now I know: I had to be good. My obedience made me worthy.

I prayed the Holy Spirit would fill our second rental home with love and laughter, use us to bless and serve our friends. I dreamt of after-church barbecues, coloured blankets on the large lawn, friends lying under the jacaranda tree.

The back door creaked as I was flinging fairy lights over the Hills hoist.

'Lou? Is that the shopping you bought on the table?'

I nodded as He descended concrete steps. I'd filled a trolley at the bulk-buy warehouse for our housewarming's Mexican feast. A tray of avocados lay on the back porch, ripening in the hot sun.

'You've got like, two kilos of corn chips. There's no way people will eat that many nachos, babe,' He laughed, rubbing my back. 'Sometimes you really don't think about what you're doing.'

I bit my lip, shrugged, and looked at Him in the bright light. 'I'm sure we'll eat them eventually.'

An hour later, I stood over the chopping board, kitchen fragrant with coriander and lime. Keys dropped on the dining table. He'd exchanged the corn chips for a giant tub of sour cream and jumbo packs of cheese, correcting my mistake. I imagined Him at the check-out: 'My wife …' Shaking his head, rolling his eyes, smiling.

Later that night, as our friends drank beers in the backyard, He corrected me again. I was telling a story wrong. 'It didn't happen like that!' I protested, as if it were all a joke. Public humiliation wasn't a grand parade but a small silent spike. Short comments of ridicule when I misbehaved. The man who loved me was the man who betrayed me.

He operated control by two preferred methods. The first, criticism, served to undermine my sense of self until I believed I could achieve nothing unless guided by Him. Every other option was impossible — or invisible. He never said, 'Louise, you can only buy the brand of toothpaste that I like.' But if I bought the wrong one, He complained, made it seem I was a fool for forgetting, or he would sigh and buy the preferred brand Himself. My incompetence became a strange inner fence, a blanket of incapacity; my limbs couldn't move unless commanded, like a possessed doll. I was terrified of making a mistake.

The second method of control, infrequent episodes of violence against objects, flowered from absurd domestic quibbles. Once I mowed the lawn 'wrong'; another time, I accused Him of using the wrong kitchen utensil. These episodes heightened to a fearsome, volcanic pitch. He refused to accept feelings as proof, questioning every statement I made, demanding evidence and logic until I spun, disoriented, lost. It was when the fights escalated that He threw things.

I was never the target, it seemed. He punched a hole in the wardrobe. He threw a cutting board on the floor so hard it broke. He slammed our front door and its glass panel shattered. These episodes — perhaps an average of one for every year we were married — are hazy and unclear in my memory, no matter how much I try to go back. But their consequence took years to untangle.

He never went to abuser school, where a muscly man with black eyes wrote an equation on the blackboard, a + b = c: *if I break things when she answers back, then she won't feel safe. And she'll learn not to question.*

But this was how it happened. This was coercive control. The intimate and private, the secret and psychological. These are the arenas where power plays out.

Compared to others who've experienced emotional abuse, my sentence was reasonably light. He made financial decisions but didn't isolate me from my friends. He gaslit me but didn't monitor my movements. He never called me names or threatened me. It was a game of subterfuge played out in non-verbal cues. I carved out spaces where I felt free — my back room with my writing table, my books — and refused to acknowledge the places I was not.

My acceptance also served to manipulate moments of intimacy I cherished. For when He threw things, He showed me a secret part of Himself seen by no one else on earth. And when the red tide of fury calmed and drew back, it left behind the small wounded boy curled up on the shore. My Husband's voice softened, His eyes lost their fire, and He nestled into my arms. After the anger came the quiet, and that was when He needed me.

Discontent grew, slow and furtive in the dark.

He thought a writing career unrealistic: I needed to make rent. So I wrote one day and waitressed four at a Croydon cafe with artwork hanging from exposed brick. He fixed up a vintage bike and painted it lavender; we named her Genevieve. One morning, I pedalled to work and tried to remember when we had stopped kissing. There were pecks, of course, familial lips-to-cheek, but I felt an urgent welling in my throat for deep, wet tongue. Early on, He'd pulled away and wiped His mouth. 'Lou. So sloppy!' His chastising laughter made my hunger ugly.

He proved He didn't want me each time He turned from

my touch. Lacking the resilience to deal with rejection, I stopped reaching out and waited until He beckoned. I endured this loneliness by sublimating my attention to available sensual pleasures: sunset clouds painted purple; lorikeets' shrieks in the jacaranda; sandy Semaphore on hot nights; an expensive gin and tonic at the fancy bar we liked. Beauty was sharpened, distilled, exquisite, in the midst of suffering.

I clattered across the Brompton train track and chained Genevieve up by the artisan bakery for another day making flat whites. I loved this job for its community; I knew the names of my regulars, and their coffees, too.

The personal trainer, for example, only had to ask me for his usual. Long black, avocado on rye with a side of bacon. An alpha male, he managed a nearby gym and wore tight Adidas T-shirts. He espoused a personal mythology in which his ancestors were Viking warriors. A taxonomy of touch: his grateful hand on my arm when I served coffee, a kiss on the cheek as he arrived, and when he left, a hug, pressing his entire body against mine. Crotch included. Once, I took an order from his table of four and he stroked my knee beneath the table. I was wet for hours, my vulva swollen on the uphill bike ride home.

He made it clear what he wanted with an aggressive, unwavering gaze. At night, I closed my eyes and visualised him shoving me against a wall, kissing my neck, and pushing his hard against my soft. We never fucked, but he was responsible for hundreds of my private orgasms.

Thus began my pattern of sexual fantasies to cope with a disinterested Husband.

The next time imagination touched reality and another person touched me was two years later, when a bushfire raged in the northern Adelaide Hills. Twenty thousand hectares had been burnt. My best friend, Gul, drove us to a music festival in McLaren Vale, and we applied diamantés to our faces in the car park. She pushed straight burgundy hair from her face, stuck sparkles around her almond-shaped eyes, then helped me arrange mine.

In the dry heat of high summer, we lay on thick grass, she in a svelte black number with thigh-high split, me in an ankle-length green dress and flowers in my hair. Cool pinot grigio, indie bands, softening sun. Fire was swallowing houses and hills eighty kilometres away, but our only reminder was smoke on the tip of the tongue and a crimson sunset that soaked the vista in blood orange. Gul and I took selfies before the burning sky.

Later, we danced barefoot to Afro beat, and I fell onto a tall man's chest. I felt Gul's scratch on the small of my back, an alarm clock, and returned to her on the dirt dancefloor. Stage lights flashed red, we swayed, electrified; as if pulled by gravity, I found the man again, his heat, his scent, his unshaven jaw; his large hand slid down the small of my back and cupped my right buttock, and I didn't dare look at his eyes but lifted my chin as he leant his face towards mine — that shoulder-scratch again, *wake up!* I scampered through darkness to collapse on our picnic blanket. My friend's long-dress silhouette approached. Sister, saviour, mother hen.

On the drive home, Gul — who had drank significantly less — pulled her car into a McDonald's drive-through. She pushed salty fries into her mouth, right hand on the steering wheel.

I took a bite of cheeseburger and lamented, 'That guy was just, there, y'know?'

Gul, always ready to rise to outraged solidarity, wrinkled her nose. 'Ugh. Did you see him as we drove away? He was against that bus, sucking face with another girl. Women are just pieces of meat to him!'

I sob-moaned, mouth full of beef and pickles. 'But it was just so *easy*, y'know?' This hunger contradicted everything I believed, everything I was. Sexual transgression could destroy my world.

She nodded, hand scrabbling in paper bag for fries, eyes forward. 'I know, baby girl. I know.'

Headlights lit the empty road. I was so full of wanting. Only kilometres away, the earth burnt.

after

Germany

Zionskirche's bell rang out over a sourdough bakery. Men in red beanies and women in culottes hurried under cherry blossoms to the gothic church. Conflicting sensations rippled through my body: goosebumps, an urge to look up, and unease in my lower belly. The whisper of the Interior Judge: *I should go to church*.

Swifts looped across Prenzlauer Berg's cheery blue sky. Soon, I'd meet up with Gul, halfway through a two-month backpacking trip with her boyfriend, Tim. They'd been in Kazan — the capital of the Russian federal republic of Tatarstan, and Gul's family's hometown — then Istanbul. They'd fly into Germany in two days.

Her suggestion to meet in Berlin was perfect. I'd explored women's leadership in my religion's history, and I wanted to see how this played out in Islam. Ibn Rushd-Goethe Mosque, a new mosque here, was founded by Turkish-born lawyer and women's rights campaigner Seyran Ateş in 2017. Men and women prayed together, and women led prayer.

After we'd met, Sister Margie Abbott had posted me the 1994 book *Defecting in Place: women claiming responsibility for their own spiritual lives*, by Miriam Therese Winter, Adair Lummis, and Allison Stokes. An ethnography of feminist faith in the USA from the 1600s to the 1970s, it contained survey responses from 4,000 Catholic and Protestant women (though the interviews had been critiqued for a lack of African American and Hispanic voices).

Fighting unequal spiritual systems was a task of survival for these women. To defect in place, the authors claimed, was to refuse to resign to the way things were; was to participate on their own terms, become agents of change, and transform elements of religious tradition *while still existing within the structure*. This could mean creating new rituals, adapting ceremonies' meanings, re-imagining God as goddess, or reinterpreting scripture.

After my failure to find Pope Joan and thus a talisman of disobedience, I wondered if I could find hope in the stories of ordinary subversive women. Those who saw the inequality and instead of giving in to helplessness, channelled their anger into productive change. Many of the people I'd met so far — Brigidine nuns, renegade queer priests in Sweden — were defecting in place in Christianity.

Could I explore the other monotheistic world religions — Islam and Judaism — to understand how female believers navigated the complexities, the contradictions, the rage in their chests? How did they do it? What was the positive direction of feminist faith?

I no longer trusted the Holy Spirit's direction but still felt an uncanny sense of inevitable compulsion, a slippery, silvery inner-knowing of what was 'right'. Just like at the start of my trip, I was being led into the dark, away from certainty, into mystery. I had to trust.

Gul and I grew up in a multi-faith friendship without it being a point of conflict. It felt fitting to look into Islamic practices while exploring a new city by her side.

I pushed open the cafe door. The barista behind the silver coffee machine had thick black glasses and a boyish grin — Sam! He had been a close friend of my Husband's, four years ago in Adelaide. He brought a filter coffee to my table: awkwardly, politely, we caught up. I was relieved when he sauntered away, chequered tea towel swinging from his back pocket, and felt astonished to have bumped into someone from home. Was God still arranging coincidences from beyond the grave? Synchronicity begged interpretation — Gul always said that everything happened for a reason, good or bad — but the dissolution of my world view meant possibilities of meaning could be endless. Or non-existent.

A stab of pain flashed. Leaving Adelaide meant I'd left behind community, especially in church; I'd shared years of joy, sorrow, and milestones with loads of wonderful people. But our contact was contingent on church attendance. Once we stopped sharing a belief, we disappeared from each other's lives. Likewise, the Pastor took me out for coffee at the end of my marriage and said he still loved me just the same. He never texted me again.

I paid and waved goodbye to Sam from a distance. On a park bench in the sunshine, I took out my notebook. Back to work. I wondered how controversial it was for a woman to lead a mosque. There were over 2,500 mosques throughout Germany, and Berlin was known for being progressive — putting aside the trance clubs, weekend-long raves, and S&M sex parties, the capital was raucously cosmopolitan, with over 200 different nationalities.

As part of the Islamic tradition of praying privately five times a day — *salat* — Friday congregational prayers were just after noon. Seen by some as a religious obligation, you perform ablution — the washing of the hands and feet — take a prayer mat to perform *salat*, and then listen to the *khutbah*, the imam's sermon. The sitting symbolised equality: rich and poor, the judge and the man returned from prison, all prayed side by side. Traditionally, women were asked to sit behind men, or in a separate section. And then an imam (male) preached and led prayer.

I pulled a copy of Dr Amina Wadud's book *Inside the Gender Jihad: women's reform in Islam* from my bag. Born Mary Teasley in 1952 to an African American family and minister father, she converted to Islam in 1972 and two years later changed her name to Amina Wadud. Now an Islamic scholar, she'd campaigned for years for female leadership. In a Cape Town mosque in 1994, she straightened her headscarf and delivered the *khutbah*.

Eleven years later, she committed a similar public act of transgression in New York. A woman sounded the call to prayer — without a veil — then Wadud led the entire service. It happened at the Cathedral of St John the Divine, as no mosque was willing to hold the event. The service was organised by American author Asra Q. Nomani, whose work focused on being an immigrant Muslim woman in America, and she held a press conference before Wadud's service began. 'The voices of women have been silenced by centuries of man-made traditions,' she declared, ignoring protest signs outside. 'And we're saying, "No more!"'

I was a little intimidated when considering how to approach Islam and analyse a religion that wasn't my own. After being immersed in Christianity for thirteen years, my judgements were legitimised by the nuance of lived experience. But I couldn't turn such a critical eye on another faith, whose complexities I was unable to fathom. I'd have to tread carefully.

The blue dot that was me approached the red pin of my destination. I looked up from Google Maps: the mosque was at the back of an old church. Marlene Löhr, Ibn Rushd-Goethe Mosque's press officer, met me three flights up. Coloured light shone through a wagon-wheel stained-glass window. With a warm, round face and shining dark hair, she urged me to sit.

Seyran Ateş, Marlene told me, was a lawyer from Istanbul who had felt alienated by the conservative mosques in Berlin that required women to pray behind a curtain. She decided to begin the community she wanted to worship in. There were inclusive, mixed-gender prayers in mosques in London and New York, but, Marlene claimed, Ateş was the world's first female director of a mixed mosque.

'In the beginning of Islam, women had all kinds of roles in the community,' she said. 'They were leading the prayer. We even had women going to war, defending Mohammed.'

Born in Mecca, Saudi Arabia, in the seventh century, the Prophet Mohammed was a merchant who married the wealthy businesswoman Khadija — fifteen years his senior. When he was visited by an angel, he asked his wife's advice, and she told him to listen to God's messages. With her encouragement and financial support, the Prophet began to share what Allah said.

'Then after the death of the Prophet (peace be upon him),' Marlene continued, 'we have over the centuries, a patriarchal system that became what is taught in Islam. But it is not consistent with the first teachings of Islam.'

In a mosque of only thirty regular attendees but with a paid press officer, it was clear a large part of Ateş's vision was to provoke change.

'Seyran Ateş always says, "I'm not fighting Islam, I'm fighting patriarchy in Islam."'

This reinforced my reading. *Woman and Gender in Islam*, by Egyptian American professor at Harvard Divinity School Dr Leila Ahmed, claims that as Islam expanded by conquering neighbouring tribal regions, Judeo-Christian Middle Eastern and Mediterranean customs were assimilated into tradition. For example: the story of Eve coming from Adam's rib — not present in the Quran but incorporated into Islamic literature; and the practice of veiling — which Ahmed said started as a practice for some upper-class women. In pre-Islamic Arabia, many marriage arrangements were matrilineal: a woman remained with her tribe, and a man visited her whenever he was nearby. Children remained with the mother, and ancestry was traced through the maternal line. As Islam grew in power, Ahmed wrote, the religion consolidated separate regions and incorporated local patriarchal practices, eventually embracing patrilineage. Which means some traditions thought to be Islamic are cultural inheritance, not religious mandates.

Similarly, Marlene believed that original Quranic texts were not patriarchal but honoured women and men as equal. A verse from the third surah (chapter) of the Quran: 'I shall not lose sight of the labour of any of you who labours in My way, be it man or woman; each of you is equal to the other.'

This was the feminist liberationist perspective. The religion's core message was the source of women's liberation.

Feminist scholars and activists from Indonesia to Spain to Egypt believed that social institutions like segregation and legal subordination restricted rights in order to retain male power, thus *contradicting* the liberationist perspective. Unfortunately, patriarchal readings of the Quran dominated Islamic theology and gender politics around the world.

Marlene sighed, her soft voice becoming hard. 'Many Muslims believe there is only one truth in Islam, and that we are deviating from it, and they have to punish us for it.'

Ibn Rushd-Goethe Mosque, she said, had received a fatwa from Egypt's Dar al-Ifta al-Misriyyah, a state-run Islamic foundation, which claimed that the mixed mosque was incompatible with Islam. Multiple newspapers reported that Seyran Ateş herself was under twenty-four-hour police protection — but it was murky as to whether this was related to her wider work as a human-rights lawyer. In 1984, while studying law in Berlin, she had worked as a counsellor at a women's centre. A Turkish bricklayer entered the centre and fired three shots at Ateş and the young woman she was counselling. A bullet hit the girl in the stomach and killed her. Ateş felt a bullet pierce her neck. She was twenty-one.

'We were threatened by the mullah regime in Iran, we were called "terrorist mosque",' Marlene said. She linked the antagonists to immigrant communities in Germany, who reproduced the conservative ideology of their home states. 'Like mosques from Turkey, because Turkish mosques are directly connected to the political system in Turkey, or we have Muslims from the Shiites, who are directly controlled from the Iran mullah regime, mosques financed by Saudi Arabia.'

I asked Marlene about their main point of criticism.

'We say women can also preach. We say women can also lead prayer. We say women can *call* to prayer. It is not exclusive to men anymore.'

The Quran did not rule on this; it came from the Hadith. (The teachings of Islam come from three books: the Quran, considered to be the direct message from Allah; the Hadith, which are sayings of the Prophet Mohammed; and the sharia, commandments on how to live a good life. Sharia was the law institutionalised in the eighth and ninth centuries, derived from Quranic texts, the Hadith, and fatwas, the rulings of Islamic scholars.)

But the biggest issue, Marlene said, was mixed prayer.

'This is why we are threatened, this is why we get insults, this is why people all over the world are unhappy. Men and women pray together, and this is forbidden in Islam. They say men cannot control themselves when they are next to a woman.'

Gender segregation was justified by the argument that a man would be aroused by seeing a woman pray before him.

'No one ever cared about whether a woman finds the bottom of a man sexy or not, heh. That is not a question they would ask themselves. And you know, we had a member of this community who is gay himself who says being in Friday prayers is the nicest thing he can do!'

I got her point — not only did gender segregation refuse to imagine a homoerotic encounter, but it also erased the potential for hetero female desire.

Our meeting over, I tapped down the dark stairwell and emerged onto wet ground, fresh from a sun shower. Limiting religious authority to men meant that male interpretation was seen as objective truth. Thus entrenching patriarchal philosophies.

While there was a long tradition of female scholarship, feminist theology was a fairly new scholarly phenomenon, having only been established as a public discipline in the past sixty years. In this philosophy, scripture could be interpreted by unfolding revelation. As society changed over time, the meaning of holy texts evolved.

I unlocked Frankie's empty flat after picking up a spare key from his friend. Sun stretched long through tall, wooden-framed windows, warming caramel-coloured floorboards. Frankie had showed me kindness in a Bulgarian snowstorm; now, I would sleep on his spare futon. The two-room flat was sparsely decorated: a record player, a disco ball, a hula hoop leaning against a wall.

I lay on a fluffy rug, toying with white tendrils, watching dust motes drift and spin, then picked up my phone and posed for sexy selfies. Sucking in a round belly, pressing out my chest to emphasise little titties. Bri had emailed the pictures from Scotland yesterday, and I surprised myself by not hating them. Perhaps I wasn't disgusting? Perhaps, draped against the mountain, arms open to the sky, I was okay? To examine a nude photo was to reckon with the body. An opportunity to begin the fragile journey of reconciling with the self.

I remembered with a sense of shame examining my pussy in the shower. Vulva-gazing was so intimate I found it ugly. But politics penetrated all levels of existence. How did political structures impose upon and define our relationships with our bodies, with the most private parts of our selves, with the deepest parts of our psyches? Women were only publicly and officially allowed to interpret religious texts in recent decades, which meant our lived, bodily experience of spirituality was absent from centuries prior. In response to the echoes of silencing, I knew I must narrate my inner experience, unspool the hidden layers, investigate the darkness and the light, and write myself and the women before me back into history.

Frankie's key in the lock late at night. He put a pillow and blanket on the futon and showed me his hula-hoop techniques. I slipped into sleep, then felt him poke my shoulder.

'Louise? You closed your eyes while I was talking. You need to listen. Did you know that you can do anything you put your mind to? Anything. It is possible.'

In the morning, he pulled on purple velvet tights and an eighties sports jacket, and we walked past bearded men pushing prams and women in loose black shirts smoking on wooden benches. After a buffet vegan brunch of scrambled tofu, beetroot tahini, and fake pickled herring, we separated. He went to a three-day-long dance party, while I spent the afternoon at the Memorial to the Murdered Jews of Europe, paying my respects to victims of the Holocaust. The 19,000 square feet of concrete slabs were arranged in a grid on undulating, sloping ground. Stark sunlight pushed down upon my shoulders.

I probed the anxiety in my ribs and tried to sit with my research and the trepidation it inspired. As a white Australian questioning Islam, how could I ever understand? The monument before me warned never to forget the danger of Othering people. I considered my own country. White Australia was created through savage colonialism, the destruction and repression of Indigenous heritage. Australian identity continued to be constructed in opposition to the Other. There was a string of perceived enemies, but when I was growing up, Muslims were our target. Australian media was an Islamophobic landscape of oppressed hijabis and violent terrorists. After 9/11, the Howard government claimed that refugees — from mostly Muslim countries — threw their children overboard. This lie was used to legitimise the imprisonment of asylum seekers, in deserts far from coastal capitals and then beyond the mainland: Christmas Island, Manus Island, Nauru. Campaigns of systematic torture aimed to strip people of dignity as punishment, to illustrate the power of borders and the might of the state.

I looked up at the summer sky. A hot air balloon hung above buildings, *die* printed on its curves. I was twelve when 9/11 happened, and grew up as veils were wrenched off in our streets, as newspapers published vilifying cartoons, as white men wearing Australian flags as capes congregated in Cronulla to chant 'Fuck off, Lebs' and brutalise people. Ethnicity and religion assimilated into a target for white Australia's rage.

Media and politicians harnessed this fury. Xenophobic senator Pauline Hanson said in 1996 that we were being 'swamped by Asians'; twenty years later, she surfed the wave of Islamophobia. In 2016, she called for a ban of Muslim immigration into Australia. In 2018, senator Fraser Anning echoed this sentiment, praising the White Australia policy and complaining that black Muslim gangs were terrorising Melbourne. 'Certainly all terrorists these days are Muslims,' he said, 'so why would anyone want to bring more of them here?'

I was a product of this white-supremacist system. It was deeply uncomfortable to admit, but this was the lens through which I saw other cultures. It was essential to keep interrogating my construction of self.

I uncrossed my legs, sharp aches in my calves, and wandered away from the memorial. The sun drifted towards the horizon, and light dropped away.

Toast for dinner as I opened my laptop, blue-lit face in dark apartment. I sifted through quotes I'd collected from Australian Muslim women who challenged the prejudice that lived inside of me.

'The question whether Muslim women can be feminists is already problematic,' said poet and activist Sara Saleh on a panel in 2019. It depended, she continued, on the belief that Islam was un-feminist. 'We need to step into a space of unknowing and unlearning.'

Yassmin Abdel-Magied, a Sudanese Australian writer and engineer who established Youth Without Borders, was demonised in Australia for being a Muslim woman of colour who spoke against Anzac Day's fraught war heroism. On the panel show *Q&A*, she said, 'Islam to me is the most feminist religion. We got equal rights well before the Europeans. We don't take our husbands' last names because we ain't their property.' By critiquing this Western social norm, and contrasting it with Islamic practice, she flipped the stereotype, presenting Islam as liberator of women.

Along the same lines, author of *White Tears/Brown Scars* Ruby Hamad wrote a 2012 *Eureka Street* article called 'A Feminist Reading of the Koran'. The worldwide stereotype of Islam as a violent, retributive religion came from the Taliban's reign of terror, she said, a fundamentalism uncommon to most Muslims.

Misogynist rights abuses existed. The Taliban shot Malala Yousafzai in the head. Iran's religious police interrogated and jailed women who didn't veil. The Saudi Arabian guardianship system meant women weren't free to move in public alone. But Australian media used these incidences to code Islam as E V I L to a majority-white audience. The scholar Edward W. Said detailed in *Orientalism* the manifest ways Western depictions of 'the east' perpetuated a sense of savagery, brutality, and backwardness, while retaining a sense of the West's own self that was morally upright and good. Projecting what we most despise within ourselves onto the Other.

And, like Hamad said, religious fundamentalism was only a small part of a pluralistic global religion. But white Australia wasn't educated to the difference between Shia and Sunni Islam or smaller sects, between conservative and liberal ideology, even the difference of opinion within communities or families. We didn't regularly hear stories of hospitality, provision, and compassion, of the millions of dollars donated to charities. In pursuit of Othering,

Western narratives amalgamated all Muslims into one homogenous group. But there were as many Islams as there were Muslims.

My love. Here, finally, her chocolate eyes, her velvet voice, her round smiling cheeks!

'Your hair! It's so cute and little!' She fingered my curls as she pulled away from our third hug, while Tim lingered, clutching the bunch of sunflowers I'd bought.

Outside Pergamon Museum, tourists whizzed on segways and students fell asleep on thick grass. As we entered the Museum of Islamic Art, Gul whispered that a gallery they had visited in Moscow told the story of an angry nun who chiselled off all the penises of a convent's religious statues. We fell into laughter like schoolchildren. Tim's long brown hair wove through the crowd, his nose ring glinting as he turned back to check on us.

Gul and I sat beside a stone carving of a phoenix — a Tatar symbol — reminiscing about high school. Did I remember, she asked, when she had me over for brunch? We'd held hot mugs of tea, resting our elbows on a plastic tablecloth, when I suddenly sighed and shook my head. 'Oh, it's so sad — I wish my non-Christian friends were going to heaven.' I told her she was going to hell while eating her scrambled eggs.

'Gul! I have *no* memory of this!'

'Don't worry about it,' she shrugged. 'Ancient history.'

I invited her to youth group, I remembered, and she came sometimes.

'My parents encouraged me to go,' she said. 'Because Islamically, it's about tolerance and respect.'

Other memories arose, times when I didn't return her respect.

Not long before I married, I invited her to dinner at my Boyfriend's house. Chicken mignon: thigh meat wrapped in bacon. She pulled out the wooden skewers, unwound the rashers, and ate the chicken in delicate bites.

'I don't eat pork,' she'd said quietly, smiling, smiling.

These memories made my stomach churn. I'd made assumptions, hadn't realised the lack of conflict between our faiths was somewhat predicated on her silence. For years, I'd sensed a quiet, secret fence, and never asked: about prayer, her mosque, family traditions. By unspoken agreement, conversation didn't cross these lines. We talked about sex, fears, desires, but her inner spiritual world was closed. While I never needed to defend my faith, Gul was required not to impose. She held her faith close to her chest, sharing with protective reticence if prodded.

Infrequently, she'd revealed the cost of growing up in an Islamophobic country: veiled aunties being verbally abused at the supermarket, knife threats at the Islamic school, graffiti at the mosque. I never considered that her extreme privacy could be self-protection against violence.

Only recently, I'd realised how she adapted herself for a white audience. Her number, in my phone, was still under GG, the name she gave to strangers, colleagues, and new friends. As our knees touched in the museum, it suddenly occurred to me: 'Is this an anglicised version, because people find Gulghina hard to pronounce?'

'For sure,' she said. 'I mean, it's like, do you have a whiteboard? How much time do you have? Remember at school people used to say Gul-gina [so it rhymed with vagina]? Now that's my DJ name!'

We burst into giggles. Beyond burning mix-CDs, Gul had never DJ'd in her life. Her sense of humour was built upon hyperbole, the absurd, and a gleeful suspension of reality.

Tim returned; the museum was closing. We left the tourist district and dawdled through wide streets of pastel-painted, nineteenth-century apartment buildings, where calm parents pushed double prams under leafy chestnut trees. Waiters wheeled TVs into the summer evening so beer drinkers could yell at the World Cup.

Our talk turned, momentarily, to my ex-Husband. Gul had seen Him at a restaurant back home. Tim fell behind us, allowing distance when he sensed emotions rising. Gul reminded me of the hat He hated, the door He broke. 'I'm still angry.'

'Yeah …' I rubbed the back of my neck. 'I'm only just learning how to get to that bit.'

Night fell, and we decided on a cheap Syrian restaurant for plates of herby falafel, garlicky hummus, and acidic tomato. Our plates were empty when a balding man nearby tilted his torso to release a generous fart, the rumble amplified by the wooden bench.

Tim had wide, astounded eyes. 'Did that really happen?' he whispered. Gul's mouth was open in silent laughter. We grabbed our bags and ran across the street, where, finally, hysteria exploded, and I laughed more than I had in months.

Zipping under enormous trees' dappled shade on hired bikes, we crossed Alexanderplatz and joined a cloud of commuter cyclists. To the sound of mechanical gear clicks and pedal whistles, we cycled by remnants of the Berlin Wall. A day-party's trance heartbeat pounded like a ghostly echo from the other side.

Gul and I left Tim and rode to Ibn Rushd-Goethe Mosque to meet Susie, the woman who led prayer. I was happy to steal some one-on-one time. Travelling with my best friend and her boyfriend was a strange experience. A couple is one body; shared opinions are expressed as *we*. I had to negotiate their *we*, to jealously insert myself and disrupt their equilibrium.

We climbed three storeys up. With a crimson veil over caramel curls, her white nose peeking from beneath, Susie faced Mecca. And sang.

The person who performed the *adhan*, or Islamic call to prayer, was called a muezzin. Among families at home, roles might differ, but traditionally at mosques, this was a man. '*Allahu Akbar* (God is Great),' Susie's voice rang out. '*Ashhadu an la ilaha illa Allah* (I bear witness that there is no God except the One God).' Her body swayed; as she shifted weight to each foot, the opposite heel lifted, soft, slow. 'So that's the call,' Susie said in a high-pitched voice, turning her head to us. 'And then we pray.' She bent to kneel, whispering, then placed her head on the ground. A rhythm to her movement as she murmured.

We left the mosque's main room and walked up another flight of stairs to the office. Beside a long meeting table, here lay the ephemera of community hospitality: bottles of water and juice, piles of coffee cups in plastic tubs.

'We are not many people,' Susie said when she saw me looking around the room, 'but we do translations in our spare time, we run workshops …' She arranged some croissants on a plate for us.

About thirty people belonged to the mosque, half men and half women, and around five showed up for Friday prayer.

Susie grew up in Berlin, brought up by German parents who weren't religious — though at fourteen she was confirmed at church, like many of her friends. She felt a definite call to religion from childhood. 'When I listened to fairy tales, I felt like a spiritual type of person.'

Her first boyfriend as a teenager was Muslim, which brought her in touch with Islam. But when she married, she and her first husband went to church together. After twelve years, they divorced, and she stopped practising.

'Two years ago, I met a man who I got very close to, and we had a lot of talks about Islam, and I got to know a very different Islam, an embracing, forgiving, loving Islam. And then I came by coincidence — which is not coincidence, of course — to this mosque. And here also I learnt that there is a different type of Islam that has nothing to do with punishment.'

Susie had only converted in the last days of Ramadan, a few weeks ago. 'I had been practising Islam for quite a while — it is a thing of the heart. During Ramadan, it became an urge to say it. I didn't do it in front of anybody except in front of my friend. We went to the mosque together at night. It was very pleasing.'

Like in France and Belgium, the veil was outlawed in public service, symbolising the xenophobia sweeping Europe. School-teachers were forbidden to wear hijabs to work in some states of Germany. In 2016, chancellor Angela Merkel had said that the wearing of full-faced veils should be prohibited in Germany 'wherever it is legally possible'. But for many people, it was an essential part of worship. Most mosques expected women to put a scarf over their hair as a sign of respect. Though I'd never seen Gul with a scarf, she wore one to mosque, because it cut out all distractions, allowed an intimacy with God.

Ibn Rushd-Goethe had no ruling on the veil, a deliberate 'political statement' by Ateş. 'When we pray, most people actually do wear the veil, surprisingly,' Susie laughed, 'but nobody tells you that you have to.'

Gul and I crossed the busy road from the mosque and debriefed over tea and lemon cake. She'd sat in on the interview, but when I asked if she had any questions, she shook her head, arms crossed. In the cafe's quiet, I realised she was angry, like a pot simmering with the lid on. She hadn't spoken out of respect.

I asked her what she thought, nervous. I wanted her to trust me, knowing there were times in the past when I didn't make her feel safe.

She brought my attention to the racial dynamics. Susie, like Marlene, had mentioned the fatwas. 'Did you hear that the communities against them are all from Middle Eastern countries? I'll admit it, some Arab and Kurdish communities in Australia have their issues, for sure. But this mosque is only afraid of brown people.'

And further, Gul couldn't abide the suggestion that if women didn't have the same roles as men, they were silenced. The focus on leadership from the front, she felt, minimised the powerful work of strong women.

'What about the centuries of tradition? The hundreds of years of women before us?' she asked, licking white icing from her finger. 'We have a hadith in Islam: heaven lies at the mother's feet. She is *worshipped.*'

Gul's own grandmother had a precious, sacred role in her life. It was at her knee that she and her brother were taught many Quranic stories. Things always seemed so simple from the outside, she said. 'Women are not measured in relation to men, but in relation to God.'

Frankie took us to a bohemian bar lit with crimson lights and a roaming tarot-card reader. I began to yawn at midnight. At the station, I took a video of Tim and Gul waving from the platform when our train pulled away. After a few hours' sleep, they would fly to Austria and continue their trip. I envied their companionship, was relieved to exit their social dynamic, and resented their leaving. If a stranger farted in public, who would laugh with me?

The city was empty early the next morning. I drew the curtain of a street-side Photoautomatik booth on Schönhauser Allee; a succession of white pops as I turned my head before dark glass. The machine dispensed a black-and-white strip. On the back of my unsmiling portrait, I scribbled, *alone again.*

Dissatisfaction descended as I watched Berlin's shopfronts through a bus window. I got the sense that women at the front — of the church, of the mosque — was a Western image of equality. Exporting a Western feminism assumes that my way is the best way, a form of cultural imperialism that imposes a 'superior' ideology. Was I, in my obsession with women in clear, structured roles of power, erasing the ancient inheritance of female authority that didn't mimic male privilege?

Over and over, I realised how limited my perspective was, how naive and self-centred I'd been. Over and over, I was discovering I had power in a situation where I'd assumed I had none. So many things needed to unfurl to reveal the truth.

The women I'd interviewed at Ibn Rushd-Goethe Mosque were converts who didn't grow up in Islam; they weren't raised with the combined heritage of culture and family like women like Gul. It was exciting to see women defecting in place and challenging religious norms, but to get a better picture of Muslim women transgressing tradition and provoking change, I needed to visit a place where religion and culture were interwoven.

And something was bugging me about Susie. She'd found

Islam through men. Why did her spirituality follow romance? Wasn't she strong enough to walk her own path?

At the airport, I raised my arms like a crucified woman. When the uniformed lady placed latex hands near my chest, my cheeks burnt and I imagined asking her to do it again.

'Is this your backpack? It's got liquid in it.' A man with *Security* embroidered on his pocket held a plastic cup of yoghurt I'd taken from Frankie's fridge.

'It's yoghurt. It's not actually liquid.'

His serious, thick eyebrows bore down upon me. 'I must ask you to dispose of it.'

'But it's my breakfast!'

'I'm sorry. It cannot go through.'

I cursed the rules and yanked my backpack from the conveyor belt, scrambled in the pocket to find a spoon I'd borrowed from an Irish Airbnb. The security man, his arms crossed, kept supervising the removal of boots and belts, but his eyes flicked back to me. I hurried yoghurt into my mouth, sullenly holding his gaze when I could, locked in a private, petulant battle with male authority in this airport, this country, this world. *Stop telling me what to do!* I wanted to scream.

I dropped the empty carton into his bin, licked the spoon, and hoisted my backpack. At the gate, I slid down a glass wall and thought again of my disgruntlement with Susie. It hit me and I groaned, pulled my knees up to my chest. How could I criticise her? Didn't I go to church because a handsome man paid attention to me? Weren't boys onstage the reason youth group was so exciting?

First call for boarding. I joined the long, shuffling line. I was just like Susie. I fell in love with Him the same time I fell in love with God.

Morocco

Men streamed towards Rue San Francisco, patterned prayer rugs tucked under arms. The mosque was full; latecomers unrolled mats in neat lines on Tangier's Grand Socco. Some on the hard street, some on the adjacent park's soft grass.

I sat on a bench beside an empty fountain, listening to the *adhan* broadcast from the minaret's loudspeaker. Hundreds of bodies bent, knelt, and prostrated in symphony. Prayer as public declaration of surrender. Cars, cats, and tourists passed.

The *khutbah* was in Darija, Morocco's Arabic dialect. The country's constitution claimed Islam as the official religion, and the king was believed to be a direct descendant of the Prophet. I cast my eyes across the faithful who wore striped djellabas or golden embellished robes, T-shirts or buttoned shirts, baseball hats or *kufi* caps; some were bearded, some moustachioed, some clean-shaven. All were men. Friday prayer was a male religious obligation, and there wasn't the same social expectation for women to attend, except on festivals like Eid-ul-Fitr.

Still in search of women defecting in place, I'd been reading feminist Islamic theologians. One of the most prominent of these was Dr Asma Lamrabet, a radiologist who had made a second career as a religious scholar. She published reinterpretations of text in Arabic and French, and luckily for me, some had been translated into English. I had emailed Dr Lamrabet a few months ago, and she had agreed to meet with me in Rabat. So I'd bought a flight.

I planned to first spend a few days in Tangier, a port city of less than a million on the northern tip of Africa, before heading south. My room in Marshan was perched high on the edge of the deep aquamarine ocean. On clear days, Andalusian mountains shimmered across the Strait of Gibraltar.

Street sellers set out glowing white shoes, sunglasses, and jeans atop neat blue tarp in preparation for the incoming foot traffic. The Grand Socco was an open square in the centre of a cobblestoned ring road, towered over by Cinema Rif's white-and-red art-deco building and skinny palm trees. Tangier was irresistible to a writer. The city's role in Western literary history swirled in my dreams, romantic and luminous. In the 1950s and 1960s, the Parisian-style buildings and tight medina were home to American and British poets, painters, and musicians, attracted by loose laws on drugs and homosexuality.

Due to the port city's position — fourteen kilometres by sea to Europe — imperialist powers had long sought economic and military control. The nineteenth century saw most of Morocco controlled by France and Spain; Portugal, America, and Britain had economic interests here, too. This incurred multiple, muddled layers of bureaucracy and governance. From 1912 until Moroccan independence in 1956, Tangier became what William Burroughs called the Interzone, a lawless territory and haunt for expat hedonism. Burroughs — who literally wrote the book on being a junkie, and whose writing documented his proclivity for sex with teenage boys — wrote that in Tangier 'you can do exactly as you want'.

Paul and Jane Bowles lived here, and it was visited by Jean Genet, Truman Capote, Henri Matisse, Joan Miró, and Keith Richards. Western travel writers emphasised a history of socialites, addicts, deviants, and spies, creating an air of treachery and sleaze. This depiction, however, has been condemned by Maghreb and Arab writers, for perpetuating orientalism.

Warm wind through my hair. A slim man in a black T-shirt sat beside me and flashed a crooked-toothed smile. '*Bonjour. Ça va?*'

I rose. At Cinema Rif's cafe, young men and women nursed mint tea and glass bottles of Coca-Cola on white cane chairs, smoking and watching the street, or sketching, editing photos on laptops, or playing guitar. Ignoring men's greetings, I wandered, gazing at shoe shiners with wooden boxes for customers to rest their feet; a row of metal workshops; piles of rams' horns lined on the pavement, curving from buckets with a vile, black odour. Behind the fish market, peacocks blinked in cages alongside ducks and songbirds.

The sun set, pink slashed across the sky. Anything could happen. On Blvd Pasteur, I pushed open the door to Librairie des Colonnes. Opened in 1949 by French publishing house Gallimard, it was once frequented by visiting literary giants like Samuel Beckett, and used as a reading room by local authors like Mohamed Choukri and Tahar Ben Jelloun. Between shelves of books in French, Arabic, and Spanish, I found an English novel. The bookseller with curly hair and a black moustache spoke Darija to one customer, French to another, and English to me.

I smiled. 'I just got here. What is there to do in Tangier?'

'Hmm … There's an art exhibition opening tomorrow at Gallery Delacroix. Meet me there at six?'

He wrote his number in my phone under 'Ilyass'.

On the hill back to Marshan, a man with fuzzy brown hair fell into step with me, alternating between French, Spanish, English until I relented and said hello.

'I stopped my car to talk to you.'

I shrugged him off and climbed the stairs to my Airbnb's rooftop, leaning against the concrete wall in my underwear, smoking, looking at constellations in the rich black sky. Had I made the right choice, in coming to Morocco? Anxiety was a tight chest, a clenched stomach. As I exhaled, my shoulders relaxed — I'd been hunching them all day. The topography of shame. I'd lived within this landscape for so long.

A shooting star dashed, then faded.

An unveiled white woman walking alone was an invitation. I swatted away calls of *guapa* and *hola bella*, and instead watched women on the street: those my mother's age with the niqab and aba in black or olive, teenagers with long T-shirts over jeans, hijabi girls with elegant flowing dresses, and young women in sleeveless tops and skin-tight jeans.

I changed accommodation, dragging my suitcase over dusty cobblestones to spend two nights (the most I could afford) at El Muniria, the hotel where William Burroughs wrote *Naked Lunch*. Its bar downstairs was decorated with Jack Kerouac quotes. I traced my mouth with blood-red lipstick, unaware that tonight I would meet everything I desired, and everything I'd tried to escape.

At Gallery Delacroix, Ilyass was wearing a violet jacket and teal baseball hat. In one room, Arabic script shone in neon; in another were life-sized prints of middle-aged women in leopard-print veils. We left and wandered the medina's tight maze, its crumbling walls painted blue and white; past tiny rooms where textile makers sewed beneath bare lightbulbs, and Cafe Baba, clouded with hashish haze.

'It's nice to walk through the streets with a man,' I said. 'Now, barely anybody looks at me.'

He grunted. 'Moroccan people are very sexually frustrated, you know. It is a basic human need, but they are not allowed, only within marriage.'

At the kasbah gate, we gazed over the rolling ocean. Brown

eyes behind round black-framed glasses, Ilyass described how he read incessantly behind his bookseller's counter. His favourite philosopher was Spinoza.

Gentle sky faded to lavender, then deep blue. Seagulls cackled in the night. The evening *adhan* wailed from competing mosque speakers.

Ilyass' family came to Tangier from Damascus 150 years ago, he said. When I told Ilyass I gave up my religion, he was confused. 'But you cannot stop what is part of you.'

We ordered mint tea in Gran Café de Paris' leather booths, where Francis Bacon once drank coffee by mirrored walls. Ilyass' friends joined us, and he translated infrequently from French, smoking, leaning his elbow on my knee. We moved to the bar upstairs, where a singer warbled into a microphone, disco lights flashing green, red, yellow. On a balcony, where we gripped sweating bottles of Casablanca lager, waiters brought tiny plates of fried meat.

'It's tapas,' Ilyass shouted in my ear. 'Free.'

I turned to his friend Rachid. He wore a red beanie slid halfway up his shaved head, and a sly, half-lidded smile. Ilyass disappeared, and Rachid took me to another bar, where a resentful blonde left us plates of fried fish. He kissed my hand. My cheek brushed his jawline.

'Do you want to come to my room?' I whispered.

'It is not so easy to go to a hotel.'

We walked a moonlit path under a glowering sky. He bought peaches from the late-night fruit stall, his stocky body bending, gripping, and clutching fruit, squeezing them for firmness.

On Rue de la Kasbah, he asked me to be quiet so as not to disturb his neighbours; we crept up marble stairs, past different-sized coloured slippers outside apartments' front doors. On the top floor, he opened a red iron door to a small room: a low gold-green couch lining three walls, books on a high shelf, a countertop gas burner with a blackened tea pot, and a teenage cat that jumped and yowled.

He poured the kitten, Sharifa, some kibble. We kissed standing up. It was probably the beer, but when we undressed, I wasn't self-conscious. I ran my hands along thick curly hair across his shoulders, arms, and back. He played electronic music that put us in a trance; we found a rhythm and kept it for hours. Rachid was aggressive. Whatever he wanted, he could have. He grabbed my hair, pulled my neck to arch my back, and took me from behind. I was nothing but whimpers and trembling.

Not long before dawn, the morning *adhan* erupted from a medina mosque. He took a peach from the fridge and fed me cool slices. Sharifa eyed us from a corner, then pounced on my hair. I yelped.

'Please, be quiet. I only moved in two weeks ago and don't want to be homeless again.'

The sky lightened, and finally we slept in a tangle of sweaty limbs. As we dressed, I picked up a copy of Leïla Slimani's *Sexe et mensonges* on his coffee table. He told me I could keep it.

Through midday bright to El Muniria, to shower. At Café de Paris, I ordered a black coffee, a boiling bitter kick in a tall glass. I was smoking more in Morocco, mimicking everyone else, who always had a cigarette in hand.

I crossed my legs, squeezed my thighs tight. My vulva throbbed. I was exhausted and thrilled. It was a long time since I'd stayed up all night fucking. This was the life I imagined for myself when I left home: an elegant, mysterious woman smoking at a cafe, leaving a string of sexy lovers in her wake.

I flipped through the book Rachid had given me, squinting at French words I recognised, then opened my laptop to find the English version. Leïla Slimani, a Moroccan writer living in Paris, had won France's most prestigious literary prize for *Chanson douce*, or *Lullaby* in English. She wrote unflinchingly about darkness, rage, and brutality at the intersection of race, gender, and class. Her third book was nonfiction, and translated to *Sex and Lies*. Slimani collected stories from Moroccan women about a society that severely restricted sexual freedom. I was grateful to find a Moroccan writer explaining social norms for a Western audience. It would prepare a foundation for my interview with Dr Lamrabet.

Ilyass had implied it was illegal to have sex outside of marriage. Slimani explained: 'In Morocco, the ban on "fornication", or *zina*, isn't just a moral injunction. Article 490 of the penal code prescribes "imprisonment of between one month and one year [for] all persons of opposite sexes who, not being united by the bonds of marriage, pursue sexual relations".'

Now I understood why Rachid couldn't come back to my hotel room: he could literally be arrested. I'd asked at El Muniria reception this morning if I could have visitors. The teenage attendant told me that last week, a guest had brought a girl to his room, and her auntie (the owner) had asked them to leave.

I clicked onto travel blogs about hotel-staff bribes, Airbnb hosts who requested marriage certificates. Somebody could be evicted, I realised, for inviting girls home — I had to creep up and down Rachid's stairwell so as not to provoke community surveillance.

Sex and Lies was an incredible documentation of women's lives under state-sponsored oppression. The ability to be sexually active was a class issue, she wrote: if you had money to pay for a hotel room or to bribe police; if you owned a car, or lived in an apartment alone or outside of your family; only then could you circumvent the law.

Like in twentieth-century Ireland, there was a gendered double standard. Men were expected to have premarital dalliances, even if it wasn't openly discussed, but social punishment for transgression was far more serious for women; it was difficult to marry if it was known you weren't a virgin.

Institutional dominance inspired self-policing. The laws were a deliberate attack, Slimani asserted, on civil rights.

'In Morocco, as in other Muslim countries, we can view this condition of sexual deprivation as an obstacle to the development of individuals and citizens. Kept in order by an iron-fisted government, men reproduce the authoritarian regime in their family circles and households. Thus we produce individuals who adapt to an oppressive system.'

Systemic injustice echoes in the flesh. Intimate experience inspires how we act in society. The structural informs the erotic, and in the opposite way and in all directions, a web of cultures, minds, and bodies.

Rachid dropped his weight beside me and threw paper bags of pastries on the glass table top. He tore them open. All of Tangier passed by the rounded windows that looked out upon the street. We talked of Nietzsche, immigration, hints of our past. His mother's illiteracy, his postgraduate degree, the Moroccan Navy, which opened fire on boats of refugees heading for Spain. During Ramadan, he said, he went travelling; he created different personas so he could legally eat in daylight or drink beer at night. In Asilah, he was a Moroccan Jew; in Essaouira, a French Algerian.

We went to a tiny restaurant to eat tagine, sweet with raisins and onions. Rachid offered me a chicken neck, and I baulked. 'This is what we feed to cats and dogs in Australia.'

'I am like a dog, then,' he grinned. And stripped meat from bone with his teeth.

Later, Number One bar played blues real loud. It was dark, I was drunk, reeling, and when Rachid leant close and whispered, 'Something special for your last night. I know a cocaine dealer,' not one inch of me said no. We bumped into Ilyass, who complained about Spanish women in bars, 'sitting on their fat asses', who couldn't handle a conversation, no Spinoza, no philosophy. I gave Rachid a 200-dirham note, and he went downstairs to meet his dealer.

'Do you want to start here?' he asked. 'You can do a line in the toilets.'

'No, Rachid, I don't know how to do it,' I whimpered, my hand on his chest. 'You have to show me.'

The bar was closing anyway, it was 2.00 am. We snuck up his stairs. Bent over his coffee table, Rachid cut lines with a bank card.

'Just don't breathe out on it, okay?' He rolled the 200dh note and demonstrated.

I did as he said and then I sucked his cock. I licked his balls, everything was sharpened with exhilarating intensity, we did things I'd never done before, he asked me and I obeyed, the whole reason of my life was to please. I never tired. He slapped my butt with well-aimed open palms, the sound rang out in thick air and I gasped low and then he came close and closed his hands around my neck, thumbs joining at my vocal cords, he pressed down, the sound of my breath desperate, pathetic, he looked me in the eye, that half-lidded gaze, those uncaring auburn eyes, watching me struggle for air.

He sat back. 'Can I take your belt?'

'Please.' Yes was intoxicating, no was unavailable. He picked up my crumpled crimson jeans, unfurled it, I didn't look, couldn't look, could only hear that slow metal clink through each loop. I was on all fours. He pressed my face to the couch, my butt in the air, he stood over me, raised his weapon, the belt hit my butt with a stinging thwack and I groaned, an animal.

We drank, kept doing lines, talked. I was a laser beam of clarified intensity. Eyes open wide. Endless cigarettes. Sucking in sharp breath. Music. Touch. Sweat. One cigarette packet crumpled, I fumbled in my bag, threw mine on the table. The first *adhan*. The sun arrived. I began to cry. He pulled a red sheet across the window against the light of day. Sometime later, we had sex again. He was above. He took the belt. Buckle-clink. He wrapped it around my neck. He pulled tight. He slapped my jaw. The sound of his voice. Black.

My alarm trilled. I swam back to consciousness, his dick was inside me, thrusting, I was sore, I placed a hand against his heavy, furry chest and whispered, 'Enough.'

'Really?' he kept pushing.

I grunted deep in my chest, 'More.'

The alarm again. Time to check out of my hotel. I pulled on jeans, threw the belt — that betrayer, that black snake with clinking silver mouth — into my bag, and wiped tears, breathless, turning away.

'Hold on, come here, I don't want you to leave like this.'

Naked, he wrapped his arms around me. I permitted his embrace, unmoving, then reached for the door.

Under brutal sun, I slid down a concrete wall at the entrance to Tanger Ville station, whimpering softly behind dark glasses, sucking on cigarette after cigarette. What happened last night? I should eat, it was almost 2.00 pm. No, I couldn't. Did I say yes? Did I say yes to everything?

Lonely air-conditioned first-class. Four hours. Dry landscape flashed past, donkeys carrying loads, mountains rose then fell, and then: a field of sunflowers, yellow and kind. A brief tide of joy, then the ocean withdrew. He didn't hurt me, really, only a few little bruises, but I was drunk and high, my first time on cocaine, he didn't ask me sober. At every station — Kenitra, Meknes — orange trees blessed the centre of platforms, luscious citrus bursting from dark green. I let a man put a belt around my neck and pull.

before

The Rewards

The treachery of Christianity echoes in the silence. The unspoken. The gaps in between. When I said, after I hit my neighbour's car late at night, that 'God protected me', I unthinkingly implied that God chose not to protect others who weren't so lucky. When prosperity-gospel pastors said economic success was reward for correct action, it meant God therefore refused to give his favour to the poor.

My fellow believers and I were devoted to lip service. 'Women are powerful,' said my Husband, my Pastor. 'They have the same rights as men.' But they worshipped the Father God, Son, and the masculine Holy Spirit. Thereby reinforcing power structures that benefited them.

And I believed what they said. The Pastor knew identity could be designed, constructed, and performed through image. That you can influence what people think of your actions through appearance and persuasive speech — or perhaps this is only true of charismatic leaders.

As his profile grew, the Pastor leveraged any opportunity for publicity. He wrote op-eds for secular media, was asked to advise government officials. He held a press conference and the prime minister attended. The poet revolutionary now wore a blazer, shirt, and tie.

We become known in the Adelaide church scene for progressive values. A few people in our community were gay; the same time the Australian marriage equality debate heated up, Hillsong fired a choir leader for being in a same-sex relationship. The Pastor suddenly saw that the church was homophobic. Our denomination's national organisation — to which we paid annual fees — declared homosexuality a sin. So the Pastor resigned us from the national and state bodies, making our church independent and removing his legal status as a pastor, completing his transformation from maverick to outlaw. He invited TV cameras to a celebratory Sunday to publicise our safe religious space for LGBTQ+ people (we weren't the first church to do so; we were just good at marketing). An interstate activist flew in. We were disrupting conservative bureaucracy, challenging outdated theology, addressing the social violence of the church. That day, we wept in joy to stand for love as people in our congregation declared they finally felt at home. They could unite their previously estranged elements of identity: religious and queer. The day was subversive justice and it smacked of congratulatory self-promotion.

It wasn't until after I left the church that I saw the horrible fact of his multiplicity: he was both a campaigner for the marginalised and a political opportunist. Both a narcissist that cultivated followers and my wise spiritual teacher. He was good. He was bad. A villain *and* a saint.

The men in my life reinforced power structures that benefited them, but so did I. The Pastor asked me to preach. I said no. A year later, he asked me again and I wrote my first sermon.

I stepped onstage, adrenaline thumping. Someone called out for me to hold the mike closer to my mouth. I was sweating. But as Sally had said ten years ago when I got my first Bible, God never gave you more than you could handle. And preaching came with rewards. I was already central in the social milieu, known and loved; now, I received the spotlight, too, the privilege of speaking when everyone else was silent.

The Pastor gave me a platform because he trusted I wouldn't rock the boat. He only allowed known quantities to speak; years earlier, he had given new immigrants in our community a go and it got awkward when they acted in line with their own beliefs. Benjamin decried the flames of hell, gripping the podium and peering at the congregation with burning eyes. And Patience, a mother of seven and respected leader in her community, condemned gay people. Because they contradicted our theology, neither of them was given the microphone again. Which was a shame, because they were some of the few people of colour who spoke onstage in our community for years.

But the Pastor let me write about whatever I wanted. He trusted I would reproduce the party line.

And so I did; adding feminist analysis, eagerly teaching peers to subvert patriarchal paradigms, but never questioning the fundamental structure of our religion. Within my sermons, I reproduced the posture of subjugation: we must surrender to the will of God. We are broken people, and need God to be whole. The Father loves us despite our mistakes.

I felt ashamed for my lack of scriptural knowledge. Weren't teachers meant to be scholars, guiding communities through close reading of holy texts? From the weekly spending money my Husband and I allowed ourselves, normally spent on burgers or Friday-night gin, I bought a membership to a Bible College Library.

I planned to educate myself with historical context and analysis of the New Testament. But when I entered the quiet, dusty library, gravity drew me to the section marked Feminist Theology;

I fingered spines of Rosemary Radford Ruether, Mary Daly, Elisabeth Schüssler Fiorenza, Mercy Amba Oduyoye. I'd muted Auntie Liz's furious emails, but her questions still led me here. Eighteen months before I left my marriage, and two years before I left Australia, this was my pilgrimage's first step.

In line with my idealised concept of leaders as infallible, I'd once thought sermons were transmitted directly from God, as if preachers were a holy spirit radio. But they actually document the sermon-writer's challenges, lived experience, privilege, and historical and cultural context. These are texts that present a track of personal spiritual questions like footprints in snow.

I marched into the car park to my chained-up bike, my backpack heavy with new knowledge. The low, late-afternoon sun painted the bark of tremendous eucalyptus trees an exhilarating orange. Something tender and new quivered in my chest, like a vulnerable seedling just-sprouted from dark soil. At this point, feminist theology didn't disrupt my faith, but reinforced it. Jesus, I thought, transcended patriarchy's bullshit. Jesus, the lamb before the lion, the symbol of the compassion of the human heart in the face of our violence; he was the answer, the answer, the answer. His message was the core of liberation, and all the other Bible verses must be interpreted through this lens.

Every two months, I loosened my waist-length curls and wore my lucky socks to preach. Despite lacking rhetorical technique, and projecting excruciating nervousness, I was well received — my messages suited the church's leftist identity. Feminist theology was a natural branch of liberation theology. And, I repeat, I did not challenge the hierarchical nature of our divine encounter.

Though Dad had no care for religion, he visited church whenever I was onstage. Like watching my teenage netball games, his visits were an act of support. He'd take me out for lunch afterwards — sometimes, my Husband came, too. Mostly, He didn't.

Early in my short preaching career, I texted the Pastor to ask for feedback.

'You did great,' he replied.

'Can we meet up and talk about it?'

'I'm in Sydney this week.'

Our discipleship meetings were over. Our dynamic shifted as his sphere of influence expanded. My rewards had changed.

Unknowing Is a Darkness

I accepted God's will but wanted to escape. I needed to be touched, but my Husband did not. I loved Him and resented Him. So I prayed, submitting these tensions to the Lord.

The front door closing, the rush of the shower. He poked His head into the back room where I was curled on the couch by my writing desk. Short wet hair slicked back, chest bare, a towel around His waist. The curve of His pectorals, delicate nipples, dark tangle of hair at His sternum.

'Hey, babe,' He smiled. 'You ready?'

'Yep!' When He turned, I rolled my eyes, threw my novel down, and followed Him to the bedroom. He pulled on clean jocks and lay stomach-down. I straddled Him, and pumped moisturiser into my hands, sliding wet palms on His skin.

'Ooh, chilly!' He wriggled His hips. I kneaded the top of His buttocks.

Ever since He started His job unloading pallets in a warehouse, He suffered from chronic back pain; when it was severe, His face grew drawn and white. But He continued to play basketball, and post-game massages were my job, to alleviate the ensuing pain.

I circled palms to His middle.

'Lou,' He whispered, turning His head. The flutter of His eyelashes. 'Would you mind going down again? I just need you to work the muscles that line the spine. If you go from inside and spread towards my waist, that feels really good.'

'Sure, darling.'

I rounded the heels of my palms, lifted my butt, and leant forward, using the heft of my body to press. I swallowed frustrated tears. When He was facedown, when I pressed my full weight, when His palms lay in supplication, even then, His hand still clasped my wrist.

We shared the bedroom's full-length mirror. He wore a slim-cut navy suit with a tight, patterned Jack London shirt; I lingered behind in a sea-green vintage dress cinched at the waist, straightening a leopard-print hat. I lurked behind Him, breathing His Versace cologne. He looked up from adjusting shirtsleeves.

'Lou, I told you. Sorry, but that hat, it looks kind of … silly.'

'Oh well,' I shrugged and grabbed our gift. 'Ready to go?'

The two-hour drive to the River Murray was spent in silence, my favourite weapon of wounded defiance. I knew He hated the hat; I wished He would stop telling me. Why did he need to view me as lesser than Himself?

But later, my heart softened as I watched the couple at the altar, my commitment to Him renewed as if I were parsing the vows myself. That night when the dancefloor heated up, I flung the hat from my sweaty head with relief. It spun onto wet grass.

I was driving, so only drank two wines, but by 11.00 pm,

for some reason — the loud music, the long drive, the heat — I was attacked by one of my terrible headaches. It would likely soon descend into dire nausea. The black air heavy with cricket tweeps, I slumped on a table and watched light globes strung over the dancefloor. They bathed jerking bodies in yellow glow, casting moving shadows onto the night garden. I leant my head on the white tablecloth. The grass looked so plush, inviting; I slid down, rested cheek upon cool green, and finally closed my eyes.

When I woke, shined boots were thirty centimetres from my face. I crawled from under the table and turned my head up to see His ironed trousers, His careful hairstyle tousled from dancing's chaos.

'Lou? What are you doing?'

I was bleary, slow. 'I didn't feel well. Are you ready?'

We crunched across the gravel car park. The moon was bright, the violet sky clear. He was woozy from beer, disturbed but irritated to have found me on the ground. He thought me pathetic in my passivity, thus justifying His disdain. 'Why didn't you tell me you wanted to leave?'

I shrugged. It simply didn't occur. I wasn't in the practice of identifying what I needed, nor asking for it. No. I waited for instruction. My voice was restricted, but more importantly, so was thought. It was unthinkable to move in contention over our agreed dynamic. Power played out among the mundane, and placed a fence around my creativity, initiative, and imagination. This was the curious, invisible harm caused by coercive control. I was blind to my own agency.

Yet by accepting His vision of me as powerless, I was safe. Assurance of incompetence meant I didn't need to try, nor face failure's humiliation. I crawled into the cage and locked the door myself.

———

Around our fourth anniversary, my Husband began working in His dad's boat shop; one day, if things went well, He might take over the business. His father expected Him to start at the bottom like any new employee. He spent days soaping fibreglass fishing boats, arriving home with hands cracked from detergent, too tired to help cook dinner.

He needed space, space, always more space. We ate dinner in separate rooms, in front of separate screens. He took long showers in the morning and evening. He hid His music, waiting for me to leave the house to practise guitar; if I asked Him to play, He protested with a sense of violation. Our private inner worlds couldn't be bridged. We bought a king-size bed with a firm mattress for His back pain. At night, under fresh blue sheets, we spread out like starfish and still did not touch.

Months of minimum wage and His dad didn't offer the promised raise or responsibility. My Husband arrived home one night. When he poked His head into my writing room, distilled sun cast golden light on His faded polo shirt, His sharp cheekbones, His sunken eyes. He was due for a haircut.

'Hey, babe.' He welcomed my arms more easily than usual, and I rested in His embrace and inhaled. That's when I smelt it: His sweat was different — sweet, sharp fear, or panic, or both.

I drew back and looked into his blue eyes. 'Are you okay, darling?'

He pulled away, sat heavy on the couch, and leant forward, hands clasped between knees. 'I told Dad. That I can't work for him anymore.'

'Wow.'

He looked at me. Dust danced on dying sunlight. 'D'ya think you could put your dreams of going overseas on hold just a little longer? It's time. I need to start my own thing.'

We'd discussed this. Having previously been a barista for four years, He wanted to open His own cafe. I sat beside Him, pressed my leg against His. I didn't consider what things cost, because we'd do it together. I wasn't required to look out for what I needed — that was His job.

'Of course, babe. Yes.'

I asked God what this meant for our lives as I sat on red plastic seats in the chicken shop, where a blonde mother disciplined her two ugly children. I knew, I thought as I pulled the greasy package to my chest, God had a plan for my life. And I was following his will. So he would look after me.

We took a last holiday together. He drove us four hours through dry shrublands and open plains. Near the Grampians, we turned up a driveway to a house atop an enormous field; at the sound of our car, kangaroos bounded across the green. The next morning when I rose from bed, the French doors were open to the valley. He was eating breakfast at the table outside, watching the roos pull tufts of grass, and beyond, the enfolding mountain range. I watched the back of His shaved head, His neck, as He bent to spoon cereal into His mouth. The lines of His body were so soft away from life's tension.

We hiked all day, and at night drank gin and tonics while waiting for pizza dough to rise. 'I picked up the key the day before we left.'

'Already?'

'Yeah. The agent said I could get it early.'

I focused on slicing tomatoes, thin as He preferred, translucent red juice seeping over the thick chopping-board wood.

'Y'know, Lou, this time is really special. It's our last moment to be together, before things go really mad.'

Baby mozzarellas were round and white in viscous liquid. I plucked a ball and placed it beneath my knife.

'The fit-out is so full on. I'm going to be working long days.' He planned to turn an empty concrete shell into a bright, functioning cafe. There was plumbing required, electricity, construction.

I turned to him, chewing soft cheese. 'And I'll do everything I can to support you.'

'Starting your own business — it changes your life. Things are going to be different.'

'I know, babe.' I pressed the side of my body against His. We'd been through this. He was a precise man, and only repeated Himself when upset.

He grasped the bowl of risen dough. 'Can you get the trays, please?'

That night we fucked. For the first time I could remember, He wanted me, He sought me out with eager fingers, eager mouth, eager moans. At dawn, I woke to piss, and when I returned to the bedroom, I pulled back the curtain, cold air bristling vellus hairs along my stomach. Blood-coloured light splashed the valley in an unearthly glow. He needed me. We were embarking on an adventure, and He needed me by His side. Kangaroos ambled across the land, lit by violent pink.

The cafe was the beginning of the end.

after

Morocco

3.00 am. Doubled over on the toilet. An urgent fire clutched me deep inside. I wrapped my arms around my belly, and pissed a couple of burning drops, groaning, then sucked from a large bottle of cranberry juice, crimson running down my chin. Please make this UTI go away, I begged — it was impossible to imagine mumbling to male pharmacists in old medina shopfronts.

I'd been torn open and rearranged. Rachid had fucked me in a new way, not the tenderness from my teenage dreams, not two souls becoming one flesh, but wild, rough, desperate pleasure. He went deeper, darker, dirtier. He found my eagerness to please, to follow instruction, to obey. Did an enlightened, adult sexuality mean sadomasochism? What did it mean if I wanted him to dominate? What had I said yes to, what had I resisted, and what boundaries had been cracked then destroyed, like water breaking through a dam?

I crawled into bed and settled. His hand swung to strike my jaw. My eyes shot open.

Breakfast in the *riad* was served on a mosaic table by a fountain. Coffee, Moroccan bread, silver-wrapped triangles of cream cheese, yoghurt, and fruit. Every day, I skipped lunch and only pushed open the compound's large door in the evening, in search of a tagine or fried-fish sandwich. In suffocating avenues, I bent my head under fat wooden planks propping up buildings that leant like elderly men on walking sticks. Locals carried furniture and deliveries on the backs of donkeys. I pushed into the crowd and kept my eyes down, ignoring the excruciating, ceaseless male gaze.

My interview with Dr Lamrabet was on Tuesday. In the anguished days before, writers were my companions. Leïla Slimani had quoted Fatema Mernissi, a feminist sociologist and pioneer in Islamic thought. I found one of her most famous books online, *Beyond the Veil: male–female dynamics in modern Muslim society*, written in 1975. Born in Fez in 1940, Mernissi grew up in a harem with her mother and grandmother (one of her grandfather's nine wives). She was a major force in arguing for women's social justice in Morocco and beyond, and only passed away in 2015. Her explanation of gender segregation gave meat to the bones of the understanding I'd gained from Slimani.

'The Christan concept of the individual,' she wrote, 'as tragically torn between two poles — good and evil, flesh and spirit, instinct and reason — is very different from the Muslim concept. Islam has a more sophisticated theory of the instincts, more akin to the Freudian concept of the libido. It views the raw instincts as energy.'

Essentially, female sexuality was seen as active and aggressive, while men were passive and acquiescent. Moroccan society depended on family and community, so was arranged to guard men from responding to women's insatiability. *Zina* was illicit intercourse, Mernissi wrote, which had the potential to incite *fitna* — chaos — and this caused the dissolution of family structures. Marriage was a 'protective device against *zina*', and was the only socially legitimate way of having sex. Men and women together led to *zina*, which led to *fitna*; therefore, genders must be segregated to protect societal stability. Islamic culture, then, utilised the threat of *fitna* to uphold patriarchal values and justify restricting women.

The broad sky darkened outside my open window, and I snapped my laptop shut. In the marketplace, a butcher with a deeply lined face threw scraps to four skinny cats prowling by his white-tiled shop. His assistant — not much more than a boy — reached into a cage of loud clucking hens and grabbed one by its feet, a knife in his hand; he disappeared into the shadows. The chicken shrieked.

I bought dinner, and on the way back, the butcher boy was pulling at a carcass. White feathers floated to the sawdust floor.

Alone on the *riad*'s terrace, I picked at my chicken kebab. A moon glowed low; the night was soft. Mutters and cumin cooking smells swam from the community of rooftops. Swifts pierced the air with sonar tweets, swooping around minarets. Tomorrow, I'd meet Asma Lamrabet: a great honour, as her work directly built upon the efforts of Fatema Mernissi.

And after Rabat?

I texted Rachid.

'I'm coming back to Tangier.'

Through the medina-maze, past a wagon laden with abundant bunches of coriander and mint. On Ave Mohammed V, taxi drivers shook their heads when I showed the address on my phone. I walked uphill to Rabat Ville station and found an older man who would take me. The back seat had no seatbelt. The driver asked questions in French, and I passed my iPhone, open to Google Maps, from the back seat. We turned onto a highway.

A van swerved, colliding with the taxi's front corner, and when the driver slammed on the brakes I was thrown forward. The van's driver, with a black beard and belly like a basketball, threw open his door to argue in Darija, grabbing the taxi driver's shirtsleeves.

A traffic warden arrived and started yelling, too; the driver got back in, apologising softly, '*Désolée, désolée.*'

When I finally climbed out, I realised Google Maps had taken me to the wrong address. I needed number 60; this street hit 58 and inexplicably began at 1 again. Ever the inept pilgrim, I had let my phone credit run out and I had no internet. Panicked, I began to wander. Flowering bougainvillea spilt over concrete fences that hid enormous houses and the invisible noise of gardeners chopping and sweeping.

40 … 28 … 10, then, impossibly: 60. Thank goddess? Dr Asma Lamrabet invited me to sit on a long, colourful lounge in her elegant mahogany study. French doors were open to the trimmed garden under stretching palm trees, looking over a shimmering blue pool. She accepted my sweaty apology for being twenty minutes late, but we would get to the matter quickly, she said, as her next appointment was with a Swedish journalist.

Her first order of business was to establish our different feminisms. 'My context is not your context,' she said. 'So if my feminism is Islamic or Arab or Berber, it is our own context. When I was young, I had a very Westernised feminism, because it was the only way I could understand feminism. I wanted to be free, as a woman I see in the magazines and in the Hollywood movies, and I said this is my dream. It was a struggle against tradition. But my context was very different.'

She'd highlighted the fallacy of the Western gaze in her book *Women in the Qur'an: an emancipatory reading*: 'The current meta-discourse of *the veiled Muslim woman, reclusive and oppressed*,' she wrote, 'is merely a ceaseless reproduction of the Orientalist and colonialist vision continually *en vogue* in contemporary post-colonial representations.'

After her youthful entry to feminism, Dr Lamrabet said, she began exploring Islam through academic theology. Her first book asked what it meant to be a Muslim woman in the current Moroccan context; now, her work concentrated on new interpretations of texts.

Just this month, she'd resigned from a post at the Mohammadian League of Scholars: she opposed her colleagues' stance on inheritance law. While the government's 2011 constitution enshrined equality between men and women, sections of the Moroccan Family Code (from 2004) saw that daughters of a deceased person would receive only half as much as male children. This rule of *taasib*, based on a hadith, was justified by the idea that men held the responsibility of their families' financial welfare, but women did not. Dr Lamrabet argued this was based on outdated understanding; according to a 2014 census, one in six — 1.2 million — households in Morocco were run solely by women.

Her maid delivered refreshments. 'Some Moroccan tea?' Dr Lamrabet lifted the silver-spouted teapot to pour from ten, twenty centimetres high into small glasses etched with gold.

Dr Lamrabet believed the spiritual message of the Quran was different to patriarchal interpretation. 'So we have to change. The text allows us to make other interpretations.' Men's interpretation of holy scriptures kept power in their hands, she explained. 'God creates men and women equal. This is in the Quranic text. But when you see the teaching, they say that God created the man superior.'

I sipped fragrant, sweet tea. One of the greatest problems in Islamic reform, she continued, was that many Moroccans didn't know the text. Illiteracy was a huge problem, especially in rural areas, though this was changing with education reforms. Still, religious knowledge was often passed through families and imams.

'There are human interpretations, man's interpretation. And there is the sacred text. We have all the right to interpret it, to contextualise and interpret the norms, man and woman.'

I thanked her for her time, and walked through unrelenting sun to a tram stop. Dr Lamrabet saw Moroccans as pushed and pulled by cultural traditions and religious norms, wrestling with the tension between Western influence and nationalistic pride, modernism and tradition. It was a schizophrenic society, she had said: education systems claimed equality for women, but moralistic traditions were rigid, outdated conventions. Islam's ethics of liberation demanded equality; Moroccan culture preferred patriarchal values. In answer, she was calling for a separation between religion and politics.

That night as I sat on my bed transcribing her interview, I understood that Dr Lamrabet was dismantling patriarchal dominance using the core message of her religion.

I clicked back to my notes. She wrote in *The Qur'an and Women*: 'Islam is the bearer, like other monotheistic religions, of a message of peace, love, and justice emanating from God, who by creating human beings, men and women alike, created them inescapably free, equal, and dignified.'

This was the liberation perspective, the lens through which she interpreted the text. A thrill ran through me. As in Christianity, feminist theology was growing as a discipline. Dr Asma Lamrabet and her contemporaries were defecting in place and transforming the patriarchal system from within.

'*Salaamu Alaikum.*' Rachid held his hand on his heart and tilted his head as the wide, heavy doorman pushed open the door to Au Pain

Nu, the restaurant named after Mohamed Choukri and his famous book *For Bread Alone*.

'*Chukrane*,' I whispered. Square tables covered with maroon tablecloths lined the restaurant's wall. There were no other women. A grandfather waiter showed us to a corner, and instead of sitting across, Rachid slid into the booth beside me. I could smell the odour of his body. Lust made it hard to breathe.

Rachid placed a hand on my leg, looking at the menu.

'You want wine?'

I nodded. Beside him again, I was intoxicated, mute.

The waiter came, and they negotiated the type and price. As they spoke, I peered at the various portraits of Choukri in frames scattered across the walls. I was back in a city dripping with literary history. And next to a man who wanted to fuck me. Both gave me a fragile sense of belonging.

I took off my jacket, shoulders bare. On the street, this would be a daring invitation, a provocation to every man to look, to follow, to ask for my Instagram, WhatsApp, to join him for a tea. When the waiter left, Rachid's eyes flickered to my tanned arms.

Two saucers of fried fish. I took a bite, pushed my plate away. How could I swallow when desire messed with my stomach? Buzzed in my limbs? I hadn't eaten since breakfast at the train station. But hunger was stolen, everything was pointed towards him, his dark stubble, his lips, my head moved in rhythm with his speech, I wanted to undress him, to stroke all of his skin.

'Do you want to kiss me?' he muttered, voice confiding. His eyes flickered to the rest of the bar. A waiter cleared fish bones and dropped plates of eggplant covered with spiced mince and bechamel.

His voice was low. 'You can kiss me now.'

I followed his instruction and pushed close to the line of neck and jaw, brushed my lips along his chin, inhaling him with trembling breath. The force that pushed our bodies together was magnetic, it was gravity, it was heat.

'That's enough,' he whispered.

'But Rachid,' I pouted, a pleading child.

'The whole restaurant can see. Enough.' He reached beneath the table. He bunched my calf-length skirt in his fist, grabbing and gathering, until he'd pulled up the material and his calm hand was on the hot skin of my thigh. Rachid looked, for a moment, at my parted lips.

'Take off your clothes. Light me a cigarette.'

Air on my shoulders, my thighs. The white-red pack of L&Ms, a lighter from the back pocket of my crumpled jeans, flicker, flame, a greedy inhale before I handed it over. Then on the hard gold-green couch he slid into my hot wet and I gasped into his mouth. We kissed endlessly, breathing each other, then a break, yes: cool peach flesh, a blunt knife pushed towards his thumb. He squeezed, dripping cold sweet between my lips. He rubbed a yellow slice on his dick, and fed it to me.

'Get on your knees.'

I obeyed. He unweaved the scarf tied around my hair.

'Put your hands behind your back.' Cigarette breath beside my ear, he tied my wrists. A noise of protest when it was too tight, so he loosened it. Slightly.

I looked up. He leant against the kitchenette with crossed arms, impassive through the weaving line of smoke, inspecting me. His black beard was rugged, thick dark hair spread across his shoulders, chest, and stomach down to threadbare grey underpants. He cupped his palm and slapped my jaw. Tears came and I shook my head.

'Okay then. What do you want?' Rusty voice. Eyes dark. Lungs pulled in smoke sharply. This was play, with its own language.

'Please, Monsieur Rachid, I want your cock.' I wavered before him, hands resting on my coccyx, balance uncentred by tied wrists. We locked eyes and I whispered, '*S'il te plaît.*'

Later, I lay on his couch, smoking, as he showered to wash off the cum that had leaked from the back of my throat. I smiled; I could never make my Husband come from a blowjob. He returned with a towel around his waist, and I laid my head on his chest, snuggling into black curls.

'Good girl,' he mumbled, stroking my hair. 'Good girl.'

We fell into a routine. I met him after work, and we drank in tapas bars until the early hours, piling up tiny plates and beer bottles, and teasing with forbidden touch before walking through deserted streets. We couldn't go home earlier than midnight, to keep his neighbours unawares. He choked me most nights. The belt came back.

Desperation had made me easy to seduce. And desperation kept me bowed. I was acting without thinking, pulled forward by water's dark current. If I slowed down the wanting wanting wanting, I wouldn't like what I saw. So I kept meeting him late, kept fucking until morning light, kept kneeling at his feet.

Most nights, I fell asleep long after dawn on his patterned couch, under a sheet dirty with cum and wine. When I woke, my chest was tight, the sternum wanting to crack. Middays, I returned to my rented room above Café à l'Anglaise, to shower in a teal bathroom decorated with a picture of the King on a waterski and a painting of Jimi Hendrix. A black coffee from the tiny restaurant, enjoyed on the blue rooftop, where the owner had discarded an easel and dried oil paint palette. Then I retreated from the heat.

These were dreamy days, lying on my unrumpled bed, French windows open. I watched cirrus cloud drift, listened to schoolchildren's shouts, women calling and laughing, the pleading, persuasive voice of old men's arguments, the whole of life on Rue de la Kasbah. Some days, I got lost in the medina, where a man in his sixties would inevitably tell me where I could smoke kif, and pull out a photo of him and Jim Morrison from a pocket somewhere in his djellaba; sometimes, I wandered to the kasbah gates and looked over the rolling ocean, refused teenage boys' offers of a puff from giant spliffs, and watched scrawny kittens scrabble across the cliff face, searching for food in rubbish.

On the fifth day, I languored on my bed in underwear and ran my hand up and down my stomach, inspecting new bruises on my collarbone, my breast, my thigh. What was happening? Good and evil weren't so easy to discern anymore. My self-image as benevolent, sensible, and sweet had cracked when I cheated in my marriage, and splintered when I laughed at the news I received in Istanbul of my ex-Husband's cancer scare. Now it was destroyed.

In returning to Tangier, had I betrayed myself or honoured long-repressed desire? I googled 'feminist S&M', but none of the articles went beyond clickbait cliches. An Irish friend said her psychologist had explained that some rape victims liked domination and submission because they could enact terror in safety. I hadn't been assaulted before, so this wasn't my truth.

And it was unsafe. I was allowing a man I'd only known for a few weeks to simulate violence upon my body. I liked the danger; I'd never been so alert, so present during sex. My naive devotion came with the expectation of him to act in my best interest. But would he truly hurt me?

And was it really just a game? From what I knew of BDSM culture, there was an emphasis on consent, communication, and aftercare. Kink established mutually agreed boundaries, fostering an encounter of vulnerability and trust. But here, there was no sober discussion. This was the eroticisation of male dominance and female submission. Rachid's contempt was a replication of the impassive violence of an abuser. Every night I knelt before him, his respect for me eroded. And I was contracting, getting smaller. I felt more pathetic day by day, allowing his disdain to seep into my psyche like thick black sludge edging under a door. He never said the words, but I believed, again, that I was stupid. I believed, again, that I couldn't make a decision. And again, I was beginning to lose trust in myself.

Every night, we performed the sins of patriarchy. Politics played out upon my skin.

Vulva-gazing: what feels good, what feels bad, in our flesh in our touch in our fucking?

I trailed my finger along the bedspread and began to talk, voice sultry from smoking all night.

'You like it when he hurts you. Because you deserve it. You are nothing you are selfish you did wrong so many wrong things you fucking piece of shit what kind of person chooses a man who hits them on the face for fun?

'Someone who doesn't love herself.'

I sat up. Huh. That was a rhetorical question, brain, you weren't supposed to answer.

I'd thought self-hatred was loud and large like a truck. But maybe it was quiet growth from seed to sapling to tree. The conviction that nothing I was or could give was acceptable. That my body was not enough. The body *is* the self; hate the body, hate the self.

Perhaps it would surprise nobody that I was led to masochism. Maybe it was common among the religious, or ex-religious, to exorcise shame and self-loathing. Rachid enforced the convictions of the Interior Judge; finally, I was being treated as I subconsciously thought I deserved. He punished me for being wrong, and then he called me 'good girl'.

It wasn't threats that sent me trembling to do men's bidding, but reward. The Pastor, the Husband, now Rachid: I granted the men in my life the power to call me worthy. I was desperate for their approval; the only price was my obedience.

I rose from my bed and sat on the floor of my balcony, lit a cigarette, trailed my finger along white curlicues. When I was on my knees, I felt the same spiritual surrender, the same blissful purge, the same orgasmic exhilaration, as when I danced to God in church. Being below reflected my not-good-enoughness; the posture of devotion was one of subjugation.

Cool wind pushed at my cheek. If God was a man, then man was God and I wanted to submit. To their power. External to me.

I stubbed out my smoke. Rachid somehow intuited desires that, until now, I'd hidden from myself. Had I summoned him? Did he see it in me when we met at the bar above Café de Paris? He saw it in me every night, when I looked up at him like a dog waiting for the whip. Had he betrayed me? Or was he giving me exactly what I wanted?

I dressed in a loose shirt, skinny jeans, and Doc Martens, and went to Cinema Rif's cafe to drink mint tea and smoke in vintage glamour. Since leaving home, I'd tried to expand, grow strong, push push push against the current, the forces of history and past mistakes. I'd tried to uphold my rules of pilgrimage, tried to follow the shining light, tried to see my vulva as a flower. But in Tangier, I'd walked into the river and tied the gag myself. I'd pushed from the water's edge and was being carried in rushing dark. I used to be holy. Now sin was all I had.

Rachid, black T-shirt and grey baseball cap, was six beers down when I met him. He ordered a bottle of red. Two of his friends burst through the door, thin men with dark, sun-kissed shoulders, explosively curly hair, and heavy backpacks. Mo was tall with a long black ponytail and wide-mouthed charisma; Adnane had a high, round forehead, fluffy hair spraying out like a sunflower, soft brown eyes, and wonky teeth. They were just off the ferry from Tarifa after a crazy weekend at a music festival. Adnane sat beside me.

We talked travel, energy, and the meaning of love, sharing cigarettes and eating tapas. A barbecued sheep's head arrived, a traditional Moroccan dish, and Rachid poked the eyeball with a fork. I told Adnane I felt powerless in a new country without language.

'Yes, but you are still power*ful*,' his raspy, gravel voice. Our bodies aligned. He began to touch my knee, a blaze of white heat shot to my armpits, and I threw a glance at Rachid, who was laughing with Mo.

Adnane reached down to stroke my exposed ankle. 'I like your hairy legs.' His eyes became wolfish.

My gaze flickered to Rachid. He was looking directly at me.

Adnane went to the bathroom, and Rachid leant close, saying in a low voice, 'You better stop playing around. I'm going to have to punish you.'

The next bar was thick with people watching a band playing Amy Winehouse and Hindi Zahra. When Rachid had his back turned, Adnane placed a straw between my lips, and I sucked cool gin, looking into open honey eyes. I pushed past him in the crowd, my chest against his, and he kissed me quick.

He drew back, placed his mouth at my ear. 'What exactly is the nature of your relationship with Rachid?'

I couldn't answer.

Rachid sat on a stool, his elbows on the bar. He adjusted his baseball cap with one hand and spat words into my ear, 'I saw this. You keep fucking playing around. I will punish you so hard.'

I played the little girl and stood between his open legs, touched his thigh. He made a fist and, ever so slowly, brought it to my cheek, pushed so that my head turned.

We drank beers with dark eyes, leaning against the bar. I rubbed my ass against him, he put a hand to my waist. I was falling through black night full of stars. We climbed the stairs to his apartment in silence.

'You want a line?' He bent over the coffee table. The tiny ziplock plastic bag was beside a discarded book of poetry and a plate with the dried heart of a peach. I shook my head, continued to undress. He pulled up a stool, and I knelt before him. He slapped my jaw. Hard, then harder. I let him.

'Light me a cigarette.'

I crawled, my ass in the air, to get the red-and-white pack from the coffee table. Every inch of my skin glowed. Finally, he pulled off his pants.

'Kiss it.'

I placed my lips on his dick, pubes freshly shaved. My tongue flicked out to taste him.

'What did I tell you?' He leant forward, slapped my cheek. 'Just kiss it.'

I jerked back. Burning eyes, angry tears. 'Rachid. Don't fucking slap my face. I can't. I can't.'

'Okay, it's fine,' he smiled. He would make me beg. 'No problem. Tell me what you want.'

'Please, let me suck it, please.' Simpering voice. Girl again.

'Please, what?'

We locked gazes, I pushed my hands up his round belly, and whispered. 'Master.'

'What did you say?'

A deep groan. 'Please, master.'

'You can suck it.'

Tender skin hot on my tongue, the smooth, firm shaft, the yeast scent of his groin; I wanted the sweat of him, the dirt of him, to take every beautiful and ugly part of him into my mouth.

He smiled down at my bobbing head, something was funny, 'I want to slap your face,' then leant back in a reverie, muttering, 'Fucking suck my dick, fucking suck it … fuck you, fuck you.'

I pulled away, eyes brimming.

'Aw,' he laughed, pulling me to stand, 'I didn't mean it.' He held me to him, stroked my hair. 'It's just part of the game,' he chuckled.

The game continued. He pushed me down again. I got lower. Ran fingertips down hairy legs. Tender lips to rough toenails. The ecstasy was unbearable. He raised his right leg. Placed His foot upon my neck. Surrender. I found God on my knees. I sucked His toes. Absolution. He pressed my head to the filthy ground. Annihilation.

—

Sea wind whipped my hair. The stench of diesel and brine. It was cold, but I refused to let Tangier out of my sight until it disappeared completely. The city's steep hills and white medina buildings piled lopsidedly on top of each other grew small. The sand-coloured kasbah faded into mist. I gripped the ferry's white metal bars as we crossed invisible borders.

The internal work of my pilgrimage — hoping, exploring, swimming through pain, sticky-taping bits together — had all been undone.

I wrapped my denim jacket tight, sucking fiercely at a cigarette. Morocco melted into the horizon. A physical urge: to bend and slap the grated metal on which I stood. To shriek: I chose it. I chose it. I chose it.

I let Him press His foot upon my neck.

before

A Taste

To transgress is to meet a buried desire.

I was ignoring signs my marriage was unravelling. I stopped liking Him. Our conversations were limited to the cafe's upcoming opening. When He took late-night motorbike rides, I fantasised about His painless death.

But I endured, because I knew I should stay, no matter what. I nailed my restlessness to the cross. Love was commitment. A choice. A sacrifice.

My needs were unmet, my emotions denied; I was numb. Until something happened, only months before the end. And everything changed.

A petite woman with wide hips in men's pants, Dani took money at the till then repeated the coffee order with a liquid-chocolate voice. My name on her tongue, Louise, not Lou, as if she knew a secret part of me that nobody else touched. She exuded competence and strength, dashing around the shop with schoolboy bravado. Thin caramel-coloured arms, black hair shaved into a mohawk. She loved to tease, was sharp and quick, and observed my delight when she complimented my hair, noticed my desperation for attention. I may have numbed the hurt of my heart, but she responded to my burning, shifting heat.

The cafe we worked in was narrow between the coffee machine and counter. Perfect for brushing up against bodies — deliberate? Accidental? Impossible to say. Dani made a joke in my ear. Slid a hand along my back.

A secret alliance grew. She knew how I liked my coffee. I spread blackberry jam on bagels for her. We winked at each other when our favourite customers arrived. I became her confidant, and she swore me to secrecy. She detailed her closeted days, her long-term partner, their favourite lesbian bar. She answered my questions about how women had sex, licking her lips, looking down at her elegant hands, looking up at me. Threat in her eyes, promise too.

Twelve years older, and the manager, I allowed her to cross boundaries no man could. Twice a week, after counting the till and mopping the floor, we pulled down the heavy warehouse door and stayed late, eating snacks, doing the crossword, sometimes drinking wine. I tied myself up in knots convincing myself we weren't doing anything wrong. Because she was a woman, it was okay for our knees to touch. Because she was a woman, I could hold her gaze.

'Wow!' Emma, my closest friend at church, pushed open the glass door and placed her hands on her hips, admiring the tiles my Husband had installed. 'You've done so well!'

He nodded and showed her the toilets, the back entrance, the wheelchair ramp. His jeans looked loose.

Two weeks from opening, the coffee machine was here and the furniture would soon arrive. Still so much to do. But our community was keen to help. Our Bible study group arrived, and He handed out paintbrushes and laid out plastic drop sheets. We turned the music up loud.

I sneaked a look at His hollow cheeks. Sixteen-hour days, blown-out costs: He was following His dream and it was killing Him. When He fell into bed at night panicked and exhausted, I would keep reading my novel. His sadness was too enormous. I lived in the midst of His melancholy's low fog. Whereas He was in a shadowy pit. Drowning.

David climbed eight feet up on a ladder to paint the entrance-frame black.

'Watch the drops on the floor, mate,' my Husband called out, before turning on His power tool. I sat on the floor to smooth door handles in the toilets, following His careful instructions not to damage the metal.

Emma popped her head in the doorway. 'Dinner's up!' Carrie dished out homemade lasagne and held out a plastic plate to Him.

'I'll get some in a sec, Caz,' He replied, and continued painting a wooden bench. We pulled up dusty stools, said grace, and ate together. He never joined the group.

At 10.00 pm, we filled a garbage bag with paper plates, then dragged it out the front door. When everyone had left, He inspected my work.

I was crouching at the front door with an armful of drop-sheet plastic when He stood over me.

'Lou.' His voice measured, quiet. I looked up. 'I only asked you one thing. To use the right cloth to clean the metal.'

My throat constricted.

'But you used the scourer. Now the metal's all scratched.' His eyes darted to the floor beside me. 'For fuck's sake. Why don't people listen? I told them to be careful about paint drops.' David had dripped spots of black from eight feet above. There was white, too, from Emma's brush. 'They might as well never have come. Now I'm going to have to clean that up, too.'

'Babe, c'mon. Everyone came to help.' Sometimes I thought He was blind. How could He care about this stupid floor?

'You only see people's intentions.' He rubbed the side of His face, scrunched His eyes. 'But I see the results.'

'Okay. Look — I'll come and clean it tomorrow.' I'd already spent hours on my knees, chipping at the floor with a paint scraper. With no practical skills, it was all I could offer. To Him, my Husband, who was in over His head.

But no matter how I pulled at His weight in the cold darkness, it wasn't enough. I couldn't fix Him. I couldn't save Him.

Leaning into my bathroom mirror, I painted black strokes of eyeliner, then unscrewed fuchsia lipstick. My heels clacked on pavement on the way to the bus stop. Tonight, I'd be interviewing an author in a university lecture theatre for the first time in my career. She was famous and it would be a full house.

Two days until the cafe opened. This morning, He'd pushed long legs into jeans and pulled His belt tight. When the door slammed, I heard the car pull away and the sediment of His struggle settled over the furniture, the curtains, the carpet. Even when I was alone, His sorrow pervaded the house.

'Will you be there?' I'd asked Him last night, carrying a plastic bag of kebabs to feed Him and a friend. They were on ladders, rigging lighting on steel chains.

Boot steps creaked to the floor. The hiss-click of a beer can. 'You know I can't, Lou.' Regretful but steadfast as he brought the red can to his mouth. The bob of His Adam's apple, the unshaven throat. 'There's just too much to do here. Thanks so much for dinner, by the way. I appreciate all the help you're giving me.'

He appreciated me. Lucky me, I thought as I leant against the lecture theatre's glass door, then shook the hand of the author. He appreciated me. If only He showed up.

The doors opened to the public, and I watched strangers and friends stream in as a tech guy miked me up. I tucked a curl into my headscarf. There was Dani. She came to me while her girlfriend found a seat. I embraced her and white-hot heat rose from my pelvis and flooded my torso.

She pulled back, looked me in the eye. 'You'll do great. Okay?'

My limbs reverberated like a metal pole struck with a baseball bat. Onstage, I could feel the heat of her glowing in the crowd.

At work, our vibe became molten. She told me to vacuum, then apologised for being bossy.

'I don't mind,' I replied, leaning against the counter so my hips faced her. 'Just tell me what you want and I'll do it.' I was terrified to look her in the eye.

I got a new job, and told Him I'd invited everyone from work for goodbye drinks. But it was just me and Dani. Finally alone. In a bar where I wouldn't see anybody I knew. She arrived with a fresh haircut, her scalp shorn close in an artful fade. For two hours, we perched on stools, sharing a bottle of Fiano and a rocket-and-prosciutto pizza, telling childhood stories, recounting dreams. Beneath her tough exterior was a trembling child: that dark, wounded vulnerability I found irresistible. Booze warmed our veins, body language said what we could not. I leant into her. Every one of my cells was on fire.

I touched her thigh. She looked at me with eyes ablaze, and with all my strength I refused to look away. She brushed the hair from my shoulder. Our boundaries dissolved.

She paid. At the next bar, I saw a missed call from Him, and put my phone back in my pocket. House music blared and we sat on wide couches beside a wall with a video of a spinning vortex; I forgot how small Adelaide was, what would happen if somebody saw, and allowed her to graze her lips against my neck. Loud music hid my moans. It was the first time I'd been touched in five months.

She hailed me a taxi and hugged me goodbye, leant her face to mine and flicked her tongue into my mouth. I fell, spinning, alone, into the cab's back seat. From the street, she shut the door. I returned to my marriage bed.

At church the next morning, dust motes danced on slants of sunlight while He played guitar onstage. I sat in my usual spot and raised my hands, floorboards creaking under bare feet. Being filled with lust was like being filled with the Holy Spirit.

For months, we texted and called, sending messages that began with 'We should stop' and dissolved into erotic promises. We met in quiet bars, feigning nonchalance. I begged her with my eyes to touch my skin, but could never form the words. For the very first time in my life, I had no interest in eating. My body was aflame and needed nothing else. I vibrated with longing. The sun burnt brighter; my jacaranda tree erupted with vibrant purple.

My Husband betrayed me by emotionally abandoning me. And now, I discovered my own capacity to betray.

I texted: 'I need to tell you something.' On tall wooden stools at an East End wine bar, I fingered my glass of riesling and took a breath. 'I'm in love with you.'

'Oh, Louise,' Dani chuckled without humour. That liquid voice. 'One day, you'll realise I've been a cunt.'

I left on shaking legs. She stopped answering my texts.

I'd been desperate for attention and she'd provided; then, I confused my sexual obsession with love. Perhaps she groomed me for her own gratification, having perceived my naive trust and self-deception. Like the Husband and the Pastor: just as I needed her attention, so she needed my adoration.

Nevertheless, when Dani had kissed me, I'd tasted a different world. My God was male, my Husband male, and I was beholden to them both. Could there be another way?

after

The Czech Republic

I chewed a smoked-salmon-and-cream-cheese bagel while swinging my legs on a high round stool. Beyond the bakery window were ornate, rococo apartment buildings. A gang of twenty tourists behind me pointed at piles of fresh pastries. Lazy golden ceiling fans stirred thick, warm air.

I felt hollow. But a rope tied to my sternum tugged these last, faltering steps: I was following a trail of radical Jewish feminism and had found myself in the capital of the Czech Republic.

Once the capital of Bohemia, Prague was a curious mix of Czech and German history, and made me feel as if I were in a storybook. Nearby, the Brothers Grimm had collected fairytales of witches and lost children, twisted forests, petulant kings. Lemon, lime, and mandarin-coloured buildings lined the Vltava River like perfect white-icing cakes. Gothic spires spiked the skyline.

There was evidence of a Jewish community in Bohemia from the early tenth century. In the First Crusade, in 1096, hundreds of Jews in this region were massacred by Christian knights. Social and religious unrest led to the murder of hundreds more in Easter 1389. The 1500s were a golden age for Jews in Prague, as enlightenment and intellectualism developed; in this time, the Talmudic scholar and Jewish mystic Judah Loew ben Bezalel — known as the Maharal, legendary creator of the Golem — lived here, and was buried in the Old Jewish Cemetery in Josefov. The nineteenth century saw Prague as the centre of German Jewish culture, and at the beginning of the twentieth century, the city was liberal and cosmopolitan. But Nazism crept in, Jewish people were ghettoised, windows were smashed, and on March 15, 1939, in the middle of a snowstorm, the city fell to Hitler's troops.

Nowadays, a small but vibrant Jewish population frequented kosher restaurants, hotels, and synagogues. Tourists sought out literary history in the works of Max Brod, Jiří Orten, and Franz Kafka. In the Jewish Quarter, metal plates in the sidewalk were inscribed with the names of victims and survivors of concentration camps. Pinkas Synagogue listed the names of Holocaust victims.

Once more, I didn't belong to this faith, so my research could only skim the surface. Christianity grew from Jewish roots: the Old Testament is the Hebrew Bible; the two religions parted ways over Jesus' resurrection. Jewish faith is a covenant relationship with God that follows sacred laws and rituals to pursue holiness. For many, faith is a cultural identity, irremovable from selfhood, intertwined with family, ethnicity, and race. And so in answer to patriarchal thought, liberal believers, rabbis, and theologians were defecting in place.

I finished my bagel and shuffled from the stool. Two tram rides later, the sun had set. In a shadowed doorway beside an absinthe bar, I shone my iPhone torch on the doorbell list. What was the name of the Airbnb host?

A Korean man with an enormous, loose black T-shirt, sharp cheekbones, and a bowl cut appeared.

'Jenny's house?'

That was her name! I grinned.

'Please.' He lifted my suitcase and unlocked the door, striding into the dark. I fumbled with my phone, then crossed the black-and-white-chequered foyer, with no choice but to trust the man stepping up the curling stairwell.

The high-ceilinged apartment was a full house. Jenny was a tall, gregarious Taiwanese art student who spoke three languages and curated exhibitions. Her uncle was frying pork in the tiny kitchen, and bowl-cut boy was staying with a friend in the room next to mine. As I hung floral scarves on the wardrobe and lined books upon the desk, I noticed my red suitcase's wheel was torn and ragged, likely chipped by Swedish gravel. I'd since dragged it over broken pavement and rough asphalt, through snow and heat. Soon, I told my battered suitcase. Soon we'd go home.

The next morning, late summer's bright sunshine poured through a dirty restaurant window, and I drank black coffee at a heavy wooden table. Students yelled and smoked, gulping deep steins of amber breakfast beer.

The interior landscape — my ribs, my pelvis — felt like blackened scrubland after a bushfire. I could barely stomach my thoughts.

A waiter delivered a plate of scrambled eggs on rye, and I ordered another coffee. Chewing, I scribbled down what I knew:

1. I chose to go back to Rachid.
2. I made myself low before him.
3. I allowed him to have power over me.
4. I gave *my* power *away*.

My stomach tightened. I pushed away the half-eaten plate of eggs. Perhaps if this was limited to the sexual arena, I could accept it. But my subordination had leaked into all aspects of my life. The question was why, after everything I now knew, had I still done it? Why did it serve me to give my power away, in my marriage and with Rachid? And *how could I not do it again?*

I flicked through the pages of my journal, frantically searching quotes from the feminist writers that were my guides, then alighted upon Carol P. Christ: 'Religions centred on the worship of a male God … keep women in a state of psychological dependence on men and male authority.'

Butter-grease fingermarks on every page. Finally, I found a scribbled sentence from Rosemary Radford Ruether: the patriarchal imagination 'makes the erotic relationship a sado-masochistic one of male assault and female submission'.

My throat felt thick with an urge to vomit the toast I'd swallowed.

I didn't know how to integrate everything, or understand the depth of my indoctrination. But I knew I wanted to be free.

Last time I'd phoned Auntie Liz, she suggested I journal about the girl who wanted to obey. The good girl.

I put pen to paper and the words became a river:

he stole my voice he stole my voice he stole my voice he stole my voice stole it stole it stole it stole it he didn't like what I said he silenced me my love took me down to the river to silence me and when he left i could not speak he said no louise be quiet he said lou now's not the time i let him show me the way yes sir i said as if my petulance was resistance as if anger could be stuffed deep but i am dredging it up pulling up hair clogging the drain clasping a hook around a dead body in a large black lake it's heavy so heavy at the end of my chain lugging it up to the surface the light it's streaming loud water, the dead body is me, bloated, blue, cold, at sixteen, at eight, the self who could throw open her arms and leap, who could shout without shame, he pushed her down, i drowned her too, she died, but now i have rescued her and as her skin touches air her body is revived, her skin tans, rose blooms on cheeks, i bend to her mouth, breathe life into my own lips

she gasps. she opens her eyes. looks at me with blue eyes. and grins. she begins to laugh.

———

A storm was brewing in my torso. Pain radiated from my hips. Then the telltale wetness in my undies. I searched for *tampóny* in the closest supermarket to Jenny's apartment, hand pressed to my belly.

Menstruating while travelling meant I'd paid toilet fees in Stockholm's libraries, I'd woken at 3.00 am in Istanbul for fear of staining bedsheets, I'd cancelled plans in Dublin because walking exacerbated pain to the point of nausea.

This was a central experience to women and people who menstruate. But Christianity didn't honour the cyclical process. Instead, it centred the masculine body — Jesus' starved yet muscular form bleeding on the cross. God birthed the world from darkness; woman was formed from the rib of a man. No sacred stories of a bloody infant crowning between a howling mother's legs. No sacrosanct breastfeeding Mother Mary, no honoured parables of a grandmother teaching a teenager what it means when she bleeds. We are unmentionable, disgusting, cast out from the holy place. We are shame, shame, shame.

And in religious culture, too, we were excluded. Some women were told not to receive communion while menstruating, were refused entry to church or asked to stand at the back. Hindu temples restricted menstruating women from entering, as did some mosques. Implying that this natural and regular function of her body inhibited a woman's connection to the sacred.

In many religions, menstrual impurity was a 'key symbolic expression of women's subordinate status', wrote sociology professor Susan Starr Sered, a former director of the Initiative on Health, Religion, and Spirituality at Harvard. Rituals involving female bodies often served an ideology of purity, and this, Sered wrote, drew attention to woman's status as Other.

But there was a Jewish ritual for menstruation. The Talmud (the primary source of Jewish law) laid out the rules of *niddah*: sexual relations are forbidden while a woman menstruates. She is separate from her husband for twelve to fifteen days — seven days after she stops bleeding. In Leviticus 25, a 'menstruous' woman was forbidden to touch a man; this is still observed by a small number of Orthodox Jews. Then she visits a *mikveh* — private bathhouse. She brushes her teeth, removes all jewellery and stray hairs, and has a quick shower. Jewish law requires her to be scrupulously clean. A *mikveh* attendant examines her, even looking beneath her nails or combing her hair. Then the woman steps into a small, shoulder-deep pool, whose dimensions are in ancient measurements of three cubits deep, one cubit wide, and one cubit long. Chest-deep in water, she prays, then immerses her entire body, including every hair on her head. The attendant ensures the immersion is done correctly, watches her go under and come up, and chants a blessing. Dunk, rise, sing, three times.

Then the woman returns home, and she and her husband become one flesh.

On the hottest day of September, I walked by the river that weaved its way through the city centre, happy to have research tasks to distract me from thinking about Morocco. The majority of Jewish people today identified as Reform, a liberal version of the religion. About 10 per cent of Jews were Orthodox, and within this group were smaller sects with slightly different rules.

I sat beside the Old Jewish Cemetery under ash trees to

read Orthodox feminist writer Blu Greenberg. Bolstered by the women's liberation movement in the seventies, her work began a new tradition of Jewish feminism. Not only did her writing voice female experience — when public representatives of her religion were traditionally men — but it also explained Orthodox rituals to outsiders.

Niddah, she wrote, meant separation; the word *mikveh* refers to being washed clean, and can also refer to the bathhouse. Men visited the *mikveh*, too, often in preparation for holy days; it was an essential element of conversion to Judaism, and brides came with female family for a pre-marital ceremony.

Mikveh was a purification ritual adapted from ancient times. Important to understand were the Jewish concepts of *tum'ah* (impurity) and *tohorah* (purity). *Tum'ah* was incompatible with *kodesh* (the sacred). Immersing in the *mikveh* allowed women to embrace *tohorah*.

I uncrossed and crossed my legs, feeling the discreet intrusion of my tampon. The ash trees shivered. Despite Greenberg's contextualising, this notion of purity appeared problematic: women were dirty because menstruation was unclean. The revulsion of female bodies institutionalised by men into law.

According to the Bible, I deserved my pain. When God punished Eve for eating fruit from the Tree of Good and Evil, he said (Genesis 3:16): 'I will make your pains in childbearing very severe; with painful labour you will give birth to children.'

But Greenberg believed menstruation wasn't punishment, preferring to read from the laws' historical context, over 2,000 years ago. Defilements and impurities mentioned in ancient scripture, she said, were related to death: contact with a dead body, leprosy, loss of semen through nocturnal emission, or loss of menstrual blood.

'Purification through the living waters,' she wrote, 'symbolises a renewal, a re-creation, a regeneration of the life forces.'

I closed the book and walked back to tourist central. From a wooden cart near the Prague Astronomical Clock, I bought a *trdelník*, fried dough rolled around a stick and stuffed with Nutella. It smelt good, but as I took my first, sticky bite, I knew it was a mistake in this heat. I wandered through the crowded square, considering whether or not to eat the entire thing so as not to waste food I'd paid for.

Menstruation's symptoms — aches, tenderness, fatigue — were a demand to pay attention to physical experience; this information was a way to understand what I needed. It was time I started listening to my body. I swallowed and chucked the pastry in the bin, giving myself permission to say no.

The heat, the walking, the slow ache in my hips; I longed for the cool dimness of my room. Pain billowed, filled the sky. I licked chocolate from sticky fingers and turned back to Jenny's apartment.

Two days later, I met Professor Ivy Helman at a pub. She wore a sleeveless, acid-washed black dress that revealed a Hebrew tattoo on her upper arm; a tiny silver Star of David studded one earlobe below short dark hair pulled into a ponytail. We gripped heavy mugs of beer in the creamy sunshine.

Ivy was a feminist scholar and activist; for the last six years, she'd contributed regularly to feminismandreligion.com. Her blogs were reflective and thoughtful, with topics like Passover, Shabbat, ecofeminism, and liberation. I chewed on greyish meat with bread dumplings, caramel-coloured sauce, and cranberries, while Ivy had a potato fritter with cabbage salad. She ate vegan at home, and vegetarian out. It was hard enough to eat vegan in this city, she said, and even harder to eat kosher — food prepared in accordance with Jewish dietary law.

She had deep-brown eyes, which turned especially soft when she was talking about her wife, a lawyer and refugee advocate. To Ivy, Judaism presented ethical challenges to be negotiated, not a set of rules.

'I've never met anyone who would follow the strictest form of *niddah*,' she said, her round face animated. Tradition was never perfect in actuality — everybody brought their own concepts and history to how they practised ceremonies. She'd done *niddah*, but not monthly.

I joked that you'd hope female partners would be synced, right? Because otherwise, with twelve days of separation each, there was only a very small window for sex.

Ivy snorted. 'I mean, I do know lesbians who do it every month. But yeah, it's all sort of based on heterosexism.'

Like all religions, she said, believers contended with inherent contradictions.

'There's a sense of *both/and*: yes, this practice is rooted in ideas that are problematic, but —' Ivy looked into my eyes. 'It's also a practice that helps me connect to God.'

We said goodbye, and I crossed the river to walk in dappled shade up Petřín Hill. The path wound its way past snack stands and a magician's hut, where a tall goateed man in a black cape stole the attention of passing children.

In the Jewish context, ritual could be a way of connecting to a cultural practice with ancient origins. When ancestors, and perhaps even relatives, were victims of genocide, ritual was a way to honour them and enact identity.

I didn't have a cultural legacy, but I did understand ritual's power. At church, we'd eaten pieces of bread and drank plastic thimbles of grape juice to symbolically consume Christ's flesh and blood. When I'd left my marriage, I burnt my wedding dress in a backyard fire. A ritual can express something that can't be confined to language or logic. Physical action as embodied declaration.

At Petřín Hill's peak, hot air shimmered and cold pain-fire inched from my hips, down my thighs, and echoed in my knees. I sat and watched families eating picnics, clowns dipping knotted ropes in buckets of detergent and swinging them through the air. A flock of bubbles swam in the air, and children jumped, their hands stretched up to the undulating orbs that vanished with a soapy pop. I rose and trudged slowly down the hill, head pounding, and returned to Jenny's house. At my desk, I opened my laptop.

Theologian Rachel Adler had argued in 1972 that menstruation embodied the cosmic cycle of life, death, and rebirth; that both *niddah*'s period of separation and sexual activity were holy phases of a woman's life.

Twenty-five years later, she rejected this perspective as a 'slave theology' that allowed women to feel good about the practice of *mikveh* while enabling their oppression. She'd come to see *niddah* as perpetuating ideas of corruption and filth, which justified misogynistic practices in the Orthodox tradition, like forbidding men to shake a woman's hand. Despite this, Adler praised women creatively reclaiming the ritual. As more women brought their own interpretation to scripture, ancient practices were being 'unravelled and rewoven'.

Writing for Jewish parenting website *Kveller*, maternal health consultant Tamara Reese revealed she'd had several miscarriages. She went to the *mikveh* while pregnant to wash away fears about giving birth. On the same site, mental-health campaigner Risa Sugarman related a similar experience: hospitalised for mental illness, she visited the *mikveh* after having electroconvulsive therapy (ECT).

'I remained immersed in the warm, cleansing water for a few more minutes,' she wrote. 'As I departed the water and walked up the stairs, the cool air was a shock to my body. I grabbed my towel and went to take a shower. I felt warm inside and content. As I walked out the door to my car, I said these words aloud: *I can leave the ECT here.*'

And Canadian Rabbi Elyse Goldstein wrote an article for *Lilith* magazine on the subversive possibilities for reappropriating *mikveh*. Women now immersed, she wrote, for a variety of self-directed meanings: the end of chemotherapy, a daughter's marriage, a ceremony of healing from sexual violence.

'The *mikveh* has been taken from me as a Jewish woman by sexist interpretations, by … a history of male biases, fears of menstruation, and superstitions. I was going to take back the water.'

Inspired, I googled progressive *mikva'ot* around the world.

Mayyim Hayyim in Boston was founded by Anita Diamant, whose book *The Red Tent* explored ancient menstrual traditions. In February 2019, Mayyim Hayyim had run a weekly course on *niddah* and queer experience, led by a genderqueer rabbi. The course was 'open to people of all genders, sexualities, and experiences with menstruation'.

I set up a phone interview with Lisa Berman, Mayyim Hayyim's education director. I asked her what immersion feels like.

'When you walk in, it's like, *aah*. The pool of water is almost the same temperature as your body, 98.5 degrees Fahrenheit. When you immerse, you have that sense you are cutting off the outside world, and feeling held by the water.

'Water is an integral part of our deepest mythology in Judaism, between creation and flood and the Red Sea. Look, my personal theory: when you immerse in the water, you have gone somewhere that is in some way imprinted on you, where you spent time before you were born.'

For the vast majority of visitors, Lisa said, it wasn't a routine practice, but was about marking a life transition. They left the *mikveh*, she said, with a more solid identity. The old was left behind in order to step into something new.

I stopped bleeding. Propelled by other-worldly energy, I threw off my blankets at 6.30 am and marched from Jenny's apartment. The world was soft and sunrise pink. Gravity drew me to the river. Along Charles Bridge, gothic gargoyle saints stood tall over a crowd of newlyweds. Photographers angled for perfect dawn light. I hadn't known Prague was a destination-wedding spot.

A bride climbed a parapet, her tartan-legged husband gripping her waist as assistants arranged the dress' billowing train. The couple gazed nobly into what, I supposed, was the future.

I walked across a square through arcs of tangerine light; medieval spires cast knife-edge shadows stretching over street cleaners and delivery trucks. Here, too, couples posed, performing happiness to attentive black lenses.

The sun had risen. I was sweating; my stomach growled. The body makes itself known. I wandered to a mint-coloured cafe in Old Town and pulled apart a croissant.

I had asked Ivy if I could go into the local *mikveh*, near Chabad synagogue.

'No, I don't think that would be allowed,' she'd replied — I wasn't Jewish, she explained, nor did I plan to convert. 'But ... you could do it yourself. All you need is, according to the text, a body of fresh water. The only thing is,' she said with a playful smile, 'you're supposed to be fully naked.'

Early-morning sun was strong and bright. Pedestrians passed; a tram rattled uphill. Anyone can make their own ceremony. I didn't need to wait for somebody to tell me what to do or what it meant. I could listen to my inner wisdom and decide for myself. My period had finished. It was eighteen months since I left my marriage. Escaping had been one thing. Liberating my inner world was another. I wanted to heave it up, spit it out — if only it were that easy to exorcise patriarchy. Could I drown the Interior Judge? Could I wash away the self-loathing, the desire for male approval, the longing to be a good girl? Could I rise into freedom? Could I take back the water?

The roadside fruit shop was dim inside. Squeezing between high shelves of pomegranates and apples, I placed three tender nectarines in a plastic bag and nestled them in the towel in my backpack. The tram to Džbán Lake wound between old stone, up the steep incline beside Prague Castle, and out beyond city limits. I alighted near a highway McDonald's, and exited car-fume fugue into an unsigned dirt path that led into a forest. Traffic noise fell away as I descended the verdant hill in green light, and emerged onto a pathway that ringed the lake. The surface was calm.

When I paid the six-koruna entrance fee, I asked the attendant, '*Nudisty?*' She pointed, giving directions in Czech before returning to a plastic chair in the sun where she leant back and lit a cigarette. I trudged past a series of decrepit concrete structures. When the Czech Republic had been a communist country, its borders were closed, thus beginning a great tradition of lakeside holidaying. Ghosts of a summer crowd hid in double-storey buildings that once housed lively change rooms and bars. Now they were rusted, covered in barbed wire and graffiti, crumbling shrines to state control.

I knew I was in the right place when I spotted a man resting a gnarled hand on his hip, his wrinkled penis dangling from a tangle of grey-blonde pubic hair. He counted out change for a beer, grasped the brown bottle's neck, and trudged down the thistly hillside, casting a glance my way.

Grass scratched my bare calves; thongs slapped against heels. Nude figures reclined and sunbathed along the decline. I sighed, nervous about undressing in public. But I hadn't come this far to turn back now. Mouth in a grim line, I paced through spiky yellow grass and laid out a crimson scarf close to the lake's bank. I sat, pulled my dress over my head, then lay back to shift weight onto my shoulders and lift my arse in the air. Off came the black knickers. I scrunched them into my bag, leant back on elbows, and tilted my head to look at clouds streaking across blue sky. Sunlight smiled upon my trembling.

I chanced a curious glance at the couple beside me. They'd made a day of it, lying on blankets surrounded by snacks and books. When the woman went to the bar — she had moles on the back of her thighs — the man stood and, to my horror, approached, arm outstretched, offering a tiny glass bottle of red liquid.

'Sorry, only English,' I squeaked, and he shrugged, replying, 'Deutsch,' his flaccid penis at eye level. Thankfully, he retreated.

Nudists, it appeared, walked in a particular style: hands on hip, shoulders back, belly forward. Display and not-display, a nonchalant confidence. I swept my gaze past couples and a group of three men at the peak of the hill who were chatting, their elbows resting on bent knees. Everybody here was white, though not quite: an impressive orange-brown. The creamy palette of my skin outed me as an outsider. One young man sat cross-legged under a tree, wearing glasses, a book open on his lap. Another with dark hair strode across the grass wearing only velcro sandals and a black backpack. This place was sweet, with its floppy dicks, its loose breasts, its bellies not-sucked-in. As well as a shared privacy, I sensed a communal vulnerability.

Because I could see their genitals. And they did not hide. What did it mean to be free? It was to live without shame. I looked down at my pointy breasts, spotted skin, the hint of labia in a forest of wayward pubes — my body, my self, in all its failure and glory.

Water lapped along a grassy shore. My heartbeat slowed, and I closed my eyes, pulled air into my lungs — the scent of dry grass, cool algae. I had been so ashamed of vulva-gazing, of examining fine details of my flesh, but now it felt urgently necessary to become intimate with the belt marks upon my skin. The wounds of our survival guide us to our healing.

My mind swirled. The sun glowed. The breeze kicked up, rustled through leaves, velvet and kind on the curve of my waist, like on the Isle of Mull. I sat to cross my legs and bit into a sweet, juicy nectarine, its yellow juice dripping from the side of my mouth to my neck, following my collarbone's line. I had eaten from Eve's tree of knowledge and could not go back.

At the lake's opposite edge, ducks gathered. I watched people navigate the sloped bank, buttock muscles tilting with each step. The lake welcomed them, and they swam into the deep. Immersion, rebirth, release.

I closed my eyes and took a full breath, then exhaled and looked up. No one else could save me. I could only save myself.

It was time to go into the water.

I stood, exposed, and stepped forward, ignoring the hillside's eyes. My tentative foot reaching into green-brown shallows disturbed a fish that dashed off with a *sploosh*. Stones were moss-slippery and round beneath my naked soles; the coolness of the water invoked goosebumps along my thighs, stomach, triceps. Tiny midges danced along the surface, where upside-down clouds waved in royal blue. At waist-deep, I bent my knees, submerged my shoulders, and pushed in, breaststroking beyond where my feet could touch. My arms gleamed gold near the surface; when I stroked deeper, they disappeared in opaque dark.

I trod water. 'In the name of the mothers, of the women who came before me: I renounce my baptism.'

Squeezing eyes shut, I dunked myself, then resurfaced, gasping from the cold. I chanted: 'I am whole.' My voice low, wavering. I went under again, and returned; this time, my voice was strong: 'I am whole.' I pushed my streaming hair from my face. A third time under, then I rose. 'I am whole.'

Cool wind whispered through the reeds. A cloud pulled away, and the sun glimmered on green water. Ripples blossomed from my body and sang across the lake. I might not be holy. But I pronounced myself whole.

Note to the Reader

Patriarchal religions are male supremacy. They use the most powerful modes of shaping and influencing abstract thought — language and symbol — to seduce believers into accepting androcentric power systems. They indoctrinate women into a slave mentality, convincing us we are naturally inferior.

Kneeling at the cross embodies subservience, which psychologically prepares believers to accept this posture in personal and institutional relationships. Coupled with inner wisdom being sacrificed at the altar of a higher power, this stance makes followers vulnerable to exploitation and abuse. As for other belief systems — well, I hope those with the lived experience will continue to dismantle similar ideologies of domination.

Addressing the fundamental misogyny of our religious imagination is of great political urgency. As feminism alters the organisation of governments and commerce and the construction of family and work, we must also liberate our spiritual lives. Emancipation from religion is an essential arc in the global movement for gender equality, and it cannot be understated.

I call on all genders to consider the consequences of worshipping a male god. Ask questions, especially the ones that scare you. Questions can unlock the psyche's hidden doors; sometimes, what you're most afraid of is the key to liberation. So speak it out. Write it down. Sing it loud. Fan the embers between your ribs into flames. This is the unsilencing. Free the voice and you free the body. Free the body and you free the self.

Vulva-gazing can be ugly. I felt varying levels of nausea while writing this book. Strange things happened to the skin of my face. My neck broke out in a rash. I needed more sleep. When I acknowledged my indoctrination, when I understood the extent of my silence and self-censorship, when I accepted that my marriage was one of coercive control and that I submitted to my husband, the knowing poured through my body, disturbed my stomach; at different times, I felt exhausted, alive, fatigued, and sore.

But then I began to meet my true self. And she was beautiful.

So let us vulva-gaze and name our victimhood.

What will follow the feminist confrontation of patriarchal religion? I myself am not ready to give up practices of ritual and devotion, contemplation and surrender. The task, then, is to foster a renewed spirituality with roots deep in fecund earth. We must create new myths and symbols, that are founded on intersectional, anti-racist, and queer visions of justice, love, and care. And we must look beyond ourselves: any battle motivated by crimes against us must be interwoven with the fight for equality for all.

Every story is different, every wound varied, every arc of healing infinitely creative. Your methods of resistance might emphasise the maternal aspects of your god. Or deconstruct the cultural notions of masculine and feminine. Your opposition to male supremacy could mean defecting in place: defying convention, reinterpreting scripture, or reimagining ritual. Or it could mean you put this book down to lie on thick green grass, watch leaves shimmer and birds float, and never think about 'god' again.

The journey of unfolding, it seems, never ends. May you begin with the questions that live in your body.

I wish you wholeness.

Acknowledgements

We live in a time where crossing borders is wrongly called 'illegal' for some. Among racist policies that imprison and punish people, it's essential to acknowledge that the unquestioned freedom of movement that formed a central part of this book is a privilege predicated upon my Western passports and white skin.

Writing a book is solitary yet impossible without community. I am indebted not just to the emotional support, care, and guidance of those mentioned below, but to the conversations, revelations, and madness of many unlisted writers, thinkers, strangers, and friends.

So thank you to my parents, Jacqui Schebella and Wayne Schebella, who made this journey possible and whose support never ceased. To my spiritual godmother 'Liz' — Demeter to my Persephone — for the teachings. My work builds upon yours. To my faithful spirit sisters, Gemma Salomon and Gulghina Gabitov, who taught me that female friendship is the world's greatest love story. To my brother, Ben Schebella, whose own spiritual quest has been parallel to mine, and who celebrated with me every step of the way.

Thank you to the worldwide network of women and queers who put me in touch with friends and helped me find my way. To the strangers in strange countries who paid for meals, provided beds or couches, gave interviews, and momentarily invited me into their lives. To those who joined me on the pilgrimage path, and walked with me a while. Thank you to the divine wisdom of Margie Abbott, the mystical nun who pointed to the road. To my supporters on Patreon, without whom I sometimes would not have been able to pay for food and board. This economic solidarity meant I was never quite alone.

Thank you to Jane Novak, my agent, whose championing propelled me forward. To Scribe and my publisher Marika Webb-Pullman for believing in my writing, and for the gentle and patient suggestions that taught me how to make a book. To David Golding, whose copyediting is thoughtful, caring, and wise. To Arts SA, whose grant allowed me to keep going. To the Wheeler Centre, whose Hot Desk Fellowship gave me a reason to go to Melbourne, my initial step away from home. To the first readers of what would become *Holy Woman*: Kylie Maslen, Sonia Nair, Veronica Sullivan, and Sam van Zweden. To Jane Howard, who gave me so many leads and knitted a jumper to keep me warm. To Chloe Higgins, Lur Alghurabi, and Katerina Bryant for the kind and excellent critique in our Zoom writing group. To so many in the Australian and Irish literary communities who opened the door.

The first draft of this book was written on Kaurna Country, the land that has nourished me since birth. I acknowledge the Traditional Custodians of this beautiful place, as well as their continuing connection to the waters and plains. Sovereignty was never ceded. Always was, always will be, Aboriginal land.

Thank you to the artists of the September 2019 Can Serrat Residency in Spain for accompanying a revolution in my creative thought. To Lauren Foley, Sarah Devereux, Trudie Gorman, and Oana Nicoara for being soul-friends in Ireland. Thank you to my housemates (including pets) for the sanctuaries, the shared meals, the yoga rooms; during the pandemic, we made kin and relied on each other in new ways. Thank you to Jamie Gorman — monk to my holy woman — whose spiritual correspondence and thought-sparks illuminated the last leg of my *Holy Woman* journey.

And thank you, endlessly, to the trees, the swans, the ocean, the moon ...

Holy Woman Reading List

Foundational

- 'Why Women Need the Goddess', *Womanspirit Rising: a feminist reader on religion* – ed. Carol P. Christ & Judith Plaskow https://www.goddessariadne.org/#!why-women-need-the-goddess-part-1/cufo
- *Sister Outsider* – Audre Lorde
- *Beyond God the Father* – Mary Daly

Ireland

- *The Serpent and the Goddess: women, religion, and power in Celtic Ireland* – Mary Condren
- *The Festival of Brigit: Celtic goddess and holy woman* – Séamas Ó Catháin
- *Celtic Christianity and Nature: early Irish and Hebridean traditions* – Mary Low
- DoloresWhelan.ie

Mexico

- *Guadalupe: mother of the new creation* – Virgilio Elizondo
- *Goddesses and the Divine Feminine: a Western religious history* – Rosemary Radford Ruether
- 'When God Was a Girl', *Divine Women*, BBC (2012) – Bettany Hughes
- 'The Virgin of Guadalupe: symbol of conquest or liberation?', *Art Journal* 51 (1992) – Jeanette Favrot Peterson

- *Guadalupe / Tonantzin, Artes de México Número* 125 (2017)
- *Ni Una Más* (blog) – Frida Guerrera
  https://fridaguerrera.blogspot.com/

Sweden

- *The Queer God* – Marcella Althaus-Reid
- 'Bucking the Linguistic Binary: gender neutral language in English, Swedish, French, and German', *Western Papers in Linguistics / Cahiers linguistiques de Western* 3 (2016) – Levi C. R. Hord

Bulgaria / Turkey

- *The Creation of Patriarchy* – Gerda Lerner
- *Prayers to Sophia: deepening our relationship with Holy Wisdom* – Joyce Rupp
- 'The Wisdom of Women Written Out of History', *The Guardian* (2012) – Bettany Hughes
  https://www.theguardian.com/commentisfree/2012/apr/10/wisdom-women-written-out-of-history

Scotland

- *Sexism and God-Talk: toward a feminist theology* – Rosemary Radford Ruether
- *Fragmentation and Redemption: essays on gender and the human body in medieval religion* – Caroline Walker Bynum
- Motherearth and the Megamachine: a theology of liberation in a feminine, somatic, and ecological perspective', *Liberation Theology* – Rosemary Radford Ruether
  https://womanspiritireland.files.wordpress.com/2015/12/motherearth-and-the-megamachine.pdf

Ireland — Repeal

- *Dublin's Lost Heroines: mammies and grannies in a vanished Dublin* – Kevin C. Kearns
- *The Republic of Shame: how Ireland punished 'Fallen Women' and their children* – Caelainn Hogan
- *Repeal the 8th* – ed. Una Mullally
- 'White Women's Mascot: Dr Savita Halappanavar and the racial politics of abortion rights', *Medium* (2018) – Dr Chamindra Weerawardhana
https://fremancourt.medium.com/white-womens-mascot-savita-halappanavar-and-the-racial-politics-of-abortion-rights-c33daf65d544

Italy

- *Women & Power* – Mary Beard
- *The End of Silence: women and the priesthood* – Karen Armstrong
- *Pope Joan* – Donna Woolfolk Cross
- *The Myth of Pope Joan* – Alain Boureau
- 'Doctrine of Headship a Distortion of the Gospel Message of Mutual Love and Respect', *The Sydney Morning Herald* (2015) – Julia Baird
https://www.smh.com.au/opinion/doctrine-of-headship-a-distortion-of-the-gospel-message-of-mutual-love-and-respect-20150226-13q2xc.html

Germany

- *Inside the Gender Jihad: women's reform in Islam* – Amina Wadud
- *Women and Gender in Islam: historical roots of a modern debate* – Leila Ahmed

- *Defecting in Place: women claiming responsibility for their own spiritual lives* – Miriam Therese Winter, Adair Lummis, and Allison Stokes
- *Orientalism* – Edward W. Said
- 'A Feminist Reading of the Koran', *Eureka Street* (2012) – Ruby Hamad https://www.eurekastreet.com.au/article/a-feminist-reading-of-the-koran

Morocco

- *Women in the Qur'an: an emancipatory reading* – Asma Lamrabet
- *Beyond the Veil: male–female dynamics in modern Muslim society* – Fatema Mernissi
- *Sex and Lies: true stories of women's intimate lives in the Arab world* – Leïla Slimani
- *The Hidden Face of Eve* – Nawal El Saadawi
- *Headscarves and Hymens: why the Middle East needs a sexual revolution* – Mona Eltahawy

The Czech Republic

- *On Women and Judaism: a view from tradition* – Blu Greenberg
- *The Red Tent* – Anita Diamant
- 'Religiously Doing Gender: the good woman and the bad woman in Israeli ritual discourse', *Method & Theory in the Study of Religion* 13 (2001) – Susan Starr Sered
- 'Take Back the Waters', *Lilith* (1986) – Rabbi Elyse M. Goldstein https://www.lilith.org/articles/take-back-the-waters/